The authors

John Silvester has been a crime reporter in Melbourne since 1978. He worked for *The Sunday Times* 'Insight' team in London in 1990, and has co-authored several crime books, including the best-seller *Underbelly*. He is currently senior crime writer for *The Age* and an expensive but strangely popular after-dinner speaker.

Andrew Rule has been a journalist since 1975 and has worked in newspapers, television and radio. He wrote *Cuckoo*, the true story of the notorious 'Mr Stinky' case, and has edited and published several other books, including the original *Underbelly*. He is senior writer for *Good Weekend* magazine and charges much more reasonably for after-dinner speaking.

They won the prestigious Ned Kelly Award for True Crime writing for *Underbelly 3*.

RATS

CROOKS WHO GOT AWAY WITH IT

Tails of true crime and mystery
from the *Underbelly* archives

Published in Australia by
Floradale Productions Pty Ltd and Sly Ink Pty Ltd
August 2006

Distributed wholesale by
Gary Allen Pty Ltd,
9 Cooper Street,
Smithfield, NSW
Telephone (02) 9725 2933

Copyright Floradale Productions and Sly Ink, 2006

All rights reserved.
No part of this publication may be
reproduced or transmitted in any form
or by any means without the
publishers' permission

Rats
Crooks Who Got Away With It

*Tails of true crime and mystery
from the Underbelly archives*

ISBN – 0 9775440 0 1

Cover design: R T J Klinkhamer
Typesetting and layout: Stephanie Buttner

> You woke up this morning. Got yourself a gun.
> Mama always said you'd be the Chosen One ...
>
> You woke up this morning all the love has gone,
> Your Papa never told you about right and wrong.

– *Woke Up This Morning (Chosen One Mix)*
soundtrack for *The Sopranos* by Alabama 3

Contents

1. The Invisible Man 1
2. The Puppet Master 31
3. A House of Cards 53
4. Mr Cruel 69
5. Deadly Secret 87
6. A Stolen Life 99
7. Swamp Fever 117
8. Beauty and the Beast 125
9. Bad to the Bone 149
10. A Dog's Tale 169
11. Rats in a Trap 179
12. Inside Job 193
13. The Silk Worm 211
14. Fishy Business 225
15. Who Killed Jenny Tanner? 241
16. Out of His Depth 275
17. The Highway Predator 287
18. It's Payback Time 323

CHAPTER 1

The Invisible Man

Like the postman who appears at the same time every day, Arthur Brown had become invisible.

THE man who found the bodies is 70 now, the oldest drinker in the public bar of the Plaza Hotel in Townsville. He's seen and done a lot of things since he left South Otago, New Zealand, back in 1952. But nothing sticks in his memory like the day he played a walk-on part, in a cruel story that haunts the town where two little sisters lived and died.

He tells it his way. A knockabout carpenter, he'd been building houses for the nickel mines out past Kalgoorlie, then got a bankroll and itchy feet and headed east across the Nullarbor in his new Falcon, camping on the way.

He'd meant to go home to New Zealand to see his family, but good intentions slipped away as easily as last week's wages. After a little work at Woomera rocket range, building a 'secret' satellite-spotting post, he turned north.

First to Coober Pedy, then further into the desert to the 'Three Ways', where a traveller has to make a lonely choice. The Adelaide road was behind, narrowing the choice ahead to Darwin and Townsville. He tossed a coin. Townsville it was, via Mount Isa. He arrived late on August 27, a Thursday, to find the sleepy coastal city in a frenzy, shocked out of its tropical torpor by the worst tragedy since the war. Two sisters had vanished on their way to school the previous morning. Their mother was under sedation, their father half-mad with unspeakable fear.

The old man puts his glass on the bar, fishes in his coat pocket for two pieces of paper – worn, grimy, folded small – that he's kept almost half his life.

It's the carbon copy of a statement he made to police the day it happened. This is what it says: 'I am a married man, 40 years of age, at the present time of no fixed place of abode in Townsville, having only arrived from Boulder, Western Australia, on the night of 27th August, 1970.

'About 8.45am on Friday 28th August 1970 I joined a number of other persons in a taxi cab … In company with two other men I was engaged in a search party for two missing girls who had disappeared whilst on their way to school.

'We travelled along the Townsville to Charters Towers Highway and made a search in various places along this road prior to going to a spot near Antill Creek. We parked the car and set off in various directions. I traversed the creek bank and dry creek bed.

'Whilst searching in the creek I saw what appeared to be child's footprints in the sand. I continued to walk along the creek bed and, about ten yards further on, I then saw the body of a child … in a small hollow and the child was in a more or less sitting, reclining position. I saw that the child was wearing a pair of panties. At this stage I was a distance of approximately ten feet from the body. The child appeared to be dead. I now know that the body which I located was the body of Susan Debra Mackay.'

SUSAN was five, the baby of the family. Judith was seven. They were 'late lambs', as they say in the bush, born well after two boys and two older girls. They were dark-eyed, olive-skinned and pretty, like many children of the far north, where indigenous, islander and Italian influences have tempered the Anglo-Celtic majority.

Bill Mackay kissed his babies goodbye as they slept, when he left for the meatworks before dawn. He never saw them again.

The Mackays lived in Albert Street, Aitkenvale, a suburb sprawled along the Ross River Road, a highway that leads inland from Townsville to Charters Towers and beyond.

Susan and Judith left home about 8.10am, after their mother, Thelma, got them ready for school. They walked to the corner, turned left into Alice Street, and vanished.

The girls would have crossed the road to wait at their usual bus stop. But when their brother, Alan, rode past on his bike about ten minutes later, they weren't there. They weren't at school either, but it wasn't until they didn't come home that afternoon that the alarm was raised.

When Bill Mackay got home from work, his wife was distraught. He grabbed photographs of the girls and went to the police. By nightfall, police and friends gathered to search backyards in the district.

Next day, hundreds more joined in. The meatworks offered its entire workforce, and police door-knocked every house in the area. By Friday, the search had spread, which is how the wandering Kiwi carpenter, called Richard Tough, and two men he didn't know, were sent to Antill Creek, a sluggish watercourse meandering across an ugly plain, 25 kilometres south-west of Townsville. It is an empty place where scrawny cattle poke through stunted scrub and feral pigs tear up the barren ground.

Tough waited by the little girl's body for an hour until the police arrived. They followed footprints in a sandbank running along the creek bed, which was almost dry. About 70 metres away, near the opposite bank, they found Judith's naked body.

The only mercy was that the pigs hadn't got to them first. Both girls had been raped and stabbed in the chest. Susan had been strangled, Judith choked from having her face rammed into the sand. It looked as if she had fled while her little sister was being killed, and was then run down.

Beside the bodies were their school uniforms – folded inside out and placed with an awful neatness. Their shoes, socks, hats and school bags were nearby.

A senior sergeant cried when he saw it. Another policeman said he wouldn't go home until they caught the killer. He was as good as his word, staying at Townsville police station day and night, with his worried wife bringing in food and clean clothes – until he died of a heart attack two weeks later.

Had he lived, he could hardly have guessed that the case would see his generation out of the force.

IN the days before drugs multiplied crime, homicides were mostly simple domestic murders, or brawls gone wrong – as easily solved as the average burglary.

But the motiveless and random killing of two innocent children produced a huge outcry and no obvious culprit.

There was intense pressure from the top for a quick arrest, when a slow, painstaking investigation was the best chance of cracking the case.

From the start, the police's problem was not that there were too few leads, but too many.

Townsville was, and is, an army town, and the meatworks had its own blood-spattered corps of itinerant slaughtermen, butchers and boners, not all model citizens. Add meatworkers to a barracks full of soldiers and there were thousands of potential suspects.

It was inevitable that the sheer weight of numbers – and of public expectation – would affect the investigation. Local knowledge, sometimes a police officer's best tool, didn't help the tedious elimination of hundreds of suspects. Ironically, it might have been a handicap, because it would encourage assumptions about who should be put on – or left off – the long list of people to check. The temptation was to take shortcuts. The risk was that they would miss their man.

Meanwhile, there was the mammoth job of piecing together witnesses' accounts – often contradictory, or apparently so.

A teacher, Judith Drysdale, saw a man driving slowly near the Mackay sisters and staring intently at them. Much later she was able to pick a photograph of the man she saw from a series of pictures.

Nola Archie, in the grounds of the Aboriginal hostel behind the bus stop, saw two small girls talking to a man in a car. She wasn't sure of the vehicle's make or model, but agreed it might have been a Holden.

Bill Hankin was driving a road-roller on Ross River Road that morning. About 8.15 he pulled over near the Aitkenvale school for a smoke and a cup of tea. He noticed a man in a car with two girls in school uniforms; while everyone else was driving children towards the school 'like ants to a nest', this man was taking children away from it.

Hankin had been a driving instructor in the army, and he

noted automatically that the driver was thin-featured, swarthy, not tall, and drove badly. He looked middle-aged, with a tanned complexion and dark, wavy hair, cut short. A face like the character 'Bo' in the television series *Days Of Our Lives*, but older, he was to tell police later.

Around the same time, Neil Lunney was running late for work at the army barracks. Just back from Vietnam, he had a short fuse, and was incensed when a car in front of him sped up and veered to block him when he tried to overtake.

'He tried to put me over the embankment,' Lunney was to recall. 'I did my cool. I was going to bumper roll him but, when I got up level with him, I saw the kids in the car.'

The older girl, on the passenger side, had shoulder-length hair, as Judith Mackay did. The younger one, sitting in the middle, had shorter hair, like Susan Mackay. Both wore green Aitkenvale school uniforms.

Lunney yelled at the driver, and looked at him hard in case he saw him in the street. He'd been taught recognition in the army; it could mean life and death in jungle warfare. This enemy had high cheekbones, short hair, and 'Mickey Mouse' ears stuck out from a narrow skull. Lunney wasn't so observant about the car, except that it was blue-grey 'like a battleship'; it wasn't a Ford but might have been a Holden, and had an odd-coloured driver's door. He did notice two 'STP' oil stickers on the rear mudguards, and venetian blinds in the back window.

JEAN Thwaite was cleaning a car in the Shell service station she and her husband ran at Ayr, more than an hour's drive south-west of Townsville, when a car pulled up. It was covered in dust and her memory is that it was 'dirty white' or beige colour, and arrived between 11.30 and noon.

The driver was thin, dark-haired, looked to be in his 40s, and

THE INVISIBLE MAN

wore a faded, fawn or off-white shirt. He seemed preoccupied, and ignored her request to cut the motor while she pumped the $3 worth of petrol he ordered.

The petrol inlet was on the left side, and she had to open a flap to get at the screw-on cap, similar to her own 1965 EH Holden. This ruled out the car being a 1950s Holden but, unknown to her, was a design feature shared with the Vauxhall Victor, uncommon in country Queensland.

Thwaite, mother of a five-year-old, took notice of two children in the car. In the back seat, a small girl who looked as if she had been crying asked, 'Are we there yet?' In the front seat was an older girl, who said to the driver, 'When are you taking us to mummy? You promised to take us to mummy.' Both wore green school uniforms.

The driver silently handed Thwaite exact change. By the time she looked up from the till, the car had gone. When she heard next day about the abduction in Townsville, Jean Thwaite was sure she had seen the Mackay sisters, but found it hard to get the local police to take her seriously.

There was so much information – some obviously contradictory and some seemingly so – that the police felt pressured to make choices: to play hunches that one lead was better than another. Unfortunately, they got it wrong about the car.

Although the descriptions of the car given by Hankin, Lunney and Thwaite varied in details, between them they had enough key information about it to find a driver whom they all described the same way.

But the police, punting on a description of a car seen near where the bodies were found, concentrated on looking for an early model Holden. Their enthusiasm to find the 'right' car rather than to build a picture of the driver caused confusion. As one legal insider was to remark dryly 30 years later, witnesses who first thought they'd seen a Vauxhall ended up signing statements they'd seen a Holden – and an FJ Holden, at that.

Worse, despite the matching descriptions of the driver – apart from his age – there was no sketch or photofit picture of him published. Instead, the newspapers and television ran pictures of FJ Holdens.

It put the investigation so far off course, it never recovered. For the wanted man, it was an unbelievably lucky break. For others, it was a tragedy, because sex killers almost always kill again.

JOHN White was only nineteen, but he'd worked alongside men for years, and knew his way around. He'd been a carpenter, bridge builder and meatworker. Now he was a trainee psychiatric nurse, working shifts at the mental hospital in Charters Towers, which is why, late on a weekday afternoon – probably the first Tuesday of September 1970, he was to say later – he was sitting in the deserted bar of the White Horse Tavern in the main street, when a stranger walked in.

White guessed the man was old enough to be his father, perhaps in his 50s, but wiry and fit. He put his height at 'five seven or five eight' (about 172 centimetres) and his weight at no more than 'eleven stone' (about 70 kilograms). He was wearing clean work clothes – a checked flannelette shirt, long brown trousers, brown hat.

The man sat at the bar a couple of metres away, produced a tin of tobacco and rolled a cigarette. He was out of matches, and he asked the younger man for a light. White didn't smoke, so the stranger bought matches from the barmaid and started talking.

He asked White if he'd been following the murder of the Mackay sisters a few days before. White nodded, and the man

THE INVISIBLE MAN

stated that the police were 'looking for the wrong sort of car'. Before White could ask how he knew that, the man kept talking quickly. 'You know,' he said, 'I killed those two girls.' White wanted to think it was a tasteless joke, but it didn't quite sound like it. So he kept talking, trying to draw out more information. The stranger said he was staying at the Crown Hotel down the street, that he was a carpenter who did a bit of maintenance work for the publican, and that he sometimes did some prospecting in local creeks.

It was as if the older man had 'a monkey on his back, and happened to choose me to get it off,' White was to muse later.

The stranger got up to leave, and White tentatively arranged to meet him next day for another drink. And, as casually as he could, he asked him his name.

As soon as the carpenter left, White borrowed a pencil from the barmaid and wrote the name on the back of the empty matchbox the man had left on the bar; then went looking for police.

He found two, locking the station to do their afternoon patrol. He knew one of them, a Constable John Cooper, and told him what the carpenter had said and where he was. He gave them the matchbox with the name on it.

The policemen went to the Crown Hotel. Next day, the carpenter turned up at the tavern, as arranged. He told White the police had spoken to him, but he didn't seem worried.

If anything, he was a little cocky. He showed White a photograph of his house, which was small and low to the ground, with sawn timber stacked neatly in the yard. Then he had a beer, and left.

White never saw him again. He ran into Constable Cooper a few days later. 'He just said he'd been to see him (the carpenter) and there was nothing in it.'

And that, as far as John White was concerned, was that. He rarely thought about the strange encounter again, though he never forgot the name he wrote on the matchbox.

Arty Brown.

IN late March, 1972, two children in north Queensland disappeared, feared murdered. One was a two-year-old, Shay Maree Kitchen, at Mount Isa. The other was a cane farmer's teenage daughter, Marilyn Joy Wallman, at Eimeo on the coast near Mackay.

It was before the state's homicide squad was formed, so local police investigated murders. Charles Bopf, prominent Townsville detective and future homicide chief, managed the Kitchen case. He quickly arrested the de facto husband of the child's mother – another sordid domestic tragedy to add to his big tally of cases solved. The Wallman mystery, outside Townsville's police district, wasn't so easy. It was as brazen as Judith and Susan Mackay's abduction twenty months before, but with no clues. No cars. No suspects. No leads. Not even a body.

On Tuesday, March 21, the three oldest Wallman children were going to school. Marilyn, fourteen, had to catch the high school bus on the main road, a few hundred metres away along the small road that led to the farm. She left, riding her bike, a few minutes before her brothers – David, ten, and Rex, eight – who went to the local primary school.

The Wallmans' road went over a hill that hid most of its length from the house. When David and Rex rode over the crest they found their sister's bike lying on its side.

The puzzled boys looked around, thinking Marilyn had fallen, bumped her head and wandered off in a daze. David went home for his mother while Rex stayed, sitting near the bike. He heard voices on the other side of the cane field next to him, but couldn't tell if one was his sister's.

Their mother came with the car. They drove around the blocks of cane, searching and calling, fear rising as the minutes passed.

The boys' father was out fishing, and someone went to get him. Friends and neighbours gathered and began a search that has never really ended for the Wallmans.

As the days became weeks, hopes of a miracle ebbed. It seemed clear Marilyn was almost certainly dead and her body well-hidden. If buried, it was deep. If put in water, it had not floated or washed ashore.

At least the Mackays had bodies to grieve over. The Wallmans prayed for even that bitter-sweet mercy. Thirty years on, they still do.

EVERY day is a private hell for the broken-hearted, but anniversaries torment most. The Mackays had moved from Townsville to Toowoomba to get away from the stares and whispers, the crank calls and the well-meaning solicitudes of their home town, but they took their grief with them. And nothing could ease that, only mask it.

On the morning of August 26, 1973, the third anniversary of their girls' murder, they woke to nightmare news. Lightning had struck someone else. In Adelaide, where the Beaumont children had disappeared seven years before, two girls had been abducted from a football game. In a public place, in daylight, like the Beaumonts and their own girls and Marilyn Wallman.

Joanne Ratcliffe was eleven; Kirste Gordon was four. At three-quarter-time in the preliminary football final between Norwood and North Adelaide at Adelaide Oval, Joanne had taken Kirste to the women's lavatory, about 300 metres from the stand where her parents were sitting with Kirste's grandmother. Neither was seen again.

A teenager selling lollies, Anthony Kilmartin, saw a man watching the girls in the stand and, later, hurrying after them near the southern gate. He lifted the young girl under his right arm and started walking fast. The older girl, whom Kilmartin later identified from photographs as Joanne Ratcliffe, had looked frightened and tried to stop the man.

Kilmartin was vague about the man's age – 'about 40' – but gave a detailed description of his clothes and appearance. He was thin, narrow-shouldered, wearing a brown broad-brimmed hat, grey-checked jacket and dark trousers.

And there was one other thing, Kilmartin was to tell police in 1973, and an inquest six years later. The older girl had kicked the man in the knee, causing him to bend down. As he did, a pair of black, horn-rimmed glasses fell from his pocket, which he snatched up. A small thing, but it signified a man too vain to wear glasses all the time, or who needed them only for reading.

Kilmartin wasn't the only witness. An assistant curator at the oval had earlier seen a man and two girls apparently attempting to entice some kittens from under a car near a shed. The man was thin, about 172 centimetres tall, and dressed in a grey-checked sports coat, brown trousers and brown, wide-brimmed hat.

Sue Lawrie, her father and little sister heard the football siren as they left the zoo, about a kilometre from the oval on the other side of the Torrens. Sue's father guessed it was the start of the final quarter of the big game. They followed the river bank towards the new Festival Theatre, opposite the oval. Minutes later Sue, then fourteen, saw a middle-aged man hurrying towards them, carrying a small girl. Behind him was a girl about eleven, running to keep up, punching him in the back and yelling at him, 'We want to go back!' Sue was surprised the man would let his 'granddaughter' hit him without chastising her. She stared long enough to be able to describe details years later that tallied with other witnesses, but the hat and the man's face caught her eye most.

In 1970s Adelaide, the most English of Australian cities, if a middle-aged man wore a hat at all in winter it was usually a tweed, peaked cap or a natty, narrow-brimmed felt. Wide-brimmed hats were not yet a fashion effected by city people – big hats were for practical protection, and worn in summer in the country. And there were regional differences even then. The only time Sue had seen a wide-brimmed hat with a low, flat crown like this one, was when visiting relatives in Queensland, where a lot of men wore them. It was, as she was to say later, 'very Queensland country'.

Next day, Sue went for a country trip for a week, and missed most of the furore over the missing girls.

When she returned, police were concentrating on events around the oval, so she dismissed what she had seen near the zoo.

It wasn't until some time later, while discussing lack of discipline in some families, that Sue commented on the young girl she'd noticed thumping her 'grandfather' in public.

'When was that?' her father asked.

'The day we went to the zoo,' she replied. As she spoke she remembered it was the day the girls had been abducted, and she realised the sinister significance of what she'd seen. But she was young, her father thought she had the timing wrong, and he didn't take it further.

For years, it played on her mind. In late 1980, married with a baby of her own, she told her husband about it. He urged her to go to the police. She told detectives about a man in his 50s with a wide hat and a thin, hollow-cheeked face she couldn't forget.

IT was the darkest secret she knew, and she'd spent half her life wanting to tell it. But it took a move to the other side of Australia and a crisis of conscience for Merle Martin Moss to make the call she'd rehearsed so many times in her head.

She was sitting alone in a flat in suburban Perth in October 1998, looking through her family 'birthday book' when a wave of revulsion hardened her resolve. On the page under May was the name of an old man who, she knew, had molested at least five female relatives among her extended family. She despised him.

It was a family secret, shared between cousins, aunts and husbands. But an inner circle – Merle Moss, her sister Christine Millier and two of their cousins' wives – suspected something even more sinister was linked to the old man's predatory ways.

Moss had bowed to family pressure not to embarrass or distress the victims by forcing them to reveal things they'd learned to live with. The problem was, if such delicacy masked the fact that the old man was a deviate, it would be hard to accuse him of murder. She had no hard evidence he was a killer. Her suspicions relied on a web of circumstance, detail and intuition spun around the knowledge that he had covered up decades of sexual offences against children. Without knowing that background, she feared, any police officer bothering to check out a telephone tip would find nothing but a couple of harmless, old-age pensioners in a neat house in a sleepy Townsville street.

But, this night Moss decided she had to act. The Crimestoppers number flashed on her television. She reached for the telephone. It took three days for the message to filter through to the Queensland homicide squad in Brisbane. Sergeant David Hickey, who had just finished investigating a baby's death, was about to open an old file allocated for a routine review when he got a note to call the woman in Perth.

As he spoke to her, the coincidence hit him ... the old file on his desk was the Mackay sisters' murder in Townsville. Hickey, a methodical investigator, isn't superstitious – but when he told the woman on the line which file he was reviewing, she took it as a sign. She poured out her heart about an old man in Townsville called Arthur Brown.

For Hickey and another detective, Brendan Rook, it was the beginning of an exhaustive investigation. Starting with a circle of the woman's relatives in north Queensland, their inquiries rippled outwards, interstate and, in one case, to New Zealand. Some people they spoke to were shocked at the allegations of sexual abuse, others guardedly confirmed them. But Merle Moss's younger sister Christine Millier and two cousins-by-marriage filled the gaps in a Gothic horror story, played out among three generations of slow-talking, hard-working, apparently respectable folk.

It seemed that, until 1982, most family members had not suspected Arthur Brown of anything except being a 'big noter' who fancied himself as 'a ladies' man'. But, that year, a tearful teenager told her parents he had molested her as a small girl, and Brown's carefully constructed cover was blown. Four other girls – sisters and cousins – had quickly admitted similar secrets. To all but a few who refused to believe the girls, he was a pariah. And some suspected worse.

ARTHUR Stanley Brown was born at Merinda, near Bowen, on May 20, 1912, one of three children whose parents separated when he was young. His mother went to Melbourne and Arthur was to spend several years there. He told people later he had been a paperboy and had got a Victorian driver's licence before returning to Queensland.

He attached himself to the Anderson family, who also came

from Bowen and had six daughters and two sons, most of them younger than Brown. Their mother and some of the girls ran 'the galley', cooking for workers at the Ross River meatworks, where Brown worked during and after the war, apart from a spell doing wartime construction work.

A beach photograph of Brown in the 1940s shows a bare-chested wiry man with the lean muscles and dapper toughness of a lightweight boxer or a heavyweight jockey. The high cheekbones, long jaw, and prominent ears below a short-back-and-sides haircut were distinguishing features that age was not to soften.

Active, fit, and a light drinker, Brown didn't gain weight or lose his hair as he got older. He was delighted when a shop assistant once mistook his first wife as his mother; a stranger could easily have mistaken him for fifteen years younger than his real age. Even in his 50s, he would show off by gripping a table edge and balancing his body in the air above the table, lifting himself up and down. If this showed a dash of the exhibitionist, there was also an obsessive neatness. He would line up his perfectly shone shoes, fold a piece of paper before putting it in the bin, and iron knife-edge creases into work clothes when others wore rumpled shorts and singlets.

Brown was to marry two of the six Anderson sisters, and was close to two others. He was first married in June 1944 – to Hester, then freshly divorced, with three small children, but whom he'd known before her first marriage. They were to live an outwardly normal life for 34 years, but Hester's oldest sister Milly, now dead, was convinced she made the best of a dreadful mistake.

Milly disliked Brown, said he couldn't be trusted. She told relations that Hester feared him, and had once confided to her about his well-known womanising: 'He doesn't just like big girls – he likes little girls too.' Hester had caught him interfering with a child and tried to prevent him from being alone with them. But she was stricken with crippling arthritis in early middle age, and was no match for the man she increasingly relied on to care for her.

Hester's younger sister, Charlotte, had also been married before and also had three children. One son bore a strong resemblance to Brown, as did another sister's boy. As Hester grew more infirm, Charlotte visited the Browns often and even went on interstate holidays with them.

Hester kept up appearances, but once she called aside a young female relative and gave her prized lacework she'd inherited from her mother, saying bitterly, 'I don't want his next lady love to get it'. Asked who she meant, she blurted, 'Charlotte, of course'. Hester, in constant pain, became confined to moving between a walking frame and bed, a virtual prisoner in the fibro and timber house Brown had built long before in Lowth Street, Rosslea, an old suburb of Townsville. Her torment ended late at night on May 15, 1978, when Brown told the family doctor by telephone she had fallen while trying to get onto the commode next to her bed, hitting her head and killing herself.

As far as the police could ascertain twenty years later, the doctor had written out a death certificate at home without viewing the body, which Brown took to an undertaker's himself. Hester Brown was cremated, which meant the injuries to her skull could never be examined.

At the time Brown pointedly told family members he'd paid for a post- mortem to be done. Detectives told them years later it wasn't true, although at least one relative insisted she'd been there when police spoke of an 'autopsy'. Hester's big sister, Milly, didn't believe the death was an accident.

'The day Hester was found dead,' another relative was to

recall, 'Arthur was shaking with fright. He wasn't grieving, because he never showed emotion. He was worried.'

Suspicion didn't appear to worry Charlotte who, family gossip had it, had been sent packing by Hester not long before her death. She moved in with Brown and married him the following year.

She was a small woman and, even in her 60s, had the odd custom of wearing little girls' pyjamas, much to the bemusement of her female relatives. When one of her cousin's grandchildren asked her once why she wore such childish clothes to bed, Arthur Brown interrupted, saying, 'Because she's my little girl'.

MERLE and Christine's mother was a cousin of Hester and Charlotte, and the girls often visited the Browns while they were growing up.

As youngsters, they accepted Brown as a jovial, talkative man who liked to be the centre of attention. But as they matured and he aged, they tired of his boasts that he knew everybody of importance in Townsville. And they didn't like his fascination with sex crimes.

He kept a collection of lurid 'true crime' magazines and showed the graphic photographs to children. He went on about how dangerous it was for young girls to be alone, and told them to 'trust nobody'. He spoke of 'silly mothers' dropping their children too early at school.

There was another side to his 'concern'. He would say he felt sorry for male teachers because girl students were 'prick teasers' and that it was too easy for girls to 'scream rape' on a whim. 'The kids of today will set you up,' he would say. 'They'll get you hung.'

It seemed to the sisters, even then, that Brown protested too much. They recalled that their grandfather had detested Brown,

THE INVISIBLE MAN

and refused to be in the same house with him. 'Pop always said Arthur was a bad man,' Merle was to recall. 'He would say to me, "See after yourself, love, and don't be on your own with him." I often wonder what he knew.'

Apart from one minor incident, Merle was old enough to be out of Brown's reach. And he didn't try to molest Christine 'probably because I had a mouth and would have fought to the death'. But, looking back on it, she thinks she was lucky. Twice.

The week that John F. Kennedy was shot in 1963, Christine, then thirteen, was staying at the Browns'. One day, when Hester was out, Brown proposed taking her 'for a swim'. She refused because she couldn't swim, and there were no other children to play with.

Three years later, on another visit, Brown came home early from work while Hester was at bingo and Christine was home alone. He suggested driving her to a mountain outside Townsville, to take some pictures with her new camera. She refused because she didn't like the steep, winding road. Much later, she realised it was such a slow trip, it would have been too dark to take photographs by the time they arrived.

At sixteen, she was too articulate to be molested and scared into keeping quiet, as younger girls had been. So what was his plan? If she had disappeared, no-one would have known where she'd gone. Brown was supposedly at work, and she would have been just another teenage runaway. But that thought didn't strike her until after 1970.

THE day the Mackay sisters were murdered, Christine was staying at the Browns'. She was twenty, with a year-old baby, on her way north to rejoin her husband at Weipa after visiting family in Bowen.

That morning, Brown got up about 7am, cut his lunch, and

went to work. Christine remembers nothing unusual about his return that afternoon, except that the radio that was usually on was switched off that night and next morning – which meant she didn't hear news of the abduction until she got to Cairns the following evening. Another relative, who trusted Brown with her children until 1982, when his sexual abuse was exposed, was puzzled at something he said a few weeks after the Mackay girls' murder.

'I could've done that,' he told her. The woman didn't go to the police, she was to explain years later, 'because I didn't think he'd be the type'. She was to change her mind in 1982, but stayed silent rather than involve his sex abuse victims.

When police were looking for a car with an odd-coloured driver's door after the murders, Brown took the dark-blue door off his Vauxhall and buried it, according to another relative. He told her at the time 'he didn't want anyone interviewing him or annoying him'. Because they thought police were looking for an FJ Holden, they accepted his explanation. Later still, he told Christine he knew the Mackay sisters' father, and that he had worked at the girls' school. He offered to drive Christine and Merle to look at the spot where the bodies had been found. They refused, and wondered at his weird tastes.

THE detectives came for Arthur Brown after breakfast on December 3, 1998. Car after car pulled up outside the neat fibro-cement house in the neat street. There were fourteen detectives – and photographers, forensic experts and army sappers with metal detectors used for minesweeping.

While the soldiers swept the big backyard for any remnant of a buried car door, the detectives painstakingly searched the house. They were especially keen on a spare room they'd been told about, which had a door fitted with a bolt on the inside. It was where Brown kept, among other things, his personal papers. Yet there was no record of registration or insurance or mechanical work to indicate he'd ever owned a blue-grey Vauxhall Victor sedan – a car he tried to deny having owned, until they produced a photograph supplied by a relative.

There was no warning of the raid, but even when the officer in charge read the warrants, detailing allegations of murder and sexual abuse, the old man did not seem shocked. 'Didn't raise an eyebrow,' one detective was to recall. When the officer reading the warrant used the married name of one of the sex abuse victims, Brown instantly queried it, nodding when the officer corrected the surname to one he knew.

Before they left to go to the police station for questioning, Brown said to an increasingly agitated Charlotte that he'd done some terrible things she didn't know about, and it was time to pay for them. It seemed an odd comment, given that she must have known about the sex abuse allegations. At the watch-house, Brown reportedly said another strange thing, later denied. 'Those Mackay sisters have me stumped,' he declared. 'I've lived in Townsville for 30 years and I haven't heard of the Mackay sisters.'

This, a prosecutor was to tell a hushed court months later, was a clumsy lie that pointed to guilt of a crime the judge himself called 'one of the most notable events in the city's post-war history', of which 'no-one in Townsville at the time would not be aware'.

At the start, detectives thought they were talking to 'a silly old bloke', as one was to put it. But when questions swung from the general to the particular, Brown's attitude hardened.

Asked if he would go to Antill Creek with police, he retorted, 'No way I am going out there with you,' then demanded to see a lawyer. Arthur Brown had never had a conviction in his life, but he'd worked at the meatworks and around courts and police stations, and he knew the drill. He got a telephone book and looked up a law clerk, who called a solicitor who made another call. Mark Donnelly, a policeman's son and one of north Queensland's toughest criminal barristers, soon turned up to represent his new client.

From then on, Brown was silent. And his wife refused to repeat in a formal interview what she had already told police informally. The police were left pondering what had come from the arrest. One thing they'd found in the bolted room was a bottle of port, which tallied with claims by some of Brown's alleged victims that he'd given them liquor before molesting them.

And something else had been locked away for years – a set of worn work clothes, musty and yellowed with age. It included a singlet with a large, faint stain that washing had not removed.

'Arthur would never wear a stained singlet,' one relative was to say. 'I reckon it was the clothes he wore the day the girls were killed in 1970. He's kept them like a trophy.'

JOHN White, late of Charters Towers, was in Brisbane when he heard a man had been charged for the Mackay sisters' murder.

'I bet his name is Arty Brown,' White blurted to his astonished partner, then told the story of his conversation with a thin stranger in his hometown 28 years earlier. He couldn't sleep for several nights, and wrote down details as they came back to him: Brown's name, the name of the tavern, the time he spoke to the police, and the policeman's name, John Cooper. Then he called Brisbane CIB.

Sue Lawrie was living in Melbourne when she saw fleeting footage of an old man in Townsville on the television news. Something about him pricked her memory. 'Where do I know you from?' she said to herself uneasily. Next morning she took a call from an old friend in Adelaide, who asked her reaction to the news. Before the friend could explain that there was media speculation in Adelaide about a connection between the old man arrested in Queensland and unsolved Adelaide abductions, Sue interrupted.

'My God! It's him,' she screamed into the telephone. The man she'd seen on television was older, more gaunt, but, in her mind, the same one she'd seen on the banks of the Torrens, 25 years before.

John Hill had been apprenticed to the Public Works Department in Townsville as a teenager in 1974, and worked with Brown intermittently for eighteen months. The first radio bulletins about the arrest brought back a memory of a 'capable tradesman' who'd once said something so strange the younger man remembered it, word for word.

They'd been driving past Townsville police station in 1975 in Brown's Vauxhall when Hill, then sixteen, had remarked that the police hadn't solved the Mackay sisters' murder. Brown, a 'big-noter' whose habit in conversation was one-upmanship, had said immediately, 'I know all about that – I did it'.

This had troubled Hill. 'It chilled me because of the way his face looked when he said it. But I didn't believe it because it was so out of character for the person I had worked with.'

Hill had a restless night, but Brown seemed at ease next day and the boy didn't ask questions. 'Being a kid, when it wasn't reinforced, I put it to the back of my mind.' But he didn't forget it, either. When Brown was arrested 23 years later, his former apprentice called the police.

He told them about an obsessively neat tradesman who sometimes wore black, horn-rimmed glasses and who had been right under their noses for years. So close, in fact, that no-one had seen him.

FROM the day Brown was arrested, he was described as a roving school maintenance carpenter. This was correct as far as it went, and it was understandable that it was emphasised: the fact Brown had worked at schools, supplied one of the planks of a copybook prosecution case – opportunity and, perhaps, motive.

Brown, after all, had worked at Aitkenvale State School, which the Mackay sisters attended. He was known to eat lunch with the children, who called him 'uncle'. None of which, unfortunately, seemed to strike anyone in 1970, despite the seemingly obvious need to interview any men who had contact with the victims, such as teachers, cleaners, or gardeners.

Such an apparently glaring oversight isn't the only reason several retired or veteran Queensland police might have been secretly embarrassed when Brown was arrested. Schools, in fact, had been a minor part of Brown's rounds. As a Public Works employee, he regularly did jobs in every state public building around Townsville ... he was a familiar face at the police station, the prison, the courthouse and the orphanage.

Brown carried some tools in his car boot, but stored other gear in an outbuilding of the old courthouse to which he had the key. He regularly parked in spots reserved for police next to the police station, and was friendly with the court registrar, the bailiff, the matron at the orphanage and many local police.

Hill recalls that when working at the old police station, Brown usually had 'smoko' with ex-police who worked in the police garage. Hill, in fact, bought his first car from one of them. If working at the courthouse, Brown would have coffee with the bailiff and discuss seized goods due to be auctioned. He was on first-name terms with court staff and police, who called him 'Arty' or 'Browny'.

When police houses needed work, Brown did it. When one

THE INVISIBLE MAN

policeman needed dining chairs mended, Brown arranged for Hill to do it. Brown was a notoriously bad driver and parked wherever he liked, but he boasted that he never got a ticket. He also boasted he knew the most senior police in town, notably Charles Bopf, the man whose brilliant career had only one blot – not finding the Mackay girls' killer.

In a state that had rewarded some senior police with knighthoods, an Order of Australia was the least a grateful Queensland could do for Bopf. Townsville's best-known detective for years, and head of the state's new homicide squad in the 1970s, in retirement he is still a noted citizen in what is an overgrown country town.

Unlike Arthur Brown, whose mind was ostensibly eroded by age, Bopf remained alert. He lectured in law at a local tertiary college, followed current and legal affairs, and easily summoned details of his career after joining the force from the railways in 1946. But no-one's perfect: the sleuth who made a living for almost 40 years with his memory for names and faces had trouble recalling a man who claimed to know him well, and he swiftly ended conversations that raised the question.

As a youngster in the 1960s, Christine Millier was walking in the street with Brown when he stopped to chat to Bopf, and made a great show of introducing her to him. Afterwards, he claimed 'Bopfy' as 'a mate' and boasted that he was chief of police in all of Townsville. This overstated Bopf's rank, and probably the relationship, if indeed there was anything more to it than Brown scraping acquaintance with an authority figure.

But the fact remains that in 1970s Townsville, Brown knew the police well enough that he blended into the scenery, and police knew his car so well nobody even noticed that it once had an odd-coloured door. They were looking for a Holden driven by a crazed killer, not a Vauxhall driven by someone they knew. Familiarity breeds contempt. Like the postman who appears at the same time every day, Arthur Brown had become invisible.

John Hill marvels at how trusted Brown was around the police station. Brown worked any hours he liked, and Hill thinks that if he'd wanted to he could have got access to records and files. Speculation, perhaps. And yet ...

When police spoke to Neil Lunney in 1998 he said he'd made a statement in 1970, but was told it was missing. They had found his name with others on an old file note, and had a record of him taking part in an identification parade in 1971, but nothing else.

It wasn't the only evidence to disappear. Samples taken from the murder scene were, apparently, lost when the police forensic section in Brisbane was flooded in 1974.

The floods of 1974 – which struck vast areas of Queensland – might also explain why there are no Public Works records of Brown's work history. There is no record of when he joined the department, no pay records and, crucially, no record of when he took leave, when he was absent, or for what periods he was not sighted by a supervisor.

With Brown, at almost 90, unwilling or unable to answer detailed questions, his working life was a mystery. He didn't have to report to work except to draw his pay and pick up maintenance requests. He was trusted to work unsupervised. The state couldn't have employed a more careful man.

JUST as southerners go north in winter, seeking the sun, northerners head south in summer to avoid it. One of the perks of working for the Queensland Government north of Rockhampton is getting five weeks' annual leave instead of four – a legacy of when it took a week to travel to and from

Brisbane by train or steamer. But, by the 1960s and 1970s, with better roads and cars, a traveller could go a long way in a week – and five weeks was enough time to visit Sydney, Melbourne or Adelaide. Relatives know that the Browns visited the youngest of his wife's sisters and her husband in Victoria more than once. No-one willing to talk about it now knows if Brown ever went on to South Australia.

But Christine Millier has her suspicions. She believes the man she's known all her life killed the Mackay sisters, and that the fact a jury did not reach a verdict in a murder trial proves only that its members could not be told everything the family and the police know.

There are coincidences that intrigue investigators, though they would never be put before a jury. Judith and Susan Mackay's bodies were found at Antill Creek at the spot where Brown had taken little girls to molest them. That place was only 500 metres from where the body of a murdered teenager was found in 1975.

Her name was Catherine Graham, and she was last seen selling encyclopaedias door to door, near Brown's house. The last night of her life, she had made a call to her mother in Brisbane from a public telephone box.

The last thing Graham told her mother was that a man was standing near the telephone box, staring at her, and that she didn't like the look of him.

Other things unsettle Millier and her sister, Merle Moss.

They believe that around the time of Marilyn Wallman's disappearance in 1972, the Browns were visiting Hester's relatives nearby, in Mackay. Their car broke down, causing them to come home by train. Brown returned alone to get the car, the story goes, and didn't come back to Townsville for some time.

All the police can confirm is that a 'chalky blue' Vauxhall was seen in the district around the time of Marilyn Wallman's disappearance.

In early 1991, Christine was working as a carer with teenage wards of the state, at what had been the local orphanage, where Brown had once been a regular visitor as maintenance man. On Wednesday, January 23, she wrote in her diary: 'Kids (state wards) and I went for walk to Strand. Arthur Brown drove by and the kids called him "rock spider", shouting it out. Eventually they told me what a rock spider was.'

'Rock spider' is prison slang, never used jokingly, for a child molester. Somehow, at 79, Brown had a reputation outside the family as a sex offender.

Some instincts die hard. In Brown, the reflex to boast about what he'd seen and done was stronger, at times, than his sense of self-preservation.

Buildings were a favourite topic. He had a carpenter's eye for the way they were made and where they were, and once he saw a building he didn't forget it.

Talk about other cities, and he'd talk about something he'd seen there. Mention Sydney and it was Martin Place; Brisbane and it was The Valley; Melbourne he knew backwards, of course, having lived there. Perth he'd never seen.

And Adelaide? It seemed to Christine that he'd been there, too.

When the city's name came up one day, he mentioned seeing the Festival Theatre when it was almost finished. He agreed when she said what a beautiful building it was, with the steps down to it, looking over the river to the oval.

Work on the Adelaide Festival Theatre, commissioned in the 1960s, started in 1970, and the first stage was completed in June 1973, when a symphony orchestra performed in it for the first time. Joanne Ratcliffe and Kirste Gordon were abducted from the Adelaide Oval on August 25, 1973. It was Australia's worst child abduction case since Grant, Arnna and Jane Beaumont were abducted from Glenelg Beach on Australia Day, 1966. Their bodies were never found.

In a corner of the prosecutor's office in Townsville is a board with half a dozen photographs on it of Arthur Stanley Brown at different stages of his life, in different clothes, bareheaded and wearing hats.

In the middle of the collection is a computer-generated sketch of a man's face, based on the recollection of the schoolteacher who saw a driver staring at the Mackay girls before they were abducted.

The similarity between the sketch and the photographs is striking.

So is the resemblance to the police sketch of the man seen taking two girls from the Adelaide Oval in 1973.

In July, 2001, 28 years after Kirste Gordon and Joanne Ratcliffe disappeared, South Australian Police had still not taken a signed statement from Sue Lawrie about the thin-faced man she saw.

• In October 1999 a Queensland Supreme Court jury was unable to reach a verdict when Brown stood trial. A retrial was ordered, but Brown was ruled unfit to face court because he was suffering Alzheimer's disease.

On July 6, 2002, Arthur Brown died a free man in a Malanda nursing home in North Queensland. He passed away peacefully, unlike his murder victims.

The retired carpenter who found the sisters' bodies at Antill Creek said, 'I'm bloody pleased he's dead. I wish he died years ago.'

The girls' father, Bill Mackay, said, 'Everyone is convinced it was him. There's no doubt about that.'

Their mother Thelma Mackay said, 'It's pathetic to think he got away with it.'

Charles Bopf, the detective Brown claimed as a friend said it was just 'sheer luck' that Brown had escaped notice more than 30 years earlier.

'Everybody's pointing the finger at him now, but no-one bothered to tell us anything about it then.'

CHAPTER 2

The Puppet Master

'She said that Philip was an evil boy'

FOR many of those who gathered at the Springvale Cemetery that muggy spring day, it was not Phyllis Hocking's death that was the shock – her health had been fading for years. It was the senseless way the old lady died – the seemingly random victim of a prowler, who found her in the lounge room of an average house in an average street in middle Melbourne.

There were hundreds of mourners there to say goodbye. It was the day before the Melbourne Cup and Mrs Hocking's birthday. She would have turned 80 had she not been clubbed to death a few days earlier.

No burglar needed to fear her, slowed as she was by three hip replacements, a stroke and failing eyesight. Yet, instead of escaping, he bashed her again and again with a tyre lever, until she was lying dead in her son's Box Hill home.

The ferocity of the assault told police the attacker had not planned to just stun his victim. The blood found splattered on the walls, bookcase and ceiling of the room, from at least three – and up to ten – savage blows showed he was determined to kill.

But why?

If robbery was the motive why hadn't he bothered to take the $400 she had in the bag she was clutching when he attacked from behind? If it was a burglary, then why was the stereo equipment still stacked in the laundry, waiting to be loaded into a robber's van?

The death of Phyllis Hocking reflects the concerns we face as we grow older. It is not so much death we fear, but that we might no longer be able to make our own way in life.

Widowed and increasingly immobile, Phyllis Hocking had to rely on others – and they let her down.

Some of the mourners noticed her adopted son, Philip, at the chapel. A friend who had known Phyllis for 50 years was to later observe: 'He didn't speak to anyone at the funeral and he left out the side door straight after the service. I couldn't understand his behaviour at all.'

Some assumed he was a grieving son who was too upset for small talk.

Others, who had known him as a child and later as a man, were not prepared to give him the benefit of the doubt.

PHYLLIS Hocking was the middle child of a close family that spent the 1920s and 1930s moving around Victoria. Her schoolteacher father, William Wannan, took country postings before settling as English and History master at University High School.

She was educated at Bairnsdale and Essendon high schools and, later, at the Emily McPherson College before becoming a domestic science teacher who, like her father, enjoyed country schools and the rural lifestyle.

While teaching at Maryborough, she met a big, stern-faced local engineer, named Jack Hocking. They married and moved to Charlton, where Jack was appointed shire engineer in June 1942. As was the custom of the time, Phyllis gave up work as she prepared for her next role – as a supportive wife and, she hoped, a loving mother.

The young couple became friends with the local newspaper owner, John Richardson, and his wife, Rena. They lived in the same street and the women became life-long confidantes. Phyllis was to tell her friend that while she was happy, there was a void in her life.

'Phyllis knew she couldn't have any children. They were going to adopt a little boy, but they only had him about six weeks when the mother wanted him back,' Rena would tell police 51 years later.

'Philip was a little boy when he was adopted, he wasn't a baby. I found out later on that he had a sister. Phyllis had wanted to adopt both, but Jack only wanted to adopt the little boy.

'Philip grew up in Charlton. He joined the Cubs and the Scouts and was very clever. He went to primary school in Charlton and then he went to Geelong College. Jack was strict with Philip but not overly so. He just demanded good behaviour.'

Older residents in the district still remember the tall and graceful Phyllis and her shy husband, with warmth and respect. Former St Arnaud mayor and editor of the *North Central News*, Ella Ebery, says Jack Hocking was not only a hard-working engineer, but a conservationist long before it was fashionable.

While the post-war, rural culture was to clear the land for

crops and livestock, Jack Hocking helped plant thousands of trees along country roads, to fight erosion in central Victoria.

'We were both environmentalists and he fought for the trees,' Mrs Ebery said.

The gums that Jack planted now stand tall along the St Arnaud-Charlton road, next to a stone monument built in 1991 to honour his foresight. Former newspaperman and long-time Charlton resident, Ian Cameron, said Jack and Phyllis Hocking 'did everything together'.

'He could be abrupt at times, but she was a lovely, quiet lady.'

While the Hockings were admired in the district, life at home was becoming tense. Big Jack was strict and the son was wilful. Philip was later to say that, when he broke his glasses playing cricket at school, he was too frightened to tell his father and used a broken piece of the lens to try to read notes from the blackboard.

According to Phyllis's younger brother Bill, Jack was 'a product of the old school tie who could be quite rigid. I think he was rather strict with Philip and was determined that he should have a first-class education and that is why he sent him to Geelong College.'

Bill said the adopted boy was always bright and quick to learn. 'We said he was a near-genius in some of the things he did.'

But even in the early years there were worrying signs. In the early 1960s Philip went with his cousin, Paula, to visit their grandmother at Portarlington.

According to Bill, his mother, Ruby, was a tolerant woman who liked children, but she had suddenly sent Philip home in the middle of the holiday. 'I don't know what happened, but she said something that was quite strange. She said that Philip was an evil boy.'

WHILE Philip later often blamed his father for a miserable childhood, the Hockings did not give up on their adopted son. In 1960, he was sent to the elite Geelong College as a boarder. His parents hoped the schoolmasters would be able to nurture the teenager's obvious, but largely undirected, talents.

It didn't work.

He ran away from school in clouded circumstances and returned to Charlton. It was another black mark in his father's book. Jack found it harder to relate to Philip as they both got older. The father was solid and dependable while the son was erratic and unreliable.

Philip was to carry the scars all his life, claiming Jack Hocking was 'an arrogant bully'. He increasingly blamed his adopted father for his own failings. 'My lack of success in many things was due to him,' he said.

The shire engineer spent all his working life fixing problems, with a combination of strong logic and hard work, but he could never repair the frayed relationship with the boy. In the end, they barely spoke.

Jack retired in July 1976, after 34 years at Charlton. The couple moved to Rye and Jack was diagnosed with cancer about eight years later.

It took eighteen months for the disease to spread into his bones and he died in 1985. His slow death was not enough to allow the son to forgive.

'I think there had been a disagreement of some sort and Philip wasn't in contact with them when Jack was ill,' a family friend said later.

As the dying man lay in his hospital bed, he confided to a relative that his greatest regret was that he couldn't rebuild his relationship with Philip.

While Jack had given up on his son years earlier, it wasn't in

Phyllis's nature to stop believing. She hoped that age would give him what his adopted parents had failed to instil – a sense of maturity and the capacity to complete a task. But he was seemingly caught in a depressing cycle of under-achievement, drifting through jobs and relationships, never being able to survive even slight problems without walking away. More disturbingly, he started to make up stories, once claiming to be a British secret service agent who had parachuted into Europe and fallen in love with a Yugoslavian woman.

In real life, he had two children from his first marriage and four from the second. By the time he was middle-aged, he had walked and then stumbled along a number of career paths, including, in his own words, 'electrical contracting, house building, manufacturing of canoes and air-conditioners and publishing'.

'I was a professional punter, I ran an information service, I did computer consulting for a while and ran an art gallery, and was a sculptor for a while.'

He had also been a musician and ran bands, but in 1993 he met a model, while sculpting. This sparked his next big idea. He would be a talent agent, managing a string of successful singers and glamorous models. 'I don't even remember how it happened.'

It just seemed like a good idea at the time.

AFTER her husband died, Phyllis Hocking went on a three-month cruise to England and she returned, determined to rebuild her relationship with her son and his four children from his second marriage.

She sold the house in Rye and bought a unit in Glenhuntly so she could be closer to her brother, Bill. Without Jack and with her own health failing, she asked her best friend, Betty Wilson, to help her control her finances – a move the manipulative

Philip bitterly resented. Soon after moving to the unit, Phyllis went to hospital for her third hip replacement. Philip was too busy to take her to hospital, but she asked if he could look after her small garden.

When she returned, it was obvious he had done nothing. She rang her son to ask what had gone wrong. According to Betty Wilson: 'Philip hung up the phone and wouldn't speak to Phyllis for about two years after that.'

She broke her leg, but this did not move him to take a greater interest in his elderly mother. Phyllis had a stroke when she was 75. Betty found her lying in bed when she dropped in one day.

It fell to Mrs Wilson to ring the son with the news. 'I phoned Philip after the ambulance took Phyllis, to let him know his mother had had a stroke. He appeared unperturbed about it. His only comment was "Oh yeah". I couldn't understand his attitude when he could take it so lightly.'

While Phyllis's daughter-in-law, Josette, a schoolteacher, and the grandchildren visited her in hospital, Philip stayed away, claiming his car had broken down. The frightened and seriously ill woman had to resort to bribery.

If her son would come to visit, she would agree to pay for the car repairs. He turned up and, according to Mrs Wilson: 'I wrote the cheque out (from Phyllis Hocking's account) for Philip, I think it was for $800.'

While she was in hospital her small unit was burgled. Little was taken except a pair of binoculars and a strongbox containing her personal papers.

Phyllis told Betty Wilson she believed Philip had robbed her, but she lacked proof. Some time later, her depressing judgment on her son's character appeared to be vindicated.

While the binoculars were stolen, the thief forgot the leather carry case. Mrs Wilson recalled Phyllis telling her son: 'You have the binoculars, you might as well have the case.' To which Philip had replied: 'Thank you, Mother.'

Bill Wannan said the burglar was looking for more than binoculars when he robbed the Glenhuntly unit. 'Basically, everyone believed Philip had committed the break-in to see if he was in the will.'

He was the cuckoo in the nest demanding more as he got older. Every financial problem would send him back to his mother and every time he wanted to launch a new project, he expected her to be the sponsor. He liked the big picture – but she had to buy the paint and clean up the mess.

She bought him two cars, paid electricity bills and lost money on the failed art gallery. It was still not enough.

It never would be.

Robyn Maile was a nurse who regularly visited Phyllis at Glenhuntly. One day she found the proud, old woman 'extremely distressed and crying'. She had just received a letter from her son claiming it would be 'her fault' if his children were denied a private school education.

She told a professional financial adviser: 'Philip is bleeding me.' She moved to change her will to keep the money away from her son, but later changed her mind again.

According to her brother Bill: 'Phyllis said Philip was a bad man and was after her money.'

But even though she had deep doubts about her son he convinced her she should move into a bungalow behind his house. She would have to pay $2000, of course, to have a shower and toilet fitted.

A few weeks after moving in, she regretted the decision and returned to Glenhuntly, but when a unit in Dunloe Avenue, virtually opposite her son's home, became available, she sold out and moved again.

She believed it would be an ideal compromise. She would be close enough to see her grandchildren regularly, but without sacrificing her independence.

And, for Philip Hocking, it was convenient to have his mother, and her bank books, across the road. When he planned to publish a book, *Guys' Guide To Girls*, he expected her to pay for the 4000-copy print run.

Not only was he a leech, but an ungrateful one. 'My mother was always generous with her money, but she always whinged about it,' he was to comment later.

When Philip started a talent agency, Phyllis became the backer. It was no surprise that he was staggeringly unsuccessful. His one singer ('She wanted to be another Madonna') ran off with the piano player and the one model had the brains to put her shirt back on and seek alternative employment.

Yet with his mother's $20,000 business 'grant' he insisted on having a secretary, an office and a registered business name. What he lacked was any clients or any way to generate money.

Philip Hocking wasn't the only member of the extended family who wanted some of Phyllis's modest savings. His son from his first marriage, Brent, had lived in Darwin with his mother, before coming to Melbourne to start a steam-cleaning business.

If Phyllis was so generous, perhaps she could help out. She lent Brent money for a truck and became annoyed when it wasn't repaid as promised. She had every right to feel used – she had handed over $6000 and asked for only $20 a fortnight in repayments.

Phyllis would have been 91 by the time the principal was repaid. As it turned out, Brent managed to pay back a total of only $400.

Phyllis's anger did not dilute her natural generosity. She gave

Brent a dining setting and two chairs, to help him furnish his home. But soon he was back with a fresh request. Could he have the placemats as well?

Despite the financial strains and her failing health, Phyllis adapted well to life in her new unit. She was driven by council transport to the Kangerong Day Care Centre twice a week and, according to one of the helpers, 'she loved it'.

She would talk about life as a young teacher and tell warm stories about her grandchildren. 'Whenever she did ceramics at Kangerong she'd put roses on them. She was known at the centre as The Rose Lady,' a staff member recalled.

She would borrow large-print books to read and although she had to use a frame or cane to move, she refused to stop enjoying life.

At the elderly citizens' centre, she bought a ticket in a raffle to raise funds for Parkinson's disease research. She won first prize – $10,000 worth of free travel. Too immobile to travel overseas again, she began to give away the prize to people she felt would enjoy a break.

Days before she died, she offered Philip and his wife a week's holiday on Hayman Island.

According to one of the carers, Carol Gent: 'Phyllis didn't talk much about her past. She was a now person.' She told her brother she was planning for the future because, 'after all, I might live another ten years'.

To Philip, that was simply not an acceptable option.

THOSE who made the decision to cheat Phyllis Hocking of her last few years of life, killed her by degrees over months, not minutes.

Police say Philip Hocking tired of taking his mother's modest savings by instalments and devised a plan to take everything.

RATS

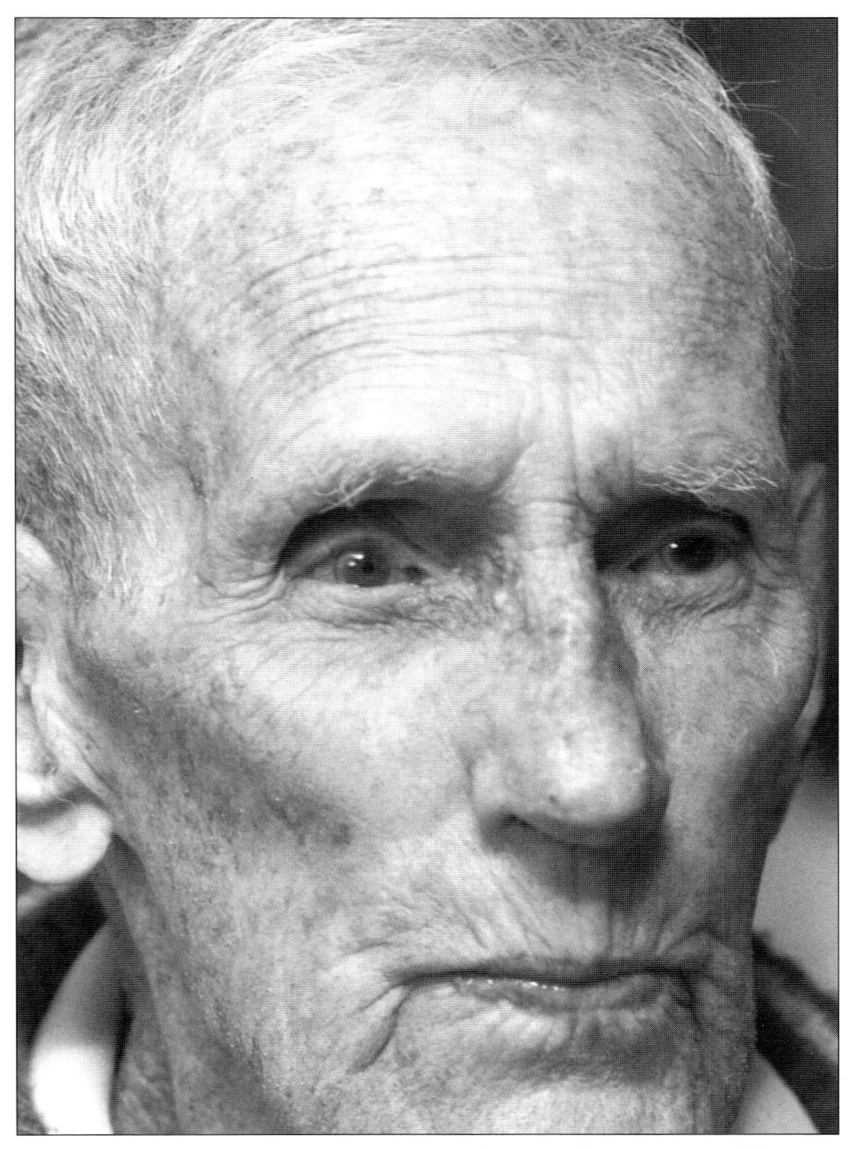

Arthur Stanley Brown ... was he one of Australia's most prolific serial killers? Perhaps he didn't remember.

RATS

If the hat fits. A young Arthur Brown in his trademark hat …

RATS

... and a sketch of the man who abducted Kirste Gordon and Joanne Ratcliffe in Adelaide in 1973. Case unsolved.

RATS

An eerie similarity? Arthur Brown and a police sketch of a suspect in the abduction of the Beaumont children in 1966.

RATS

Judith (left) and Susan Mackay ... abducted and murdered near Townsville in August, 1970. Brown was charged, but died without standing trial.

RATS

Philip's son Brent (above) ... convicted of killing his grandmother on his father's orders.

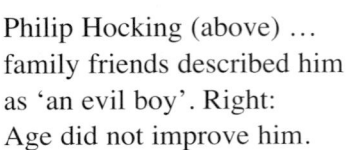

Philip Hocking (above) ... family friends described him as 'an evil boy'. Right: Age did not improve him.

RATS

Phyllis and husband Jack ... adopted a son. It would destroy them both.

RATS

The first attempt to kill Phyllis Hocking ... she escaped this fire in her home unit.

RATS

Philip Hocking ... sailing to freedom while his son sits in jail.

RATS

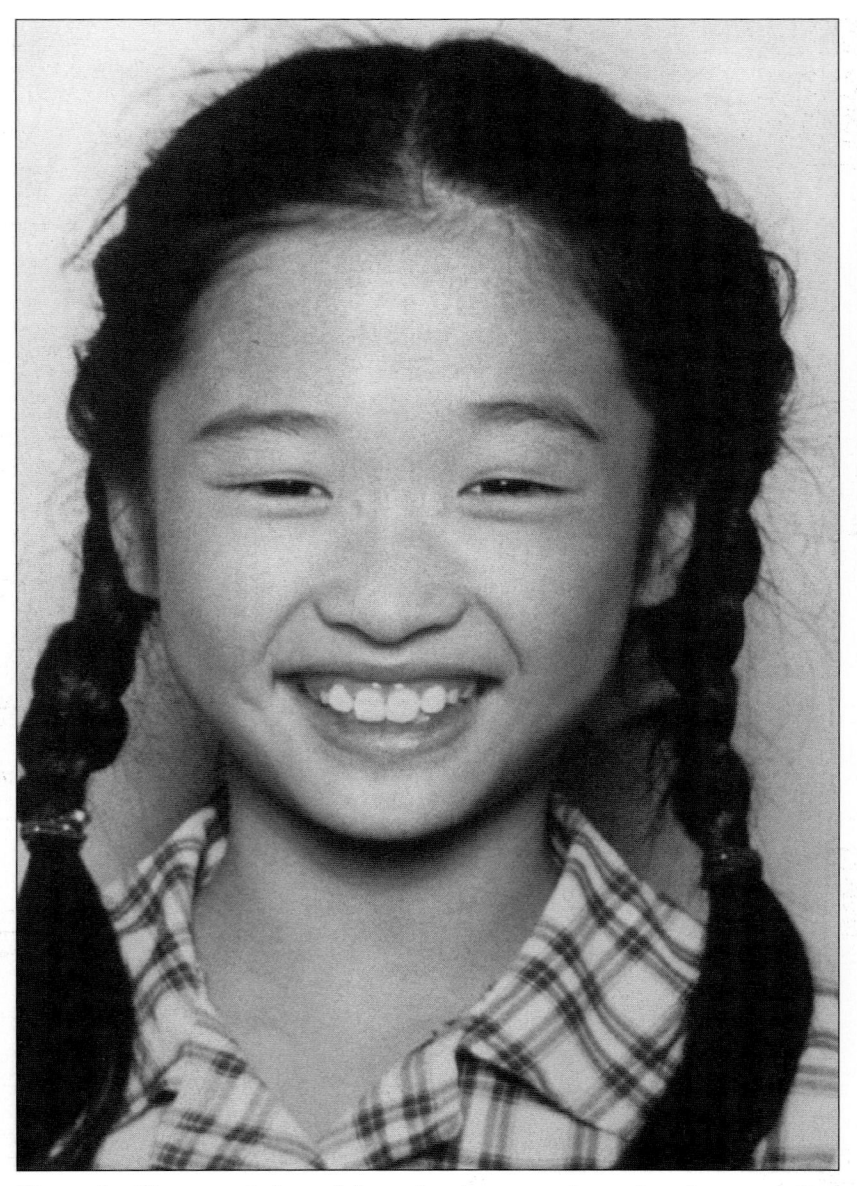

Karmein Chan ... abducted from her home and murdered.

RATS

Karmein ... the mystery remains.

RATS

Easey Street victim Suzanne Armstrong and son Gregory. Her friend Susan Bartlett (inset) was also killed.

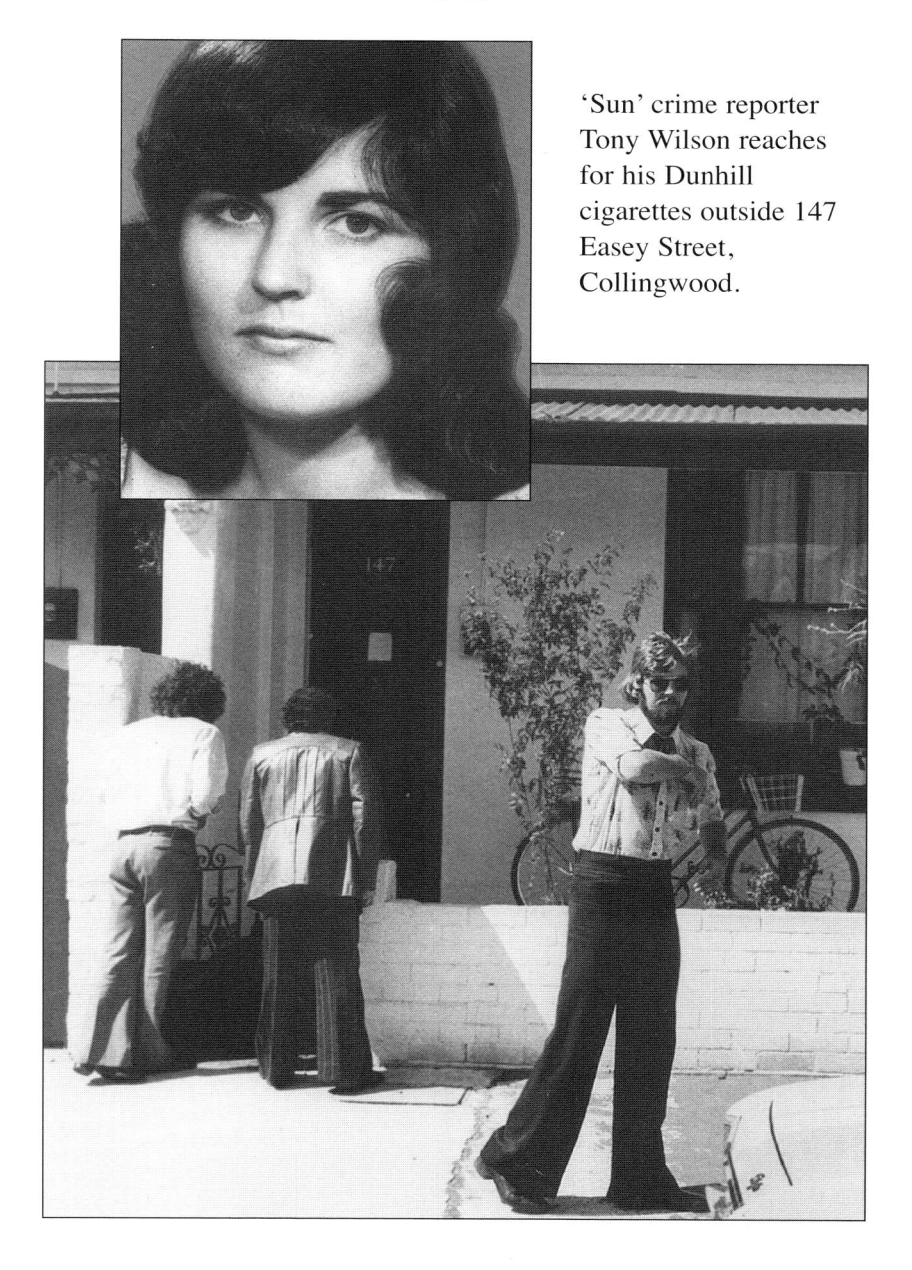

RATS

'Sun' crime reporter Tony Wilson reaches for his Dunhill cigarettes outside 147 Easey Street, Collingwood.

RATS

RATS

Rogue barrister Robert 'Rolls Royce' Vernon ... the closest he got to silk was women's underwear.

RATS

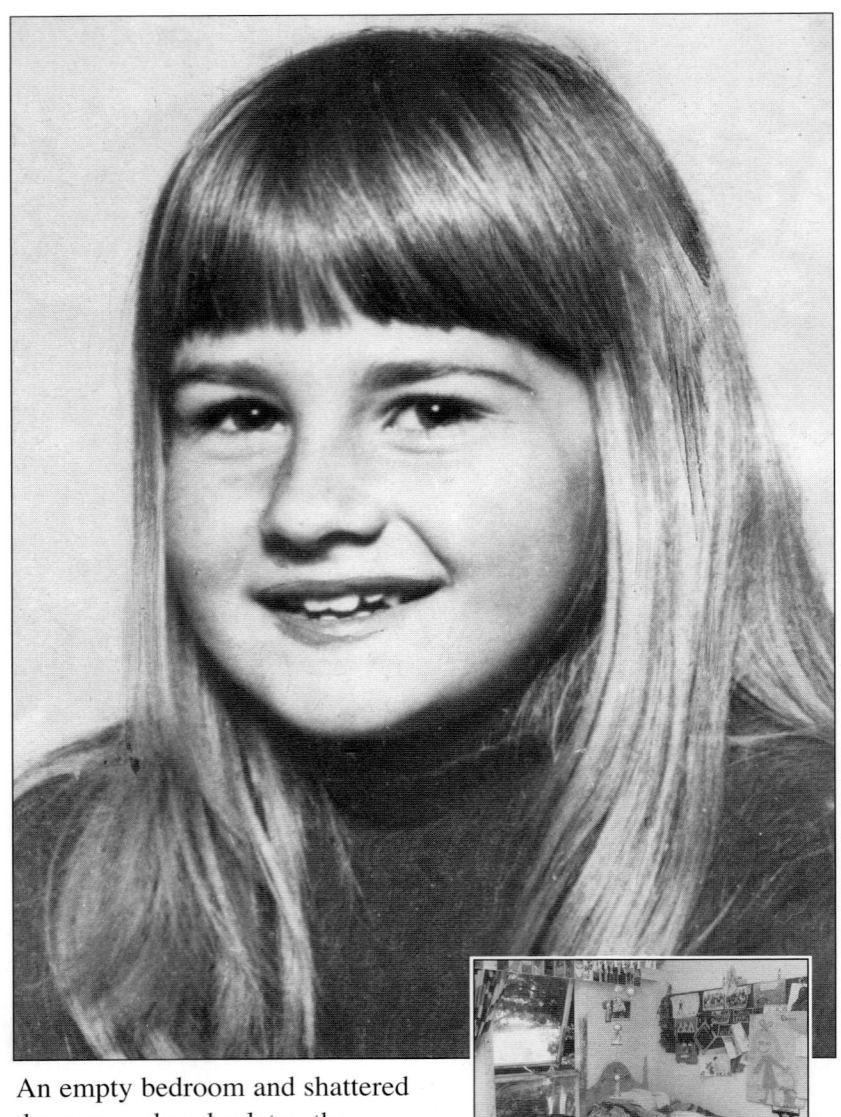

An empty bedroom and shattered dreams ... decades later, the disappearance of Eloise Worledge still haunts.

The first step required the woman to be scared out her Box Hill unit and into a home. But he needed someone he could manipulate. He turned to his adult son from his first marriage, Brent – the one who'd got his grandmother's dining table, chairs, placemats and a $20,000 loan.

While the son desperately wanted his father's approval, the daughter from the first marriage, Rachael Ovelsen, could see through the big talk and slick manner.

'I could not stand my father and he actually gave me the creeps. (But) Brent idolised our father, Philip, and wanted to be like him. He (her father) was always interested in money and scheming to make money. I would describe him as greedy. Money is all he ever talked about. Despite this, Brent still had great affection for our father and saw him as an entrepreneur.'

Years later, Brent was to confess that his father instructed him to break in and trash Phyllis's unit, making sure the burglary looked as if it had been carried out by teenagers.

Brent said his father told him to break into the Box Hill unit and: 'Mess it all up and she'll get such a fright she'll want to move out. He said: "If you scare her, we'll be able to get her to move in to a home and then I can access her money".'

Like a good son, Brent did what he was told.

On July 16, 1993, he broke into the unit, grabbed some cash, a little jewellery and a stamp collection. But what really hurt the houseproud woman was that the intruder poured soft drinks and alcohol over the carpets.

According to friends at the day care centre, she was devastated. Betty Wilson said Phyllis asked her professional carpet-cleaning grandson to help deal with the mess. After all, she had helped fund the business.

He was happy to help – at a price.

'She mentioned she was going to give him $300 initially, but then she wasn't going to give him that much,' Mrs Wilson said. Phyllis Wilson had lived through wars, depressions, droughts and the death of her husband. A minor burglary, no matter how traumatic, was not going to frighten her off her property. For the scheming, adopted son, it was time for 'Plan B'. He would burn her out. According to Brent, his father said: 'I want you to throw a fire-bomb in there.'

'I said: "If you want me to do that, I'll do it".' According to Brent, the plan was no longer to scare but to kill. 'He wanted to burn the house down and she would pass away.'

The father and son team did not know that Mrs Hocking had recently fitted a smoke detector in the unit and had the habit of keeping the key in the internal lock on the front door.

On August 8, Brent Hocking spray-painted the words 'Piss off Poofs' on a garage wall near the units – an attempt to lead police to conclude the attack was directed at a homosexual couple living nearby.

He then threw a firebomb – made of a petrol-filled stubby with a material wick – into his grandmother's home. When the smoke alarm sounded, Phyllis opened her bedroom door to what Betty Wilson said was a 'wall of fire ... if she had've been fumbling for a key, she would have never have made it out. Even her hair was singed.'

She survived, but her unit and her independence were finally destroyed. She had no choice but to move across the road to her son's house the next day. Even though she had spent $2000 to renovate the bungalow, Philip decided it was inappropriate for her, as one of his sons and a dog were living there.

She was put in the lounge as 'the only room really available' in the modest weatherboard home.

The house was owned by the generous brother of Philip's wife, who only asked for enough money to cover rates and electricity on the property – $123 a month. When Phyllis moved in, her son couldn't resist the chance of a profit and charged her board of $100 a week.

Philip Hocking was to tell police that he loved his mother and she was happy in his home. 'It has been about three months, but it feels like it was only three weeks. She really was a pleasure to have around.

'For example, we had a dishwasher, but we didn't even use it for two months, as she would do the dishes. She would also help with the housework and tidying up.

'My relationship with my mother was excellent ... I was her life.'

But Phyllis was to tell another story. Ten days before she died she went to see a friend who asked how she was coping, living with her son. 'She just spat out the words, "I hate it, but I'm all right".'

'Phyllis used to tell me very often that she thought there was something wrong with Philip.'

Mrs Wilson drove from Rye to Box Hill every two weeks to check on her friend and watched as the once strong and independent woman became increasingly frail, vulnerable and frightened.

'She was most unhappy staying at Philip's.'

Her spirits lifted on Mrs Wilson's visits. She asked her son to get some sandwiches for the special occasion.

'When I was there, Phyllis handed Philip $20 for the sandwiches and Philip just took it and put it in his pocket.'

IF Philip Hocking's plan was to drive his adopted mother into a retirement home, then his life-long failure to grasp economic realities was again exposed.

The elderly woman began to look at alternative accommodation and was taken with a home that required an up-front payment of $50,000 with a small monthly rental.

According to Brent, his father was 'really pissed off and he told me: "You've got to make sure you get her" and, you know: "That's not good enough".' Philip considered killing his mother and hiding the body in a concrete-filled hot-water tank. He then told Brent: 'I'll chuck her down a mine shaft.'

But Philip knew enough about the law to understand that if his mother just disappeared, the estate could be tied up for years. 'He decided he didn't want that ... her going missing was no good because it'd take forever for him to get the money,' Brent said.

Brent said that Philip wanted his son to pretend to be a burglar, then: 'Get a steel bar and just whack her over the head.'

Brent said his father promised him $20,000 from the estate for a new steam-cleaning machine, if he went ahead with the murder. Dad would keep the rest.

On October 26, 1993, Phyllis was taken to the nearby senior citizens' club and her grandson, then just 21 and armed with an iron bar, waited in the bedroom for her to return. 'My father drove me there and backed me in the drive in his car.'

The back door was forced with a screwdriver and electronic gear was stacked near the laundry to make police believe a burglar had entered the house.

Philip went home about 1pm. He would later tell police he needed to pick up a video for work. He checked the letterbox and found a little bonus – a $2000 cheque made out to his mother from the insurance company, as compensation for the break-in at her unit three months earlier.

He then went back to work for lunch with his secretary and they discussed at length the problems she was having with her boyfriend. He was his usual self, showing no signs that he knew his mother had less than an hour to live.

Council driver, Michael Cowden, drove Phyllis home a few minutes before 2pm and watched her walk slowly up the driveway to the back door.

Brent knew she was coming. His father had set up a homemade alarm system, so that a buzzer sounded when an infra-red beam was broken in the drive. When she entered the lounge, he struck her from behind at least three times on the neck and head. He later dumped the tyre lever in a river.

Philip Hocking left work as usual around 3.20pm to pick up his two young children from school. It was a warm afternoon and he had every reason to be in a good mood so he stopped at a local milk bar to treat the girls to icy-poles.

When he got to the rear of the house, he saw the door was open and spotted tiny scratch marks around the frame. He walked in and saw stereo equipment stacked in the laundry and said he thought: 'Looks as though we've been burgled again.'

Despite the fact he and his mother had been burgled five times and her unit had been firebombed, he remained calm.

Hocking had personal experience of how dangerous burglars could be. The previous year he'd found an intruder armed with a knife, in his own kitchen. He said the man attacked him and knocked him unconscious.

Yet, despite this, it did not apparently dawn on Hocking that the burglars could still be inside, even though he could see his gear stacked near the back door.

Then he did something puzzling. He let his two youngest children into the house and made them go upstairs to watch television. He felt they may be distressed if they discovered a 'mess' downstairs.

He didn't seem to think the burglars could have made a mess upstairs or could still have been in that part of the house, where they could grab his children.

He either wasn't thinking clearly – or he knew exactly what he was going to find.

He said he was in such shock when he found his mother covered with blood that he couldn't remember his wife's work number and eventually rang the emergency 000. 'From there it all became a little hazy.'

Blood was found all around the room, next to popular novels, including *The Jackal*, and next to her Bible. When police opened the Bible they found it had been cut so she could hide a gold necklace.

There was a movie poster in the front hallway. It was of the Kevin Costner hit, *The Bodyguard*.

CHARLIE Bezzina had been a policeman for twenty years and a homicide detective for four when he walked into the crime scene where Phyllis Hocking lay dead.

Years of experience as a suburban detective and a senior investigator told him this was no burglary. 'The cords on the stereo gear stacked up had been cut. This meant the thief would not have been able to re-sell the gear,' he said.

He said police checked local burglary patterns and spoke to local thieves. 'It didn't make much sense.'

Phyllis Hocking was wearing a watch, which was smashed. It had stopped at 2.05. Later tests proved the watch was not working and had been smashed somewhere else, then put on her wrist.

Police believe the watch was supposed to provide Philip with an alibi, as it was set at the time he was to see prospective clients in his office.

Philip Hocking was an obvious suspect and he was interviewed at length on the day of the murder. 'While he had an alibi he remained one of a number of suspects,' Detective

Senior Sergeant Bezzina said. 'We tend to start from those closest to the victims and then work out in larger circles.'

Police wanted public help to catch the killer and they asked Philip if he would talk to the media to push the cause. Never shy, he jumped at the chance. Less than a day after discovering the body, he was on air with 3AW's Neil Mitchell, playing the role of the grieving son.

'She was 80 next week. We were organising her birthday party,' he said. 'Well, you know, I'm on here Neil, because I think that somebody probably knows who did this and I think they should stop this person.'

Later that day he went to a media conference at the CIB headquarters in St Kilda Road to plead for help to catch his mother's killer.

He said that when he found the body: 'I went to pieces pretty much ... one push and she would've toppled over ... she couldn't hurt a fly really.'

In an interview with journalist, Tara Brown, on *A Current Affair*, Hocking accepted he was a suspect for his mother's murder. '(It) doesn't surprise me at all. I'd be very surprised if I wasn't.' He said he was an obvious suspect because 'Our family stands to gain financially.'

When Charlie Bezzina learned of the firebombing and burglaries when Phyllis lived across the road, it further discredited the burglary-gone-wrong theory. 'We thought she was either the unluckiest lady in the world or the victim of some vendetta.'

The obvious question that police wanted to know was who would benefit most from her death. It was Philip Hocking.

DESPITE a $50,000 reward, the case stalled and in 1995 Charlie Bezzina took promotion and transferred from the homicide squad. But when he returned two years later, he was quick to pick up the investigation again.

On August 25, 1998, a woman arrived at the St Kilda Road office of the homicide squad with information on the murder of an old lady. The informant was Kathleen Andrews, Brent Hocking's former wife. She told Bezzina the couple had split, but on January 27, 1996, they went to a Fitzroy restaurant to discuss a reconciliation. They decided they should make a fresh start.

'We had about two glasses of red wine each and Brent said that he wanted to be totally honest with me because of what he'd put me through.' He spoke of previous affairs and mistakes before they decided to try again.

It was a warm night and as they strolled back to Brent's two-storey town house off Brunswick Street, he continued his new display of honesty. He turned to her and said: 'By the way, it was me that killed Granny Hocking.'

One of Brent's former business partner and friends, Matthew Vicendese, was then to tell police of a conversation they had after a bottle of bourbon whisky.

They discussed building the carpet-cleaning business, then moving into art dealing and running giant dance parties – but they needed money.

Vicendese jokingly said: 'We could bump off my grandfather for the inheritance.'

Hocking's mood changed. 'He went all serious and told me not to do it. He then said he had done "something similar" five years ago and it had been the cause of constant bad luck since.'

Vicendese asked a few questions and Hocking said he hit his grandmother three times with a metal object. 'It was that easy.'

'I was shocked at what he had said and he appeared very moved and was crying when saying to me that his father pushed him into it.'

Brent, who had changed his name to Japaljarri after he began selling Aboriginal art, knew he was the target of the fresh investigation into the murder. Friends would ring him to say Charlie Bezzina and his team of homicide detectives were asking new questions. Japaljarri went to see his sister, Rachael Ovelsen, on February 21, 1999, and confessed that he had killed Phyllis.

'Our father had been brainwashing Brent for months, telling him how evil Granny was and how badly she'd treated our father when he was young,' she would tell police.

Brent said he knew he might still have been able to get away with the murder but he wanted 'to tell the whole truth'.

Ms Ovelsen rang the Hawthorn police and asked them to come over. As soon as a policeman and woman arrived, Japaljarri told his story. 'My father finally asked me to knock her off while she was staying at his house and so one day when she was alone, I went over there, knocked her over the head with a steel bar and killed her.'

They rang the homicide squad and Charlie Bezzina took control. Japaljarri said: 'I'd rather clean the slate and I also wanted to bring my father into this, because he's the person that coerced me into doing it and I want him brought to justice as well, and I understand that I know I'll probably go to jail, but that's fine.

'He's a con man and he's addicted to making money and addicted to not caring whether it's legitimate.'

Within hours of Japaljarri being arrested, Philip Hocking rang Rachel from New Zealand. 'He tried to press me into telling him what Brent had told the police, but I refused. I was cold and direct to him and he seemed nervous and he hung up.'

Japaljarri was charged with murder, and during his committal hearing at the Melbourne Magistrates Court, his father was called to give evidence. Far from being frightened or concerned for himself, the serial under-achiever seemed to relish the attention when he first entered the witness box.

He didn't want to answer certain questions and was dismissive of legal procedure. During the lunch break he employed a lawyer who told the court during the afternoon session that Hocking would refuse to testify on the grounds of self-incrimination. He was excused. Several people in the court said he turned and smirked at his son, who was facing life in prison.

Months later Philip's lawyer contacted the homicide squad wanting to find Hocking. He had failed to pay his bills.

WHEN, in the spring of 2000, Justice Frank 'The Tank' Vincent sentenced Japaljarri to a minimum of fifteen years for the murder of Phyllis Hocking, he gave the impression he wouldn't have minded if Philip had been in the dock with his son.

He said Japaljarri claimed his father originally asked him to break into his grandmother's Box Hill unit 'so she'd go into an old persons' home and he could get hold of her money earlier'.

'I accept that there is a high probability that this was the case,' Justice Vincent said. The Supreme Court judge said he also believed the firebombing was Philip's idea. 'I accept your claim that your actions on this occasion were also carried out at your father's request and partly to assist him in his endeavours to secure access to your grandmother's assets.

'It seems that your father was incensed by the failure of the arson attack and became even more determined to have his mother killed.

'I think it is likely, as you claim, that you were driven by your father to his home and some joint activity then undertaken to create the impression the burglars had been disturbed. He then left and returned to his business premises.'

Justice Vincent gave the clear impression he hoped the investigation would not stop with just one conviction: 'I have also taken into account in your favour the fact that you are prepared to give evidence against your father should he ever be charged in relation to Mrs Hocking's death.'

When Phyllis Hocking died, she left a will and an estate worth $350,372.56. It included nearly $200,000 in five bank accounts; the Box Hill unit, valued at $120,000; and $22,000 from insurance claims from the fire and burglary. Her list of assets was meticulous, including $106.55 from her TAB phone account.

In a clear-cut case of leaving a fox in charge of the henhouse, Philip (and his blameless wife, Josette) was named as the executors.

Phyllis declared she wanted $3000 and a lounge suite to go to her good friend, Betty Wilson, and a claw-and-ball-foot table to another friend. It is unlikely that any of her furniture survived the fire. She also wanted $10,000 to go to the Charlton Retirement Section of the bush nursing hospital.

The bulk of the estate, more than $335,000, went to Philip Hocking and his wife. Shortly after the will was cleared Philip gave his son $20,000 for the steam-cleaning machine as he had earlier promised.

After all, a deal is a deal.

The Hockings' marriage did not survive and, without the burden of immediate financial pressure, Philip broadened his horizons. He bought a luxury yacht and took up sailing.

He settled in New Zealand with another partner. After his son was convicted, he rang a lawyer at the Office of Public Prosecutions inquiring about the result.

Phyllis's brother, Bill Wannan, is a prolific author and a respected journalist who has used his logic and curiosity to solve many mysteries – including finding the Petrovs, the Russian spy couple who made headlines during the Cold War.

Mr Wannan has no doubt that Philip Hocking planned the murder and duped his son into being the killer. 'Brent killed Phyllis but what was his motivation? What was there for him to gain and who could possibly pay him to do it? Philip was the only one who would gain from her death.

Justice has only half been done and the real instigator is still at large and that seems wrong.'

Philip's daughter, Rachael, also has no doubt that the real instigator has escaped justice. 'He is incredibly evil,' she says of her own father.

And the detective – Charlie Bezzina? He said that while there was insufficient evidence to charge Philip with murder at present, he was a patient man.

'We have not given up hope. It is our view that this case is not closed. Murders don't go away.'

But sometimes cold-blooded, selfish, greedy, self-obsessed killers do. Without a fresh breakthrough, Philip Hocking will get away with murder.

CHAPTER 3

A House of Cards

*'Karma will get the bloke behind it.
He's stewing in his own juice.'*

IT'S not easy to break a man's arms and legs. It must have taken two men – big, powerful men – to do what they did to George Brown before they killed him.

It was impossible to tell, afterwards, in which order the killers broke his bones. Impossible to tell how long it took, or why they did it that way. Were they trying to get information from him, or sending a warning to others? Or, most barbaric of all, were they inflicting pain for its own sake?

This much is known. Whoever killed George Brown systematically tortured him first. They twisted his left arm until it was wrenched from its socket and the bone snapped. His right arm was shattered above the elbow. 'Like a green stick,' recalls a policeman whose thoughts still often turn to the far-off night he was called to a nightmare.

They used a blunt instrument – probably an iron bar – to do the rest. Both legs were broken above the knee. Death, when it came, was from two savage blows that fractured the skull.

They put Brown's broken body in his old green Ford and drove into the country for almost an hour, followed by a getaway car. There, on a deserted freeway, late at night, they rolled the Ford down a gentle slope about 50 metres off the bitumen.

They doused it and the body in the front seat with what police call 'an accelerant', probably petrol, and set fire to it. Then they drove away – and vanished.

This was not a gangland slaying in Chicago or a drug war in Miami. George Brown was not some Mafia hitman being repaid in kind. He was an Australian horseman.

It happened on an autumn evening in Sydney, in the hours before midnight on April 2, 1984. In the years since, no one has been charged with the murder. And in the racing world to which Brown belonged, where he was liked and is still mourned, the betting is that no one ever will be.

But few talk about who killed him, or why the case remains unsolved. They are too frightened.

THE long road that led a bush boy who loved horses to the big city and violent death, starts in the outback. George Charles Brown was conceived in war but delivered in peace. He was born at the bush hospital in the tiny Queensland town of Miles on December 6, 1945, the last of his parents' four children.

His father, Alan Brown, had fought on the frontline in the Middle East, then New Guinea. During the war, his wife, Margaret, and three older children had lived in Brisbane.

Alan Brown was a bushman, and when he was discharged he used a war-service loan to buy a property called Warramoo, 3500 hectares of lonely country, 20 kilometres from Miles.

A HOUSE OF CARDS

The baby was eleven years younger than the youngest daughter, Jean. Next was Alan junior, known as 'Manny', then Lesley, the oldest.

When George was 15 months old, his mother died. Jean, then 13, became mother, teacher and playmate to the infant with the fair curls and blue eyes. She taught him his first words and, later, to read and write.

She didn't have to teach him to ride. Like his big brother, one of the best horsemen in the district, George loved horses. He sat on a pony before he could talk, rode all over the property behind his sister's saddle at three, and struck out on his own soon after.

There was no telephone, no radio, no television, and no school for Jean and George. Their father and brother often rode off for up to a fortnight, droving cattle, leaving the two home alone.

A lifetime later, Jean's voice quavers as she describes the bond between them. At night, when she was frightened, the little boy would sleep with her. By day, they weren't bored or lonely.

'George rode a pony called Nellie,' she says. 'If he fell off he'd get straight back on. He'd always catch her himself. He was so small he'd climb up on a gate to bridle and saddle her. He never had toys or any other children to play with. He had animals.'

The motherless boy's favourite was a motherless foal he'd reared. He also had a dog, a cat and a calf, and talked to them the way other children talked to each other.

The Browns rarely saw outsiders. George, like Jean, grew up painfully shy with people outside the family.

In 1952, when George was seven, his father died. The property was sold, Jean went to work in Toowoomba, and George went to live with his married sister, Lesley, in the nearby district of Drillham.

He missed Jean. Like many a lonely child, he survived by nursing a dream. He wanted to train horses.

Meanwhile, his brother Manny, a top rodeo rider, had gone to England and become a minor celebrity by training as a bullfighter, an ambition that ended when he was gored at his debut in Spain. Manny returned to England to breed and break in racehorses. In 1962 he married. George, then 17, sailed to England to be best man. He stayed five years.

MANNY Brown got his little brother jobs with good horse trainers. He graduated to the stables of Major Peter Cazalet, where he strapped a horse called Different Class, owned by Gregory Peck, and schooled the Queen Mother's horses over jumps. Within six months, he was riding in steeplechases.

After 30 rides, and a broken collarbone, he gave up race riding to concentrate on training. He was, he decided, getting too big to be a jockey, anyway. About 1967, he decided to come home.

Brown became foreman for the then prominent trainer Brian Courtney at Mentone and, later, Caulfield. He met a country girl, Rose Effting, at a dance in 1969. He was polite, barely drank and didn't smoke – a rarity in racing stables. They married at Cheltenham in 1970; the first of their three children was born the next year.

At Courtney's that year, Brown was pictured in a turf magazine holding two of the stable's best gallopers.

One, ironically, was the crack sprinter Regal Vista – later the medium of one of Australia's most celebrated ring-in scandals, when he was substituted for the plodder Royal School, at Casterton.

Soon after, Brown went to Brisbane to work for trainer Fred Best, at Hendra.

He worked with another Queenslander with the same

surname, Graham 'Chunky' Brown, who remembered him as 'one of the kindest men with a horse you've ever seen'.

When George Brown left to try his luck with a trainer's licence back in Victoria, his mate wasn't to see him again for almost 13 years – until the day they met before a race at Doomben that was probably George's death sentence. But that was later.

Brown's first winner was an old horse called Mark's Kingdom, at Nowra races, trained from stables behind a house his father-in-law owned at Darlington Point, in the Riverina. He worked a few cast-off gallopers, broke in young horses for other people, dreamed of being a city trainer.

The chance came when he landed a job as a private trainer for a retired bookmaker and wealthy owner, Jack Mandel, who had stables next to Randwick racecourse. The boy from the bush was now a bit-player in racing's Hollywood, training alongside the biggest names in the game: T. J. Smith, Cummings and Begg.

A couple of years later he took the plunge as a public trainer, working from rented stables around Randwick. It wasn't easy. Skill and dedication aren't enough to win success in the toughest business outside the boxing ring.

For all his experience, the shy horseman didn't have the flair for self-promotion, the head for figures or the ruthlessness shared by the big names. He landed more than his share of wins with a small team, but winners weren't as regular as the rent and fodder bills.

Brown's dream of making it as a trainer didn't wilt, but his wife did. Rose Brown said later she knew he loved the children, but if it came to spending his last ten dollars on a bag of chaff instead of groceries, the horses would get the chaff. Rose hated racing's uncertainty.

They parted amicably. Rose, her daughter and two sons went back to Darlington Point. They kept in touch, and when George could, he'd send money. 'I couldn't fault him, only that for him the horses came before everything else,' she was to recall. 'I still wanted him to be successful.'

SUCCESS came, but slowly. Despite getting a few city winners, Brown struggled to balance the books. Two of his owners, Geoff Newcombe and Dick Keats, arranged a bank loan so he could pay fodder, float and farriers' bills.

'He'd eat bread and jam three times a day to feed his horses properly,' recalls Keats. 'He'd ride work himself. I remember him riding a rogue horse he had. He'd wrap his legs in newspapers for padding to stop the blistering, because he didn't want to spend money on long boots.'

Yet it looked as if Brown was making it. He was getting bigger owners, and had some boxes on the course as well as rented stables in Tweedmouth Street, Rosebery. He had been earmarked for a twenty-box complex 'on the hill' on the racecourse – a sign of recognition.

Photographs don't do George Brown justice, say those who knew him. For all his travels and his craggy face, he had a naive quality that prompts Brisbane trainer Laurie Mayfield-Smith to say of him: 'He struck me as somebody out of The Sullivans. He wasn't the gangster type. He never bragged about betting, or anything else.'

But Dick Keats noticed changes in Brown in 1983. One was that he started to wear better clothes, giving up the fusty suits he'd stuck to in the tough times. Keats guessed the trainer was spending cash he hadn't had before. He couldn't guess where it came from. And it was clear Brown was worried. By the end of that year, Keats and Newcombe had trouble talking to him, and

A HOUSE OF CARDS

he looked haggard. 'His weight dropped right away. He wasn't happy,' Keats recalls.

BY late 1983, Queensland racing stank. The smell hadn't yet hit the public, but interstate bookmakers were nervous about bizarre form reversals in Brisbane.

The once-fearless Mark Read and several other big Sydney bookies cut Brisbane bets to a quarter. They knew that when certain people plunged large amounts on Brisbane races, they always won. The first public whiff of scandal came in early 1984, when two horses, Wishane Myth and Aquitane, were scratched after being nobbled.

Meanwhile, George Brown was more quiet and moody than ever. He wasn't the type to pour out his heart, but relatives caught hints of inner turmoil in telephone calls.

He told his sister Jean and his brother Manny he was getting threatening calls. Specifically, he had been told that his horse, McGlinchey, 'won't win', on at least two occasions. He told Jean he didn't know 'who would want to do this to me'.

Some time in the two weeks before his death, he told his estranged wife he was worried because he'd been approached to ring-in a horse in Brisbane. He'd been offered 'big money', but didn't want to do it. She asked him who'd made the offer. He said he 'couldn't say'.

Rose Brown was uneasy. On an earlier trip to Sydney, for the children to see their father, she had taken 'a couple of funny phone calls' at his flat.

When she had told him about the calls, he passed it off as a former lover of Pat Goodwin, the woman described as his de facto. He blamed the same man for attempting to burn his car in the street a few months before. In light of later events, Rose doubts he meant it.

KAREN Godfrey was only eighteen, but in the year she'd worked with Brown – 'he was more like a workmate than a boss' – she'd proved herself. So when he sent three horses to the Brisbane autumn carnival in late March 1984, she got the job, with a veteran stablehand called Jackie Paull.

Star of the trio was Different Class, a city winner named after the horse Brown had strapped for Gregory Peck in England. The others were a promising maiden called Young Cavalier, and a bay filly called Risley.

Risley had won two weak races in Sydney the previous year but was not, on form, any better than the 14-1 quoted against her winning the last race at Doomben on March 31, a Saturday.

Brown flew from Sydney for the races. He met his old workmate 'Chunky' Brown. They had a drink 'for old times' sake'.

If George Brown was surprised – or worried – that Risley's registration papers hadn't been checked early that day, or at trackwork during the week, he didn't show it. When stewards called for the papers not long before the race, he said they were at the stables nearby. He went to get them, and was fined $50 for being late.

As he saddled Risley, he told Godfrey there was 'a bit of money' for the filly, but that he didn't like her chances. It was some understatement. Risley was backed from 12-1 to 8-1 in Brisbane and Sydney – and, curiously, from 14-1 to 4-1 at Wollongong. Someone down south liked her chances. Someone who wouldn't be happy when she ran second last.

When Brown checked the filly after the race, 'he was really quiet', the strapper recalls.

Brown's sister, Jean, and her husband were there that day. They later recalled he was concerned by Risley's poor run, and had criticised the jockey.

A HOUSE OF CARDS

They drove him to the airport after the races. They never saw him again.

ARTHUR Harris is an odd man out in Sydney racing. Known for mathematical skill and a phenomenal memory, he is no ordinary racecourse tout, in character or style.

A psychology graduate, philosophy expert and prize-winning classics scholar, Harris turned to setting race markets instead of bridge or chess. For a decade he was a form analyst for bookmakers Bill Waterhouse and his son Robbie ... until late 1984, when the Waterhouse father and son were warned off every racecourse in the world over the Fine Cotton scandal.

David Hickie, a Sydney investigative journalist, publisher and racing expert, says of Harris: 'Arthur carries the history of the last 30 years of NSW racing in his head.'

Both Hickie and former AJC chief steward John 'The Sheriff' Schreck describe Harris as honest, and with racing's interests at heart. That assessment, combined with his passion for keeping records, makes his recollections of some events very interesting.

When Risley went to the barrier at Doomben, the Sydney races at Rosehill were over. Harris was amazed by the amount of money being bet on the unknown filly. He was also surprised to learn first-hand that a well-known bookmaker had backed Risley.

In a statutory declaration Harris swore in September 1997 for the NSW Thoroughbred Racing Board, he stated several intriguing things. One was that he considered backing Risley himself because of the confidence of a bookmaker, but decided not to, 'as I formed the opinion that on its ratings it would be hard-pressed to win ...

'I did, however, watch the horse closely on the closed-circuit TV. After the race I went to (a bookmaker) and said: "It did absolutely nothing".'

GEORGE Brown was rattled. On the Sunday morning after the Doomben race, the small daughter of a friend walked into a loose box where Brown was treating a horse. He screamed at the child. Her father was shocked; they had never seen him behave that way.

Next morning, Brown met another trainer, Les Bridge, at the track to return a borrowed saddle. Years later, Bridge was to choose words carefully as he recalled it. 'He was concerned about some race in Brisbane. He said he was disappointed with the way the horse ran.'

Bridge talked of how much he liked Brown, then added suddenly: 'I know he was unhappy with what happened in Brisbane.' He paused. 'I hope they dig up something.' Another pause. 'You hear different things ... but you hear a lot of things in racing.' End of interview.

That Monday night, Brown was due for dinner at Pat Goodwin's house, a few streets from his Rosebery stables. He didn't make it.

Goodwin later told police she had called him about 6.50pm to say there'd been a call from Brisbane. She said he told her: 'It's been a quiet night ... I will leave here at eight o'clock. I have to drop in on ... '

Then he had paused and said: 'I'll be there at ten past eight.' Goodwin claimed not to know who he intended to see.

An owner, Ted Hendry, rang him twice, about 7.20 and 7.40, and they spoke briefly. Rose Brown rang either just before or just after Hendry's second call. She needed money to take their son Wayne, then eleven, to Sydney to see a specialist. It was a request he would never usually deny, no matter how broke.

But this time, she says, he 'wasn't himself'. He curtly accused Wayne of 'bunging on' the illness. They were staggered. He had never acted like that before.

A HOUSE OF CARDS

'It didn't sound like him,' she says. 'I wonder now if he was with whoever killed him.'

TRAFFIC was light on the F6 freeway at Bulli Tops, near Wollongong, in the hour before midnight. But one driver noticed a car on fire about 50 metres off the northbound lane, and reported it at the toll booth, 23 kilometres away.

A freeway patrol came, but reported the fire was no threat to traffic. Later, someone called the fire brigade, which relayed the call to the Bulli volunteer brigade. It was 28 minutes past midnight.

After putting out the fire, the volunteers saw something in the passenger seat of the blistered green Ford. It was a body. Or what was left of it.

When Senior Constable Peter Strik, of the crime scene unit, arrived, the body was lit up by floodlights, but barely recognisable. The hands, feet and forearms had been burned away.

'It was just a lump of charcoal,' Strik was to say. 'There was no way it could be identified by sight.' Although he didn't know about the broken bones until the post-mortem was done, he could see the stump of the left arm twisted from its socket. He automatically treated it as murder.

'It just didn't look right. I've always wondered why we never got anywhere with that one,' he muses.

ARTHUR Harris was asleep in the unit he used as an office on Tuesday, April 3, when the telephone woke him at 6am. It was Joe Amphlett, who worked for the Australian Jockey Club. He sounded alarmed. He said police believed a body found in a burned-out car overnight was George Brown, and that he'd been murdered.

About 7am, Harris declares, he called a racing identity at his home. Towards the end of a discussion with him, Harris recalls saying: 'Incidentally, there is a scandal at Randwick. The police are everywhere. They think trainer George Brown may have been murdered.' According to Harris, the racing identity said: 'I know about it.'

At Randwick races later that week, Harris approached a man called Jerry Kron, who bet heavily on Brisbane races when big plunges were being landed.

In a statement tendered later at an inquiry, Harris swears: 'I asked him (Kron) what he knew of the George Brown murder. He said: "He was supposed to do a ring-in ... He got cold feet and did not switch horses. The money went on SP and they lost heavily. They sent a couple of men around to teach him a lesson. They were high on drugs and went too far".'

Two years later, in the homicide squad offices, Harris says a detective called Jim Counsel told him the same story, of two Tongans 'who flew from Brisbane on the Sunday before George Brown was murdered and flew back the morning after he was murdered with plenty of cash. They purchased a new sports car'.

RARELY had so many police worked so long on a murder case and produced so little. From the start, the case was clouded by two flimsy theories that attracted headlines and fed rumours.

One, easily discredited, was that Brown owed SP book makers $500,000. Friends and relatives told police he'd always been a small punter, rarely betting more than $50 for himself. Experts said Brown's financial affairs showed no sign of big punting.

Then there was the theory – pushed hard by certain racing and media people within hours of the killing – that it was a 'crime of passion', a brutal variant on the staple homicide police call a 'domestic'.

In fact, the cold-blooded abduction, torture, murder and

public display of the broken body, had the hallmarks of an underworld execution by two or more killers with the intention of creating fear. Some domestic.

A detective who worked on the case still claims his inquiries showed only $3000 was bet on Risley nationwide. Therefore, he says, the murder was probably not connected with a ring-in gone wrong, and was more likely a 'crime of passion'. Intriguingly, 13 years after the murder, the then head of the NSW homicide unit, Jeff Leonard, said the possibility that it was a domestic was still a viable theory.

David Hickie, who checked with bookmakers at the time, says tens of thousands would have been bet on Risley to force interstate odds from 14-1 to 4-1.

John Schreck, later in charge of cleaning up racing in Macau before moving to Hong Kong, dismisses the chances of Brown's murder being a domestic as 'a million to one and drifting'.

A MONTH after the murder, a journalist, Errol Simper, interviewed many racing people, then wrote a story that included these telling paragraphs:

'Besides sadness, there is a considerable amount of silence among those who knew the trainer. They prefer not to discuss his death and, if they do discuss it, many refuse to be identified.

'Some are seemingly – and understandably – very nervous. If nerves aren't the explanation, then the matter may be even more strange. Taut, blanket silence is hardly a typical reaction from people who have just seen an innocent and respected friend and colleague outrageously murdered.'

A generation later, the silence lingers. Racing people once close to Brown are still nervous, tight-lipped and anonymous.

'Money got a bit short for George,' explains a former Sydney trainer cryptically, 'but he got cold feet. Honest people find it hard to do dishonest things.

'Nothing will ever be opened up. It's too big. I think you're better off letting sleeping dogs lie. Karma will get the bloke behind it. He's stewing in his own juice.'

Another friend of Brown says he is angry with what happened, but scared. 'What you are doing is terrifying,' he told the author. 'I have made phone calls and been told to drop it. It's too dangerous for me and my family ... It's too big, too political, for the police.'

But they all agree on one thing. That George Brown died because he did not substitute another horse for Risley.

The identity of the proposed 'ring-in' has never been revealed. Some speculate the so-called masterminds had grown so cocky that they ordered Brown to attempt a brazen substitution of one of his geldings – Different Class or Young Cavalier – for Risley. This, despite the fact they were different shades of bay, had different markings and were the wrong sex.

It sounds farcical. But no more so than the brazen attempt to ring-in Bold Personality as Fine Cotton a few months later. An attempt that arguably failed only because too many people knew, information leaked, and an avalanche of money was bet on Fine Cotton all over Australia and Papua New Guinea, arousing so much suspicion that racegoers were jeering 'ring-in, ring-in' as the horse came back to scale.

WAYNE Brown, now in his 30s, blond and blue-eyed, is hauntingly similar to his father, George. Often, at the races, people stare at him, then introduce themselves as 'friends of your father's'.

They feel sorry for him. Some, he senses, are even ashamed that racing somehow led to the terrible thing that happened when he was eleven. Back then, his mother says, he would sometimes ask her: 'Mum, how come they can find all these murderers, but not dad's?'

Wayne, as his father did, has an ambition. He wants to be a horse trainer. Like his father, he's worked with horses since before he left school: strapping, riding work, the lot. He has driven horse floats for a living, and is now driving semi-trailers to save the money to help set himself up. He's married to an accountant who worked for the Bart Cummings stable and they have young children.

Some day, he promises, he'll train at Randwick. Some day, he'll get stables on the course the way his father was going to. Meanwhile, George Brown's boy has a friendly word for almost everyone. To learn his trade and make a living, he says, he'll work for anyone in the racing game.

Almost anyone, that is.

• *The NSW homicide unit requests that any information about George Brown can be supplied anonymously on 1800 333 000.*

CHAPTER 4

Mr Cruel

Is there a psychologist, doctor, priest or counsellor who shares his secret?

JOHN and Phyllis Chan would have had few concerns about leaving their three young daughters home alone that night. A two-metre fence with electric front gates protected their eighteen-room house built on a triple block in the sprawling Melbourne suburb of Templestowe.

It was a Saturday night, the busiest at the family's popular restaurant in Main Road, Eltham. Their loyal customers expected Phyllis to be front of house as usual. The tiny woman with the loud voice had become part of the package – as much a part of the night out as the better than average Cantonese cuisine she had served for years. She would flit from table to table, intruding on conversations, urging diners to eat and enjoy. She loved to be surrounded by laughter and noise.

John was quieter, content to remain in the background. Some

would later tell police that Phyllis 'wore the pants' in the family. Others would say that his quiet facade hid a tough and uncompromising businessman.

John Chan had moved from Hong Kong in 1975 and, with Phyllis, had worked to create a successful business network built on restaurants and property development.

The couple worked hard and were prepared to make sacrifices, such as not being able to spend as much time with their young children as they would have liked.

Like many first-generation migrants, they wanted to build a wealth base for their children. This meant their eldest daughter, Karmein, at the age of thirteen, had to become a second mother to her younger sisters.

She did not complain and saw it as part of her family duties. She knew no other way.

In return, the family had something that money could not buy in Hong Kong – space and security. Their double-storey house, set on half a hectare in Templestowe's prestigious 'Golden Mile', had five bedrooms, a study, three bathrooms, a gym, spa, sauna, three-car garage, pool and tennis court. They were also able to afford to educate their three daughters at Presbyterian Ladies College in Burwood. Life was hectic, but satisfying. At least on the surface.

The Chans could have been the poster family for multi-cultural Australia but they were to make headlines in tragic circumstances that have never been resolved.

IT had been a typically busy day for the Chan family. John Chan dropped Karmein at her tennis lesson at the Camberwell Tennis Centre, in North Balwyn, about 9am. She had been taking lessons for a year and, while no champion, seemed to enjoy the sport.

She was picked up by her mother at 10.05am. They had breakfast at the Bulleen Plaza Shopping Centre before she was taken to the library to complete research for a school project. She was picked up by family friends, who then collected her sisters from their Chinese language lessons and drove them to the Chans' Eltham restaurant for lunch.

The three daughters stayed with their mother during the afternoon, playing outside the restaurant until a staff member drove them home about 6.30pm. They had just fifteen minutes with their father before he drove out through the electronic gates in his Mercedes, for the ten-minute trip to the restaurant.

It was the way the Chans lived. They had a suburban mansion but little time to enjoy it together. Family moments at home were measured in minutes. There was always work to be done. The parents had become more business partners than a married couple and had taken to sleeping in different rooms.

Karmein read stories to her sisters, aged seven and nine, before they began to watch a Marilyn Monroe special on television in Karmein's bedroom. During a commercial break, about 9pm, Karmein and the nine-year-old slipped out of the room to grab a snack in the kitchen.

As they walked into the hallway, they saw a man in a green-grey tracksuit and dark balaclava, holding a long, silver carving knife. He grabbed both girls by the hair and told them to 'go to the room', pointing to the bedroom they had just left.

He pushed them into the room. The seven-year-old had heard the noise and hid behind the door, but the man saw her and told her to 'come up here'.

He showed them the knife, but assured them, 'I won't hurt you'. He asked if they had any money and they said they didn't. He then asked, 'Where's your mum and dad?' and they told him they were 'at their restaurant'.

He said, 'You two little ones, get in the cupboard.' He opened the cupboard and they got in. He then dragged a bed across the door to block any escape.

They heard Karmein call out, 'Don't do that, don't do that!' The two girls called out for their older sister, and about two minutes later the man came back and asked, 'Are you okay?'

They said they were. It was the last time they saw him.

About ten minutes later, they forced open the door, pushed the bed away and rang their father at the restaurant.

DAVE Sprague wanted an early night that Saturday – April 13, 1991. He had only recently moved to what was then called the rape squad as a detective inspector after a long and exhausting stint in homicide.

Sprague had been joint officer in charge of the task force that had investigated the murders of Steven Tynan and Damian Eyre, two young police officers shot dead in Walsh Street, South Yarra.

The young policemen were ambushed by members of the underworld on October 12, 1988 as a payback, after detectives shot dead armed robbery suspect Graeme Jensen thirteen hours earlier. The taskforce worked under enormous internal pressure and intense public scrutiny for more than two years. On March 26, 1991 – less than three weeks before Karmein Chan was abducted – a jury found the four men charged with the Walsh Street murders not guilty.

It left the taskforce investigators gutted. They had worked hundreds of hours of unpaid overtime and had given all they could. Most – Sprague included – left the unit wanting to reclaim their private lives. The last thing he needed was another long-term investigation. Then the phone rang.

A thirteen-year-old girl had been abducted. At the time, police were hunting a man suspected of up to ten abductions and sexual assaults since 1985. The unknown offender was originally dubbed 'Mr Cool' but later became known as 'Mr Cruel'. It might have been better if 'he' had not been given a name, as it reinforced an impression that there must only be one offender, and that he must look 'cruel'.

As Sprague headed out to Templestowe, he had no way of knowing he would, again, be dragged into a long-term, murky and ultimately frustrating investigation.

Sprague would once more have to sacrifice family and friends to chase shadows. He would be ordered to head another taskforce, this time codenamed *Spectrum*, and told to find the man (or men) the media loved to call Mr Cruel.

The *Spectrum* investigation would last 29 months and cost almost $4million. The taskforce of 40 investigators would examine 27,000 suspects, deal with 10,000 tips and check 30,000 houses. They would arrest 73 people on a range of offences, many relating to sex crimes. But they would never find the man they wanted.

But that was later. As Sprague drove across Melbourne on a rainy Saturday night, detectives at the Chan house were already piecing together what happened during the abduction. They found that while the electronic front gates were shut, a second pedestrian gate was not secured. They also found that doors in the house were unlocked. Strangely, although the intruder could have walked in any door, police believe he cut the flywire screen in the lounge room and forced the wind-out window.

Investigators established that he took Karmein out through the sliding kitchen door. A police dog tracked her scent from the kitchen, through the garden to a gate at the tennis court, then across the court, through a second gate to a side fence and a drop of almost two metres.

The dog followed the trail for almost 300 metres to a temporary driveway, surrounded by trees on a vacant block – a perfect place to conceal a car. Police believe it was at that point the man placed Karmein in a vehicle.

Detectives believe the kidnapper must have planned the crime. 'The offender had ample time to survey the grounds prior to entering the house as there was little or no security,' according to a confidential police report.

'(There were) no outward signs that children reside at the premises – no outside play equipment, no bicycles etc. Mostly confined to indoor recreation.'

There was also another clue. At the front of the house was Mrs Chan's Toyota Camry sedan. Daubed on the bonnet and windscreen were the words, 'Pay back, Asian drug dealer'.

On the driver's side, sprayed in black paint, was 'More and more to come'. Police concluded the graffiti was written by a right-hander.

Investigators guessed the offender wrote the message on the car to leave a false trail for detectives. But if that was a false trail, where was the real one?

When children are abducted in a seemingly random pattern from their homes it creates real fear. Without knowing how the offender selected his victims, there was no way of knowing who would be next.

THERE were several obvious similarities between Karmein Chan's disappearance and other abductions attributed to the offender dubbed Mr Cruel.

Mr Cruel would break into homes, sexually assault or abduct residents and go to extremes not to be identified. He often tied victims the same way and cut phone lines before leaving.

Police had been looking for a man they called the 'Hampton

rapist' who, they suspected, abducted a fourteen-year-old from her home in February 1985. They believed the same man was responsible for attacks in Caulfield, Hawthorn, Brighton, Dingley and Donvale.

He was an opportunist who would break into houses looking for money, but who would sexually assault victims if he had the chance.

The 'Hampton rapist' was believed to be the same man responsible for later attacks, including Karmein Chan's. Much later, after thousands of hours of fruitless investigations, police were to conclude there were probably two offenders – possibly one a copycat.

While some of the Hampton assaults had striking similarities to the later ones, police finally established that the first-known attack by Mr Cruel was in Lower Plenty, in August 1987. In that crime, a man armed with a knife and a gun removed a pane of glass from the lounge room window and broke into a family home about 4am.

He forced both parents onto their stomachs and tied their hands and feet before he locked them in a wardrobe.

Their seven-year-old son was tied to a bed, and the eleven-year-old daughter was then attacked. He cut the phone lines and left after two hours in the house. He used knots favoured by truck drivers and farmers who need to secure loads. He also used sailing knots and others used by anglers and for restringing musical instruments.

The second-known attack was in Ringwood, on December 27, 1988, at 5.30am. This time, the masked intruder, armed with a small handgun and a knife, broke in through the back door. He again forced both parents onto their stomachs and bound and gagged them. He disabled the phones and demanded money. He grabbed their ten-year-old daughter, placed tape over her eyes and stuffed a ball into her mouth. He abducted the girl and released her at the Bayswater High School, eighteen hours later.

On July 3, 1990, he attacked again, this time at 11.30pm, in Canterbury. Again, he was armed with a knife and a gun, broke in through a window and forced one of his victims onto her stomach before tying and gagging her.

He again disabled the phones and searched for money. He placed tape over the eyes of a girl, 13, and drove her to another house, where he kept her for 50 hours before releasing her in Kew. This was no opportunistic burglar turned sex offender. Housebreakers prefer empty homes and soft targets. He appeared to have researched his victims and was prepared to confront parents during the crimes.

IT was always going to be a difficult investigation. The victims were young and the offender was smart. He seemed to have a basic knowledge of forensic evidence and went to extremes to ensure he left no traces. This led some to think he could have been employed in the law enforcement or criminal justice fields.

But one of his victims was able to remain clear-headed during her ordeal. She provided detectives with remarkable information and perceptive observations.

She was re-interviewed in England over five days in late 1991, and her statement was to become one of the main struts in the massive investigation. She was able to say that while the kidnapper wanted to appear in control, he betrayed nerves and his hands shook when he tried to bind his victims.

The young victim gave police details of the house where she was taken. More than a decade later, certain observations that have never been made public remain the most likely chance of police ever finding her attacker.

She told police: 'He appeared to be acting out a fantasy like he was married to me. He showed this by the affection he showed me and how chummy he was to me.' He flattered and flirted with her, seemingly oblivious to the fact he kept her manacled to a bed. He told her she was prettier than the photo released to the media. She was terrified, yet her captor treated the teenager as if the whole event was quite normal. This while he kept her chained by the neck to what police call 'the detention bed'.

He even chatted to her about the investigation and dwelled on media reports.

'When he was reading from the newspapers, he seemed to think it was quite funny that he was being related to these other abductions in the newspapers. He seemed pleased that he had the police in a twist.

'He told me he hadn't been in Victoria eighteen months ago and so he couldn't have committed one of the abductions. I don't know whether he was genuine or not, but I do know he wanted me to believe it.'

The kidnapper told her exactly when she would be released, indicating the crime was planned in detail well before he broke into her house. The girl told police that while she was in the house, she heard planes at low levels, and believed they were coming in to land. The man didn't mention the noise, which led her to conclude he had lived in the house long enough to become used to the aircraft, in the way people who live next to railway tracks no longer hear the trains pass.

More than that, she told police the aircraft were not light planes, but commercial jets. She also said the noise was of planes coming into land, not taking off.

Detectives noted the girl had lived near another airport and concluded she knew what she was talking about. Police were later to check almost 30,000 houses on Melbourne flight paths. It may have been a live lead, but it was to prove to be just another dead end.

WITHIN weeks of Karmein Chan's abduction, police asked experts from the FBI Academy in Quantico in the United States to provide a profile of the kidnapper.

The profilers were adamant: the wanted man was nothing like his public image. They said the Mr Cruel tag would harm the investigation because the public would look for suspects who appeared strange and twisted.

The serial-crime experts said they believed the man was exactly the opposite. He was likely to be well-respected, good with children and seemingly community-minded.

'We believe the offender may reside in the vicinity of the first assault (in Lower Plenty). This is further strengthened by the fact that the offender returned to that same general area in the fourth assault (Chan).

'In cases of serial sexual assault, this type of clustering indicates an area of great significance to the offender. Usually it indicates the offender lives there, while in other cases it reflects his employment.

In this case, we believe it is more probable that the offender resides in that area. In view of the fact that these incidents all occur during school holidays ... we suggest there is a high degree of probability that the offender is involved with a school. He may be employed there or connected with a school in some other capacity.

'The offender has an intense interest in children, especially children in the age group he is assaulting.

'He will spend a great deal of time with these children in what appears to be selfless dedication to students. This apparent dedication may well have earned him recognition and awards (teacher of the year, coach of the year, exceptional volunteer, etc). These types of awards may make the offender appear above suspicion to those who know him.

'It is imperative that the material to be released publicly dispels the myth of the "monster". Citizens have a misconception regarding child molesters ... those who know the offender at this time believe him to be a "nice guy", one who is genuinely interested in and dedicated to helping children and therefore is currently above suspicion. He will have home-made pornography as well as commercial pornography, including bondage and slavery themes.'

The *Spectrum* taskforce concluded that the offender was so well-prepared before every attack, he would have set up alibis to protect himself.

In an internal report sent to police around the state, *Spectrum* investigators said: 'Most offences have been committed during the school holidays or within a short period leading up to the holidays.

'Each offence has been well-planned, indicating the offender spends a great deal of time conducting reconnaissance and surveillance on his victims. If checked by police he will, more than likely, have a pre-planned script to explain his presence.

'The offender is well versed with regard to forensic evidence.

'The offender is cool, calculating and goes to extraordinary lengths to ensure that his victims do not physically see him, his vehicle, or the place of detention.

'He is well-prepared for each offence. Evidence suggests that he carries a kit containing housebreaking implements and other items needed to tie, gag and blindfold his victims (i.e. handcuffs, nylon cord and wire). It is highly likely that the offender responsible for these offences has been disturbed, or even checked by police during his planning process but ... they have not been thoroughly investigated or adequately recorded.'

IT was almost a year after Karmein was abducted that her body was found. A man walking his dog along Edgars Creek in Thomastown found some human remains on April 9, 1992. Police later found her grave. She had been shot three times in the head in an execution-style murder.

Experienced detectives say the method of her death was not consistent with the type of offender they had been hunting. Mr Cruel pretended to be concerned for his victims, using terms of affection such as 'worry wart' and 'missy', and stressed to some he didn't want to hurt them.

Checks through Australia and the US found no cases in which victims in similar crimes had been shot in the same way.

But Phyllis Chan was to tell police that like many young girls in Melbourne her eldest daughter was aware, through media reports, of Mr Cruel. Karmein said if she was ever grabbed she would fight and run.

Perhaps she did and Mr Cruel panicked and shot her. He carried a gun, and despite his veneer of friendliness to his victims, was a violent, vicious sex offender.

And while he liked to appear to his victims that he was in control, he was always terrified of being caught. Two of the girls told police he was shaking violently when he bound and gagged them and only calmed down when he had them in his car and later in his safe house.

While the *Spectrum* taskforce concentrated on Mr Cruel because of the many similarities with the previous abductions, it was increasingly obvious that there was a second possibility that had to be pursued.

As in any investigation, police had to look at all possible

motives. Now it was clear they would have to look at the theory that someone had abducted Karmein to punish her father, John.

Mr Chan was quiet and friendly but had made some enemies in the business world. He could be ruthless and hadn't been successful in building his companies by being a soft touch.

A police report said he was 'lightly questioned ... and offered any assistance into any legal or financial investigation. Appears that he is in a stable financial situation'.

Police investigators found he was an honest man, but like many people in the entertainment and restaurant industry, he had a wide variety of associates, some of whom, apparently unbeknown to Mr Chan, had criminal connections.

John Chan was wealthy. He had a small mortgage, two restaurants, a luxury house, three children at a private school and two Mercedes cars. In the culture of Asian crime it is not unusual to kidnap the eldest child, preferably a son, and then extort money.

For example, in 1996, Le Anh Tuan was abducted from his Glen Waverley home and murdered, as part of a plot to extort money from his wealthy mother.

The Chans didn't have a son. But Karmein was their eldest child. Some police thought it was possible Karmein's abduction was a straight kidnap, but the plan collapsed before the extortion demand could be made because of the massive public exposure. The theory was that the criminals had no idea their kidnapping would be linked to Mr Cruel and would become front-page news.

They expected their demands to be met with no publicity and when it became a major investigation, they killed the girl and buried the body to escape detection.

But there were undeniable similarities to cases connected with Mr Cruel. Many of the key investigators remain convinced it was the one offender.

Karmein's sisters gave descriptions of the man, which were similar to those other victims had given. They said he was aged in his early 30s and was between 168 and 175 centimetres tall. And, despite the disguise, the girls believed he was a white Australian – not an Asian kidnapper.

IF Mr Cruel was responsible for the murder of Karmein Chan, then what happened? Experienced police say that serial sexual offenders rarely stop until they are caught or die. They say the offenders become more confident and more dangerous. Mr Cruel's crimes fitted that pattern.

He began by attacking a girl in her own home, then progressed to an abduction that lasted less than a day, then to holding a girl for more than two days, and finally, to murder.

Why then, did he stop? Was he shocked at his own violence? Did he seek professional help, and is he on medication? Is there a psychologist, doctor, priest or counsellor who shares his secret?

Police have checked jail records and monitored overseas crime reports, but nothing has helped lead them to Mr Cruel. Some police think the only logical explanation is that he is dead.

Perhaps he was a seemingly respectable member of the community who, after he killed Karmein, feared apprehension or what he would do next. Perhaps he hopped in his car and simply 'lost control' while driving and hit a tree. Then he will have taken the secret to his grave – seemingly the victim of a tragic accident. More than fifteen years after Karmein's murder, there is no shortage of theories – just no new leads.

PHYLLIS and John Chan's marriage could not survive the loss of their eldest daughter. Their finances also collapsed and Mrs

Chan was only just able to save her restaurant with the help of her Hong Kong-based brother.

In January 1995, she was severely bashed in an unrelated robbery attempt. Many of the regulars drifted away. But some stuck with Phyllis and became loyal friends. They included former Chief Commissioner, Kel Glare, and (the late) Assistant Commissioner, Frank Green.

Green and his wife Norma would sometimes go to the 100-seat restaurant and find themselves the only diners.

Over the years, Phyllis Chan has fought her way back and the customers have returned. She reverted to her maiden name, Phyllis Lam. She became a devout Christian, attending weekly bible studies classes. She became fiercely protective of her two surviving daughters, wanting them to have full and happy lives.

She didn't want them only to be known as Karmein's sisters. Kelvin Glare says of her:

'Phyllis is a remarkable woman. She has taken knocks that would have flattened any other person and she just refuses to give up.

She is a person who has lost her daughter, her marriage, has suffered financial troubles and has been severely assaulted, but has been able to come back. She continues to show amazing strength of character.'

Frank Green died on Christmas Day 2000. At his funeral at the Police Academy, a small Asian woman was overcome by grief. It was Phyllis Lam.

Later she opened her restaurant for the wake. She was there at the front of house – urging people to eat, drink and enjoy.

Just like the old days.

FIFTEEN years after Karmein Chan was abducted, the files had been boxed and the taskforce long ago disbanded.

Despite the thousands of leads, hundreds of public appeals and a $300,000 reward, it had all the signs of a dead-end case.

But there remained a deep fascination with the man they called Mr Cruel and there was always a continual drip feed of tips from the public that inevitably led nowhere.

During the long investigation police kept one nugget of information to themselves. The one clue they hoped would nail the offender if they ever found the right name.

Mr Cruel, the man who went to extraordinary lengths to cover his tracks, did something that would link him straight to the crimes.

He filmed his victims to keep as trophies of his 'victories'.

Detectives believe the serial sexual predator set up a video camera in the house where he took his victims so he could later relive his attacks.

One of his victims told police she saw a tripod and camera set up at the end of the bed where she was held prisoner after her abduction. She was unsure if it was a still or video camera.

Investigators kept secret the information that Mr Cruel filmed his victims in the hope that when he was identified they would also find the irrefutable evidence. An FBI profiler urged that the information remain secret. 'These items will have great personal significance to him and he will not destroy them unless he believes that law enforcement officials are aware they exist. Because of the profound evidentiary value of these items no mention of this should be made publicly.'

But after fifteen years without a breakthrough detectives agreed to release the last-known lead in the hope of a belated breakthrough.

Detectives believe that if he is still alive he will have kept the tapes and/or photos and will still collect, and possibly swap, child pornography.

They say he almost certainly continues to collect pornography through the internet and may communicate with children using chat lines. During a worldwide swoop on computer child porn in 2004, police found that many offenders kept their incriminating collections even after they became aware they were likely to be questioned.

They would hide the material but rarely destroy it, even though they knew if the evidence was found they faced public exposure, humiliation and jail.

Spectrum detectives discovered a list of around 150 men, including some prominent individuals, who subscribed to mail-order child pornography.

All were questioned over the abductions.

The serial sex offender Mr Cruel was meticulous in trying to destroy forensic evidence. He bathed two of his victims before releasing them, and wiped sinks and bench tops to remove fingerprints.

One victim told police he bathed her, 'like a mother washing a baby'.

Shortly before releasing one victim he thoroughly cleaned the bathroom and then laid down a sheet on the lino floor to avoid leaving footprints.

In one case, he took a second set of clothes from the girl's home to dress her before she was freed. In another, he dumped the girl in garbage bags so police could not test her original clothes.

The level of planning was shown when he told one of the girls he abducted exactly when he would release her – 50 hours after she was abducted.

A former senior investigator with the *Spectrum* taskforce, Commander Steve Fontana, said, 'He was a cold and calculating offender. Perhaps we spoke to him and that scared him off'.

THE FBI PROFILE

1. He is in steady employment, a good neighbour, polite, quiet, somewhat introverted, but may be involved in certain community-minded projects.
2. He would typically live in a single-family residence, one with a garage or carport.
3. If he lives with someone, he would be absent during critical times.
4. If he is involved in a sexual relationship, the partner would be aware of sexual dysfunction on the part of the offender.
5. Those who work with the offender would notice a change in his behaviour after the incidents. He would have trouble coping, would be likely to miss work and would appear rigid and distant to workmates.
6. Some may notice that soon after the offences the offender appears stressed and changes his use of alcohol, either drinking more or abstinence. He may show a short-term interest in religion.
7. In the offender's mind there is no intent to harm the children.
8. The offender appears normal and above suspicion to those around him.
9. He will attempt to alter his behaviour on the basis of newspaper reports on police profiles of the offender.

––––––––––––––––– CHAPTER 5 –––––––––––––––––

Deadly Secret

Within days, homicide detectives had gathered what facts they could. Almost thirty years later, they don't know much more.

IT had come to this. After 22 years and countless false leads, the hunt for the answer to one of Australia's most notorious unsolved sex killings had taken two Melbourne homicide detectives across the world.

The murders had happened at the height of an Australian summer, in January, 1977, in a street whose name – Easey Street, Collingwood – was to echo down the years in Victoria. Now it was December, 1998, in the depths of an English winter, and the Australian pair shivered as they waited to play the last card in a game they hoped would trap a killer with a dreadful secret.

With the Australians were two Scotland Yard detectives, who'd narrowed the search to the building they were now watching: a drab office in a drab street in Margate, a shabby holiday town on the Kent coast smelling of fish-and-chip fat and poverty.

They didn't know their quarry's exact address, but computer checks showed he had been collecting his dole money from this particular office. It was payday. He was a certainty to turn up.

Sure enough, the man collected his dole, and the detectives collected him. Detective Sergeant Steve Tragardh and his boss, Chief Inspector Rod Collins, had agreed to let the Scotland Yard men do the talking, so the nomadic Australian wouldn't be alarmed by knowing immediately why he might be wanted a world away.

They took him to the local police station, the Yard men saying all they needed was a tiny blood sample – a routine precaution, they said soothingly, which would eliminate him from an inquiry. The suspect gave it willingly, so willingly that Tragardh and Collins wondered right then if it was a wild goose chase.

Tragardh pocketed the vial of blood, and they returned to London to extradite another murder suspect, which was the official reason for their flying visit. The detective kept the blood sample safely in his possession until he handed it over to the staff at the Victoria Police forensic science centre back in Melbourne.

Days later, a forensic expert compared the DNA code in the English blood sample with DNA from what was coyly called a 'body fluid' taken from the crime scene almost exactly 22 years before. The fluid was semen, and it had been found underneath the bloodstained body of Suzanne Armstrong in January, 1977.

Suzanne, 27, had been stabbed 29 times, and raped. Her housemate, Susan Bartlett, had been stabbed more than 50 times, presumably after coming to her friend's aid. With the same knife, police believe, although they never found it or the man who wielded it with such savagery.

The scientist checked the result. It was negative.

Four months before, the homicide squad had eight outstanding suspects on a shortlist for DNA testing against the semen sample, which had been found in 1997 with other Easey Street exhibits in a storeroom. One by one they'd been eliminated, and each time the tension ratcheted another notch. But now there were no more. The investigation was back exactly to where it was when the bodies were found on a warm day in 1977, but the trail was colder than ever.

SUZANNE Armstrong turned 21 in 1970, as Susan Bartlett had a few months before. The new decade belonged to their generation.

A year after Woodstock and two before Whitlam, Australian baby boomers plunged into an era that spawned its own anthem, the Skyhooks song *Living In the Seventies*. It caught the mood of the time, an edgy mixture of alienation, self-gratification, sex, drugs and rock'n'roll. It was a time of full employment and changing social values, and the young and restless could skate from job to job and bed to bed, across the thin ice of a suddenly permissive age.

Some fell through.

The two Sues – Armstrong and Bartlett – had been friends from schooldays at Benalla High. When Suzanne was twenty, in 1969, Susan Bartlett's mother, Elaine Bartlett, had written a reference, which read, in part: 'I have known Miss Suzanne Armstrong for five years. She has been a close friend of my daughter Susan since their school days. I know her to be a conscientious and capable young woman.'

Suzanne, oldest of Bill and Eileen Armstrong's four children, raised at Strathbogie in the hills above Benalla, was intelligent and popular. She found friends and jobs easily, and had plenty of both. She had long brown hair, a good figure and a friendly smile. Men liked her, and she liked them.

Whereas Susan Bartlett went teaching, and saved up to travel, Suzanne Armstrong travelled constantly, picking up work and boyfriends as she went. First around Australia and, then, the world – in 1972, and again in 1974, working her way through exotic destinations from South America to South London.

After the second trip, she came home with a baby boy, born in the Greek islands. His Greek father had wanted to marry her, but she had refused to be tied down to village life. Some say she named her son Gregory, after a television cameraman, Greg Molineaux, who had been a favourite boyfriend before she left, but she often wore a ring with her Greek lover's name, Manolis, engraved inside it.

Susan Bartlett, who called Suzanne 'little Sue' and was taller and much heavier than her friend, was described by one boyfriend as 'a large girl with a beautiful face'.

She had almost married a fellow teacher at Broadford High School, north of Melbourne, in 1973, but had gone overseas on sabbatical leave instead, before returning to teaching, this time in Collingwood.

After Suzanne returned from Greece in 1976 she moved to Collingwood, and picked up a little work minding the baby daughter of a barrister friend, Judith Peirce, whom she had known earlier when she had worked as a courier for Peirce's husband. She rode a bicycle around Carlton and Collingwood, her toddler strapped on a seat behind her. In late October, she and Susan Bartlett, who had been living in a nearby flat, rented a house together.

It was a neat brick single-fronted Victorian 'one-of-a-pair', of the type already popular with inner-suburban renovators. The address was 147 Easey Street, two doors from Hoddle Street. The former school friends were happy, but not for long. Ten weeks later they were dead.

ON Tuesday, January 11, their closest neighbours, Ilona Stevens and Janet Powell, who lived in number 149, found Suzanne Armstrong's part-labrador pup, Benjy, loose in the street. No-one answered when they knocked next door, so they left a note and took the dog home for safekeeping.

By Thursday morning, January 13, the note was still in the door and Ilona and Janet's curiosity had overcome their fear of being labelled stickybeaks. They heard little Gregory whimpering, and went down the lane on the other side of 147, through the open gate and the unlocked back door. Ilona went first.

'I noticed that the kitchen and bathroom lights were on, but none of the others at the back of the house,' she was to say. 'In the passage, near the front door, I saw Susan's body. She was lying on her stomach, face down ...'

She yelled to her friend –who had paused to look at the note on the kitchen table – to ring the police. Susan was wearing a green nightie. There was blood down one side, on her legs and on the walls. In the front bedroom, Suzanne's body was on the floor. 'She was lying on her back, legs apart and knees drawn up, and there was a lot of blood ... She was naked except for what seemed to be a skivvy pushed up around her neck.'

In the middle bedroom was sixteen-month-old Gregory – pale, distressed and dirty, but alive.

The first job for police was to piece together the dead women's last-known movements, and a list of their friends and acquaintances. It was a long list, and it kept them busy. Most murder victims are killed by people who know them, and there were many potential suspects among the men the two women knew.

Within days, homicide detectives had gathered what facts they could. Almost 30 years later, they don't know much more.

It went like this. Suzanne Armstrong had got up early on

Monday, January 10, and shared breakfast with Susan Bartlett before Susan went shopping with her mother at Georges, then Melbourne's elite establishment department store. Mother and daughter lunched together and, according to one account, Mrs Bartlett told her daughter it was time to end 'old associations' and concentrate on new ones – a heavy hint about what she probably saw as the young woman's increasingly bohemian lifestyle. After lunch, Susan went back to Easey Street. It was the last time her mother saw her alive.

The two Sues spent the afternoon at home. Susan made a yellow frock to wear on a date with her latest boyfriend, a salesman she had met at the Argo Inn in South Yarra. Then she cooked dinner for themselves and her brother Martin Bartlett and his girlfriend, who often visited.

After the meal, the women watched the long-running serial *The Sullivans* while Martin set up a stereo system he'd lent his sister. He and his girlfriend left not long after the show finished at 8.30pm. Later, Suzanne went to bed in the front room, which overlooked Easey Street, and Susan went to bed in the third bedroom, down the hall. Gregory was in his cot in the bedroom between. They had never changed their trusting country ways, leaving the back door open and the side gate into the cobbled lane unlatched.

Suzanne was reading a collection of Roald Dahl's short stories, *Switch Bitch*. It seems that something or somebody interrupted her, because it was found, open at the middle pages, on the bed. It seems likely she put it down to open the front door because somebody she knew, or thought she knew, came knocking.

Either that, or the killer came up the passage from the back door to get to her room. The story she was reading was called *The Last Act*. For her, it was.

DEADLY SECRET

FOR two full days, no-one knew. Amazingly, three men came into the house in that time but didn't see the bodies at the front of the house and didn't hear the thirsty baby. A fourth man stayed next door on the night of the murder. Each was let go after long interviews, but each was on the suspect list until the DNA tests finally cleared them beyond doubt half a lifetime later.

Barry Woodard, then 31, was and still is a shearer, an easy going country boy who later grew heartily sick of having his name tossed up every time Easey Street was mentioned. But, at the time, he wasn't shy about his tragically short-lived friendship with Suzanne Armstrong, whom he'd met on a 'blind date' just before Christmas, less than three weeks earlier. They'd had a couple of outings, and had dinner at his sister's place in Northcote the night before she died.

Barry telephoned twice on Monday, evidently when the girls were out, and several times on the Tuesday and Wednesday. Puzzled because no-one answered, he and his younger brother, Henry, went to the house about 8.30pm on Wednesday, January 12, came in the back door and left a note on the kitchen table. Henry wanted to have a look up the darkened hall, but Barry thought it bad manners to be so nosy, so they left.

When news broke next morning that two women had been found murdered in Collingwood, he rang Easey Street again, from his sister's house. The telephone was engaged, so he assumed the women were safe. But when his sister called the same number five minutes later, a detective answered. Within minutes he, Henry and their sister were picked up, then split up for several hours of intense questioning.

Their stories tallied, but Barry Woodard felt that a question mark hung unjustly over his head for 21 years. Until one afternoon in August 1998, when he came home from work to his house in a country town to find two detectives waiting for him. They asked for a blood sample. He was, like his brother and six other men, pleased to give it.

The other man who had been in the house without seeing the bodies was the tobacco salesman who had met Susan Bartlett the previous week. Like the shearer, the salesman was worried because no-one answered his calls, so he drove to Easey Street about 10.30 on Tuesday night – with a male friend, luckily, who was able to verify his story.

After knocking on the front door, he walked down the side lane, climbed through the unlocked window of Susan Bartlett's empty bedroom and copied the house's telephone number on a cigarette packet before climbing back out the window, all without seeing the bodies a few metres up the unlit hall.

The fourth man was a crime reporter, John Grant, known as 'Grunter' and one of the hardest of the hard cases working for the then popular tabloid scandal sheet, *Truth*. Tough, street-smart, and with a reputation for wild living that could have got him a job in the armed robbery squad, Grant had 'crashed' for the night in the hallway of Ilona Stevens's house, number 149, on that Monday.

The homicide squad spent a long, hard day questioning him but established only that he'd heard nothing through the double-brick party wall. What intrigued detectives, and other reporters, was the ghastly coincidence that Grant had also been one of the last people to see Julie Garciacelay, a twenty-year-old American, apparently abducted from her North Melbourne flat in 1975, and almost certainly murdered.

He was cleared of any involvement in either case but he, too, had to live with innuendo until the DNA tests cleared him. Still wary, perhaps, after his earlier experiences with the law, he had a lawyer with him when he gave his blood sample in 1998.

There were other leads in 1977 – too many, probably – but they all came to nothing.

A knife was found at nearby Victoria Park railway station at 10.30 on the night of the murders. A man with a history of sex offences was interviewed after stabbing a farmer in Tasmania; he had been living near Collingwood at the time of the murders, and had crossed Bass Strait days later, taking a car with a bloodstained knife, boots and shirt in the boot. And then, the dead women had known a lot of men who, in turn, knew other men.

The case frustrated the then head of the homicide squad, Detective Inspector Noel Jubb, who was to retire still tormented about what had really happened that night. It also fascinated Tom Prior, a veteran crime journalist and prolific author.

After retiring from daily newspapers in the early 1990s, Prior re-investigated the case to gather material for a definitive book. As it happened, he was diagnosed with a potentially terminal disease before he finished, and was forced to publish *They Trusted Men* in 1997 knowing it was a work in progress, not the book he'd planned.

But the old sleuth made friends with Greg Armstrong, by this time a young man, and helped find his natural father on the Greek island of Naxos, where the two were reunited.

Greg was raised partly by Suzanne's sister, Gayle Tilton, who had a son almost exactly the same age, and partly by Gayle's estranged husband, a farm manager. But the big influence in his life, Prior believed, was his grandmother Eileen, a kindly woman who had remarried after divorcing Bill Armstrong. Bill too, had remarried and moved to a farm near Bairnsdale, but died after being burned fighting a bushfire almost exactly a year after his daughter's murder.

There are other postscripts to Easey Street. One is that,

because he was illegitimate, the infant boy who lost his mother was not entitled to crimes compensation to pay for his rearing and education. That is, until his mother's barrister friend, Judith Peirce, ran a campaign that resulted in the premier of the day, Rupert Hamer, changing the law. Judith Peirce set up a trust fund to handle the compensation payment and money donated by members of the public touched by his plight. Some of the money was used to send him to boarding school in his teens, the rest being left in trust to help him through university. His studies include modern Greek, a language he practises when he visits his new-found father and relatives.

From tragedy, she says, Greg has grown into a remarkable success story. 'He is very much like his mother. Sue was a happy-go-lucky person who could roll with the punches in a way a lot of people can't.'

Before his death in 2005, Tom Prior continued to think a lot about the case. For a long time he kept coming back to one name – which, like several others, he changed for legal reasons when writing his book. This is what he wrote of the man he suspected: 'He had had an association with Suzanne Armstrong but claimed he spurned her. He had been to 147 Easey Street and knew the location of the various rooms. He had a violent temper. His marriage had broken down, and a number of previous sexual associations had failed. He had assaulted a woman before ... He was known to be drinking at the time of the murders, but had not drunk alcohol for a long time after them. He had given contradictory accounts of his movements during the 'murder' week. And he was not really investigated because he was 'trusted' as a former associate of police.'

What Prior didn't write was that while he was researching his book, a man telephoned his house at 2am one morning and abused and threatened his wife. The caller warned that Prior should 'stop asking questions', and ended the conversation with 'I know where you live'.

Prior believed the caller was a former policeman whose name he'd raised with detectives. Prior couldn't help thinking someone in the force must have tipped this man off that Prior was asking about him. Prior said he hoped nothing like that would have interfered with the integrity of blood samples for DNA tests, which had cleared the former policeman along with the other seven suspects.

Unsolved cases are never closed, but some gather dust while time and effort go into solving more recent cases. In the Easey Street case, the homicide squad has to decide whether to look further afield for possible suspects for blood testing.

The two Sues knew a lot more than eight men. Teachers and salesmen, labourers, roof tilers and meat workers. Many had visited them and might have talked to others about the friendly girls in Easey Street. Any one of them could have been the killer.

CHAPTER 6

A Stolen Life

She would never see her daughter again.

SHE would be an adult now. Maybe, like her younger sister, she would have married and had children of her own. Creative and talented like her mother, she might have grown up to build a career in the art world. Almost certainly, she would have outgrown her childhood asthma and schoolgirl shyness. But she was to be cheated of the chance.

Eloise Worledge was just eight when she was taken from the safety of her bedroom in a seemingly secure bayside family suburban home. She was never to be seen again.

It was the case that made families in Melbourne shut their doors and wonder about strangers in the street.

Despite the biggest missing persons search in Victoria's history and a $10,000 reward posted in 1976 that remains unclaimed, no trace of Eloise has ever been found. The photograph of the smiling little blonde girl remains an image of its time that scarred a generation. When homicide 'cold-case' detectives began re-investigating the case in 2001, they were surprised to discover the picture of Eloise was instantly recognised by many people more than 25 years after her disappearance.

IT was January, 1976. Milk was still delivered to homes, pubs shut at 10pm and poker machines could only be played over the border in NSW. Tertiary education was free and Gough Whitlam had been voted from office just weeks earlier. Political bumper stickers carrying the slogan It's Time were being replaced by freshly printed ones imploring voters to maintain their rage.

Patsy and Lindsay Worledge had been married slightly more than ten years. With three healthy and happy children, they appeared the perfect family.

Patricia Ann Watmuff had been a student teacher when she met New Zealand-born Lindsay Worledge, who was three years older and starting an academic career.

They met in 1963 and married two years later. Eloise was born on October 8, 1967. Anna followed in 1969 and then Blake in 1971.

By the time Eloise was born, the family had settled into a four bedroom weatherboard home in Scott Street on the corner of Gibbs Street, near Beaumaris beach, in Melbourne's southern bayside suburbs.

There was little through traffic in Scott Street. It was the Australian dream – an affordable home by the sea, an outdoor lifestyle, and shops, schools and work close by. Above all else, it was safe.

The area was filled with young, middle-class families with

similar aspirations. Couples made friends in the surrounding streets. Their kids played together and families grew close.

Eloise went to the nearby Beaumaris Primary School, just two streets away, and was due to start grade four in weeks. She was shy but intelligent and – like her mother – had an artistic flair. Everyone liked Patsy. She was energetic and enthusiastic with a strong interest in art. Lindsay was introverted, bookish and clever. And, according to associates, he didn't mind letting people know it. 'He was often described as thinking of himself as intellectually superior,' a police review of the case was to note.

And there was something else. After a decade of marriage, the Worledges found they were drifting apart.

Patsy immersed herself in her children, local friends and her passions for art and craft. Lindsay spent more time at the Caulfield Institute of Technology, where he was a lecturer. He was also completing his masters degree in business administration at Monash University.

The marital tensions became obvious. Friends noticed Lindsay's sarcastic comments to his wife becoming increasingly heavy-handed. Some friends became uncomfortable in his presence and felt he was damaging Patsy's self-esteem.

She thought they should try counselling, a move her husband refused. But Patsy went ahead and, while it did not improve their marriage, it helped her accept the crumbling relationship.

She pursued her own interests, which, according to police, 'only increased Lindsay Worledge's resentment towards her'.

By 1975, their relationship was in free-fall and they began to build independent lives. As their marriage was dying, both found comfort with others. Their personal troubles would have remained private if their tragedy had not been so public.

In September, 1975, four months before Eloise's abduction,

Patsy started talking of a separation. Lindsay agreed in principle, but in practice tried to delay the inevitable.

The timing, he said, would have to be on his terms and the split would have to wait until he completed his academic studies that November.

It appeared that it would be a civilised arrangement. She would stay in the marital home with the children and he would have unfettered access to them. Neither parent wanted the split to hurt the children. They agreed to stay together over Christmas for the sake of the children and then he would move out. They set a date. Lindsay would leave by his wife's 33rd birthday on January 10.

As the day approached, Patsy broke the news to the children. According to Patsy, Eloise had already realised the coldness between her parents. Patsy observed that Eloise had grown distant from her father because of the obvious tension in the house. Nonetheless, her daughter 'took the news in her stride'.

THE plan for an amicable separation collapsed when Patsy's birthday arrived and Lindsay had not left. What his wife did not know was that he had secretly begun to prepare to move. He inspected a rental property in Carnegie that day, telling the agents he needed two days before making a final decision.

According to police: 'There was little communication between them and it appeared they were leading separate lives although living under the one roof'.

Jane Mirvis, Patsy's friend from across the road, offered to host a birthday dinner for her on the Saturday.

About ten people were invited, but Patsy went without Lindsay. It was a public statement of independence. Some feared it was also a private declaration of war. The friends knew enough about the Worledges' domestic problems to be concerned the snubbed husband might react badly. 'A general feeling, that this was a humiliating act and that a serious confrontation could result, pervaded the group,' police found. 'During the course of the evening, some of the members of the group felt that someone was spying on them through the windows.'

Twenty-five years later, Lindsay was to deny this allegation, although he did admit he walked the street, inspecting the vehicles of the guests who attended the birthday celebration. 'He indicated he was only curious and denied being motivated by jealousy or suspicion that Patricia Worledge may have been with someone at the party.'

It was 2am before Patsy walked across the street to her home. Lindsay was awake and 'a heated and spiteful argument between them ensued', according to police records. It went for nearly two hours, with the screaming and yelling reaching a point where neighbours considered calling the police 'out of concern'.

No-one did. They didn't want to intrude on the Worledges' business. But within days that business would be front-page news.

Lindsay liked to appear in control but he would later admit he was bitter about the planned separation and had become severely depressed.

When he woke on Sunday, January 11, his mood hadn't lifted. Patsy wanted to know when he would finally leave and he promised to make arrangements by Monday.

He took the children to the beach and returned that afternoon to contact the estate agents, committing to rent the Carnegie property. He said he would sign the contract the following day.

On Monday morning, he went to Honeywell Securities, where he was a guest speaker. He had lunch with an executive, returning to the Caulfield Institute about 2.15pm. The summer break meant that work was still quiet at the college, so he joined members of the faculty for drinks at a local hotel. He had shared a carafe of wine at lunch and a jug of beer at the pub.

About 4pm, he rang the real estate agent to cancel his meeting, rescheduling for the following day. He left the hotel about 4.45pm and went home for dinner. Patsy did some sewing while Lindsay played Monopoly with the children. Around 8.30pm, she went to her regular jazz ballet class.

Eloise left her bedroom around 9.15pm for a glass of milk. She then went into the television room and sat on her father's lap while he quietly explained his side of the marital break-up. He later told a friend he was relieved he had cleared the air with his daughter.

Eloise went to bed around 10pm, wearing a two-piece, yellow, baby-doll pyjama set with 'Rock 'n' Roll' on the front and a musical clef emblem on the back.

Lindsay had continued drinking at home. He had two scotches and a bottle of wine with dinner. He drank port while watching television and eventually fell asleep.

Patsy walked home from jazz ballet and stopped at Jane Mirvis's house across the road.

She then went home to get a dress she was sewing to show Jane. Lindsay was in the lounge room in darkness with the television on. Patsy told him she was going back to Jane's.

She returned home at 10.30pm. She would later tell police the outside porch light was off, and the front flywire door was closed but not snibbed.

According to police: 'The front door was unlocked and wide open. It was not an overly hot night.' (The temperature dropped to about 12 degrees Celsius).

Her husband was still in the lounge room. She thought to shut the front door but forgot. It was around 11pm. She took some ironing to Anna's and Blake's rooms. Then she went in to Eloise, straightened her covers, kissed her good night and went to bed.

She would never see her daughter again.

Around 11.40pm, Lindsay said later, he turned off the television and went to bed. He said he checked on the children, but Patsy would later tell police that this was unusual for him.

He did not shut the front door because he did not know it had been left open.

According to Patsy, the passage light was left on for the children and then switched off by the last parent to bed. But this night, police say, 'Lindsay Worledge did not turn off the passageway light.'

At 4.45am, Patsy got up to go to the toilet. She then noticed the passage light was off. Almost certainly, Eloise Worledge had already been taken from her bed.

PEOPLE under extreme stress can have different recollections of the same events. Statements taken from armed robbery victims or witnesses to car accidents can and do vary wildly for innocent reasons.

It is not necessarily remarkable, therefore, that Lindsay and Patsy Worledge would give confusing and, at times, conflicting versions of what happened the morning their daughter disappeared.

In his original statement, Lindsay said he woke at 6.30am and, as he went to the kitchen for a drink of water and orange juice, he noticed his daughter's door was shut. On it was a sign – 'Eloise's Room'.

He went outside to collect the milk and paper, returning to bed to read the day's news.

According to Lindsay, Anna and Blake came into their parents' room and began playing. Blake said Eloise was not in her room, but neither parent took any notice of the chattering of their four-year-old. At 7.30am, Patsy got up. She began to get worried when she could not find Eloise.

Lindsay then rose and met Patsy at the doorway of their daughter's room. He looked in and immediately saw the curtain was pulled to one side, the flywire screen had been cut and the window was open. Ten days later, during a re-enactment, he said he woke to find Blake was already in his parents' bed about 7am. Anna arrived about ten minutes later. Lindsay asked his children to get the paper, but when they ignored him he went to get it himself.

He said that when he got the paper, the front door was closed. He noticed the clock in the kitchen. It was 7.15am.

In her statement, Patsy said she was woken at 7.30am when Lindsay came back to bed. She said this was unusual because it was his habit to send the children to collect the paper.

She said Blake hopped into the bed at the same time and said that Eloise was not in her room. Patsy said she left her bedroom about 7.55am and went into the hallway where Anna ran up and said Eloise was missing. In her statement, ten days later, she said she had a shower and then Anna alerted her.

In Patsy's version of events, she was checking the front part of the house when Lindsay said he had found something in Eloise's room.

She followed him to the bedroom where he pointed out that the curtains were pulled to one side, the flywire was cut and the window open. At this point, she realised her daughter had been taken.

She rang her sister, Margaret Thomas, and, 'panic-stricken', ran across the road to Jane Mirvis's home. Lindsay chose to ring the local police rather than the emergency D24 number. At 8.27, Margaret Thomas, who had arrived at the Worledge home, rang D24 and gave the phone to Lindsay.

'On doing so, Lindsay Worledge indicated in an unemotional and almost offhand tone that there had been a break-in at his house and that the only thing missing was his eight-year-old daughter,' according to police.

He told police his wife was the last person to see Eloise. He did not mention he had checked her after Patsy had gone to bed.

Eight minutes after the call to D24, Sergeant Cyril Wilson from the Beaumaris police station arrived. He knew that children sometimes slipped away from their families for hours, but once he saw the cut flywire screen, his instinct was that this was no runaway. He called for back-up. Within 30 minutes, local detectives were there.

Blake became an important witness. He said he heard someone in Eloise's room during the night and heard crackling noises that police say were consistent with steps on the seagrass floorcoverings in the bedroom.

Police formed a fifteen-strong taskforce, controlled by Detective Superintendent Fred Warnock, who said he was confident Eloise would be found.

More than 250 police, including search and rescue, the mounted branch, the dog squad and the independent patrol group, searched for nearly three weeks – the biggest operation of its type in Melbourne.

They checked parks, the foreshore, golf courses and local streets. Inquiries spread overseas, with reports Eloise had been abducted but was still alive. Police chased leads and rumours; they even consulted clairvoyants. They found nothing.

A diviner turned up at the Worledge home saying he could help. He was given a sandal belonging to the missing girl and then drove around the neighbourhood with Lindsay. He stopped and pointed at a vacant house, saying the girl had been there. Police broke into the house and found nothing. By coincidence, perhaps, Eloise had been visiting the family next door to the empty house a few days before she disappeared.

Police scientific experts checked the scene and concluded the flywire screen was probably cut from the inside. The wind-out window had been opened to its maximum 38 centimetres.

It was a narrow opening, difficult for an adult to climb through, especially carrying an eight-year-old.

The flywire was cut from a height of 195 centimetres. Dust and cobwebs around the window were undisturbed. Tan bark from the garden was found in the room.

The abductor would have had to wind open the window from the outside, lean in, cut the fly wire and roll the wire on the inside – a difficult but not impossible task.

Investigators concluded: 'On balance, based on all the information on hand, it appeared more likely that the person or persons responsible for Eloise Worledge's disappearance had effected their entry and exit through a point other than her bedroom window.'

In other words, someone tried to make it look as if Eloise was grabbed through the open window.

RANDOM child kidnapping cases shake the confidence of the community. Like the disappearance of the Beaumont children in Adelaide a decade earlier, or Karmein Chan from Templestowe fifteen years later, the Worledge case appalled and fascinated. The factual void was filled with rumours, half-truths and gossip.

Police briefed the press every day. 'Such was the magnitude of the media coverage that her image continues to be recognisable to the public at large, some 26 years later. The story generated immense public interest and led to thousands of separate pieces of information being reported to police by the public,' the later police investigation found.

The original investigators began by saying they were confident Eloise would be found alive. But they also asked the Worledges to delay their separation, wanting to keep public concern at its highest.

It was a sham. The parents gave separate interviews to the media. Patsy spent most of her time across the road at the Mirvis house. The Worledges became even more distant and, like the Chans and the Beaumonts, eventually separated. Lindsay moved out to a rented flat. Both later remarried.

From January 21 to 23, police canvassed 6000 homes in the area with a prepared list of questions. They were able to log 200 suspicious incidents that occurred on the night she was abducted.

At 10pm on January 12, Wayne Cheeseman of Scott Street heard a prowler outside his house. At 7.15 the following morning, he discovered the tool shed in the backyard had been broken into. Three chisels, an oilcan and a pair of garden shears had been left on his nature strip. Police later decided the shears had not been used to cut the flyscreen.

At 10.30pm on January 12, a neighbour at 57 Scott Street saw a car travel down the road with the headlights off. At 11.40pm, Patricia Cunningham of 26 Scott Street saw a green Holden station wagon parked near the Worledge home.

Around midnight, Ann Same of 64 Scott Street saw a young man walking along the Worledge fence line. She felt so uneasy she crossed the road to avoid him.

Around the same time, Molly Salts, at number 9, saw a young man run in front of her car as she drove along Scott Street near the Gibbs Street intersection. She saw him jump the fence into the Worledge property. Just after midnight, at 12.16, Andrew Jones of 41 Scott Street heard noises outside his house that he thought were made by a prowler.

At 2am, Daphne Owen-Smith, at number 66, heard a child's cry and the sound of a car door slamming. Anne Same also heard a car door slam at that time.

Months later, Catherine Marling told police that she had seen a green 1966 model Holden in the street on January 6, 1976 – a week before the abduction. Police found a car fitting the description had been stolen from Carlton in December 1975, but it was never recovered.

IN child abduction cases, police believe there is nearly always a link between the victim and the offender. In the Worledge investigation, there were two theories: she was the victim of a random attack; or she was taken by a friend or associate of the family.

Patsy initially hoped her husband might have been involved because he wanted to create a reason to stay in the house. As a result, police say, 'she was confident that no harm would come to Eloise Worledge'.

Because it was unlikely that Eloise was taken through her bedroom window, both parents were initially treated as suspects, although police soon began to concentrate on the father.

According to police: 'His unemotional and seemingly cold demeanour in dealing with the situation only added to the investigators' concerns. A case in point: when they learned Lindsay Worledge contacted the real estate office only a few hours after the disappearance ... to cancel his 4pm appointment, suggesting to staff in an off-handed manner they should read the newspapers to find out why.' But Lindsay Worledge's perceived flippancy might have been a simple self-defence mechanism – a shield for a frightened and grieving father.

Detective Superintendent Warnock believed he was unfairly judged. 'Mr Worledge, I think, has been seen in a bad light. A lot of people think he has acted callously. He's not the kind of person who wears his heart on his sleeve. Deep down, he cares about his children and he is very distressed about this whole business,' Warnock said nine months after the abduction.

Lindsay believed a stranger took his daughter. At the time, he said, 'I can't buy the theory that it was someone she knew. She would not have gone willingly with anyone in the middle of the night. Eloise has a timidity. She is not adventuresome. She would not go out on the street without her brother or sister. She is a shy, sensitive child who suffers asthmatic bouts.'

On the day the abduction was discovered, Lindsay asked police to give him a lie-detector test.

They refused the request but on day four, he was taken to the Russell Street police station and interviewed – this time as a suspect.

He had studied psychology at university and, when he was left alone in the interview room, he felt it was a 'subtle psychological trick'.

He described the interview process as 'a fairly terrifying experience'.

Both parents were hypnotised about a month after the abduction in the hope that new information could be found.

Less than a week after his daughter disappeared, Lindsay felt he had to deny unsubstantiated stories that he was involved in the abduction. 'These rumours will be answered when the truth finally emerges,' he said. But it never has.

The police review of the case found: 'At the conclusion of

investigations into Lindsay Worledge, no evidence in regards to his involvement has been uncovered.'

POLICE looked at ten general types of suspects: known sex offenders in Melbourne's south-east, any sex offenders within Australia involved in child abductions or who broke into houses, known prowlers in the area, local service providers, babysitters, tradesmen, door-to-door salesmen, staff and parents at the Beaumaris Primary School and government agencies with any contact with the family.

They also interviewed more than 100 family and extended family members in Australia and overseas, more than 200 friends and associates of the family, neighbours, work colleagues and students of Lindsay Worledge.

On February 20, 1976, the Worledge taskforce was disbanded. The file was sent to the local detectives at Moorabbin and any new tips were investigated and added to the thousands already gathered.

In the early 1980s, the Moorabbin CIB closed down and the Worledge file went to the Hampton CIB. Years later, the file was sent to the homicide squad and archived as a missing persons case.

Despite it being one of the highest-profile mysteries in Australia's history, when police began to re-investigate the Worledge case, they found key evidence and vital files were missing.

But the re-investigation did unearth two new suspects. The Worledges had once been connected with a Beaumaris amateur theatre.

In 1975, a man drifted into the group. Police now know he was a convicted child molester.

Detectives also know that a man convicted of child sex

offences worked at a nearby milk bar. But police have found nothing to link either man to the abduction.

They also investigated any possible links with double murderer and serial sex offender Raymond 'Mr Stinky' Edmunds. They could find no connections.

On February 6, 2002, homicide squad detectives formally interviewed Lindsay. He told them he did not know what happened to his daughter.

The day Eloise disappeared Lindsay had offered to take a lie-detector test; 26 years later, police finally agreed. On February 14, 2002, he was connected to a polygraph machine and asked questions about the abduction. Like so many elements of the case, the results were not conclusive.

Detective Senior Sergeant Jan Lierse worked on the Worledge case for almost two years and has lived with it ever since.

'We are no further advanced now than when the balloon went up when she was first reported missing about 7.30 in the morning,' she said 27 years later. 'I have no suspects whatsoever.'

The open window and the cut flywire remain a mystery. But she says: 'I believe she was taken out the front door, which had been left unlocked.'

THREE decades after his daughter disappeared, Lindsay Worledge is 'constantly' reminded of his loss. When he is introduced to strangers, they still often ask if he is related to Eloise.

'I am amazed at the reaction, even now,' he says.

Lindsay knows he was treated as a suspect by police not because of evidence pointing to him but because of the lack of evidence pointing elsewhere. He simply filled the void. 'It was all circumstantial.'

Forensic evidence suggesting she was not taken through the open bedroom window meant Eloise's parents had to be investigated. 'We were tangible. There was little else.'

He agreed to take the lie-detector test in the hope he would finally have the concrete proof that he was a father who lost a child, not a man who abducted one.

'The results were inconclusive. It did not produce a result which would satisfy police curiosity.'

He says that after the test he researched polygraph testing to find that ten per cent of tests are neutral. 'If I had known that then, I would not have had the polygraph. It is a very weak science and that is why the tests are not admitted in Victorian courts.'

Lindsay answers questions in a polite and measured manner. He has been asked them all many times before. There are no surprises, no new twists, no new evidence and no new hope.

He says he is a 'double victim' because of the constant speculation that he was, in some way, involved in the abduction, but he knows that he is powerless to alter perceptions.

'It (the speculation) was hardly pleasant. It was not of my making.'

Police say there is no evidence linking him to his daughter's disappearance. Some who worked on the case have their own theories, but they don't believe they really know what happened that night.

Happily remarried since 1980, Lindsay left tertiary teaching to establish a successful management consultancy, retiring in January 2003.

He says he was able to rebuild his life because 'there is a powerful stimulus to go on trying – to go forward'.

Like his former wife, he did not believe the new investigation or the coroner's inquest would provide any fresh insight into the case. He was right. 'I was dubious. It is essentially the recycling of memories, which are over 25 years old.'

He says he has his own thoughts on what happened that night, but they 'are an interpretation of nothing. They are just theories'.

PATSY Worledge still lives near the sea but no longer in Scott Street, Beaumaris. She is not angry and does not see herself as a victim even though she has twice been touched by tragedy, as too has Lindsay.

The Worledges' youngest child, Blake – the little boy who was first to realise Eloise was missing – grew to be a well-liked young man who worked as an information technology and quality manager for a forklift-truck distributor.

He died when struck by a car while crossing Whitehorse Road in Nunawading on a wet night in August 1997.

His mother says, 'You don't get over it, you just have to go through it.'

She spends much of her time with her art work, paintings and textile pictures, and caring for her daughter Anna's three children.

In the weeks after Eloise's disappearance, friends and family encouraged her to keep hoping, but a counsellor gently told her she might have to come to terms with never seeing her daughter again.

For about twelve years, she did keep hoping and wanting to know what had happened. But, as years passed, she accepted that Eloise was gone and she would probably never know what happened that night. 'It was time to move on. People still see me as a victim but I don't live like one.'

She knows that the case has fascinated many and resulted in

her being the subject of bizarre rumours, including that she was related to Lindy Chamberlain, whose baby Azaria was taken by a dingo in 1980.

The media, she says, have tried to pigeonhole her as a victim, turning up to seek interviews on the anniversaries of the abduction, when Eloise would have turned 21, or for routine quotes to pad out stories about mystery disappearances.

'Nothing has changed since January 1976. I don't have any guilt. I didn't leave my children somewhere or send them down the street. She was safely tucked in her bed. It is a jigsaw with a piece missing. And it is still missing.

'The inquest has stirred up a lot of emotion that we didn't need – personally or as a community.

'I long ago realised that I didn't need to know what happened on that night.'

On July 7, 2003, Coroner Frank Hender held the inquest. Despite the fact that the Eloise Worldege case had been fuelled by decades of speculation, his written finding was less than three pages.

'Widespread media coverage caused public awareness to the extent that thousands of pieces of information were reported to police and investigated,' he said.

'Exhaustive inquiries in respect to prowlers, known sex offenders, neighbourhood inquiries and vehicle checks have not advanced this inquiry.

'Eloise was a shy girl who would not have voluntarily left her home with a stranger.

'It is not possible on the evidence to find who were the person or persons responsible or when and how Eloise met her demise but her disappearance and presumed death remain suspicious. I therefore return an open finding.'

CHAPTER 7

Swamp Fever

'Everything seemed to point to him as the killer.'

THE secret behind one of Australia's greatest crime mysteries, the Lady of the Swamp murder, has now gone to the grave – twice. Or three times, if you count an unmarked burial site that no living person knows how to find.

More than 40 years after Margaret Clement – a one-time socialite who became a recluse in her decaying South Gippsland mansion – disappeared without trace, police quietly reopened the case. They always believed at least one person, besides the suspected murderer, knew what really happened, but that she refused to make a statement for four decades because of loyalty ... and fear.

Detectives had long given up hope of charging the killer, but they still believed the mystery could be solved if that one witness would tell what she knew.

But in September, 1993, the case was closed for the last time when Esme Millicent Livingstone, then 77, died in a nursing home in the Latrobe Valley town of Morwell, in eastern Victoria.

The policeman who had been in charge of the case since 1978, Detective Senior Sergeant Bill Townsend, had hoped Mrs Livingstone would have been prepared to tell him what he and others had always suspected – that her husband Stanley was the killer.

'I believe that she has taken the secret to the grave with her,' Townsend said afterwards.

The eccentric Miss Clement, then 72 and a virtual recluse, went missing in suspicious circumstances from her 810-hectare property, Tullaree, on May 21, 1952.

Senior Sergeant Townsend interviewed Mrs Livingstone when he took over the case after he was posted to the homicide squad in the 1970s.

He was convinced she knew what had happened to Miss Clement, but was afraid to speak.

'When I spoke to her, she said: "I'd like to help, but I'm too frightened." I am sure she was frightened of what her husband would do if she talked,' Bill Townsend was to recall weeks after his potential star witness died.

Stanley Livingstone, aged in his late 70s, died in October 1992 after suffering a heart attack while fighting a small bushfire on one of his properties in Queensland.

He owned most of Curtis Island, near Gladstone, had substantial rural property interests, and – if police were right about the Lady of The Swamp murder – he proved that crime does occasionally pay.

He died a millionaire, and had laid the foundations of his fortune by obtaining Tullaree at a bargain price from Miss

Clement, then improving it and reselling it for a handsome profit.

Bill Townsend was one of the few people still able to connect Stanley Livingstone with the mystery from South Gippsland. But the death of an elderly landowner in Queensland was not big news, and by the time Townsend, then the officer in charge of a suburban CIB, learned of Livingstone's death, it was too late.

Confined to a wheelchair and in ill-health, Esme Livingstone returned to Victoria after her husband's death. For almost eleven months she was in the nursing home, free from the intimidation of her husband.

Perhaps then, she would have been prepared to say what really happened in the swamps of South Gippsland in 1952. But no-one ever asked.

She died within weeks of Townsend learning of her husband's earlier death in Queensland.

'Now that she has died, I think that closes the last chapter of the mystery,' the policeman said.

IT was a story that had begun in World War I, when Miss Clement and her sister, Jeanne, inherited the beautiful and productive Gippsland pastoral property from their father, Peter Scott Clement.

The former bullock driver had made a fortune as a director of the once-famous Long Tunnel Mine in Walhalla, which was the richest gold mine in Victoria.

As well as the property, he left his daughters the then massive amount of £50,000 each.

The two women, then in their twenties, spent the next fifteen years travelling overseas, meeting royalty and rubbing shoulders with Victoria's squattocracy.

But, while the young women were away, unscrupulous managers let the property run down, secretly selling prize cattle and replacing them with second-class stock.

The drains on the property were allowed to silt over, and eventually most of the lush farm returned to the swampland it had been before white settlement.

The Clement sisters, used to easy money and unused to work, began to sell off tracts of land to pay growing bills. In 1950, Jeanne died.

The fourteen-room Victorian homestead had fallen into disrepair and was infested with bats, rats and snakes. Her beauty faded, her friends gone and her eccentric ways becoming more pronounced, the surviving sister, Margaret, carried a walking stick and wore gumboots to wade through water in the rising swamp that circled the house.

She spent her evenings reading crime mysteries by the light of a kerosene lamp.

The property was eventually mortgaged, but Miss Clement kept a caveat preventing the transfer without her approval.

In 1951, a neighbour, Stanley Russell Livingstone, persuaded Miss Clement to allow him to buy Tullaree for £16,000 on the proviso he built her a two-bedroom house near the original homestead.

It was a shrewd buy. Twelve years later, after draining the property and restoring it, he was to sell Tullaree for £126,000. Meanwhile, there had been much speculation about the old woman's disappearance and presumed murder, but nothing could be pinned on the domineering Livingstone, who was renowned for feats of strength and his notorious filthy temper.

THE speculation might have remained exactly that as the years passed, with only the thinning ranks of old local residents remembering the Clement sisters and Margaret's strange disappearance in the swamps she knew so well.

But in 1978, an earthmoving contractor, preparing some newly subdivided blocks of land for sale at Venus Bay, noticed some strange bones exposed by his machine about a metre below the surface. He investigated, and the police were called.

Tests showed that the bones were human. Careful searching revealed a rotting purse with four shillings and a sixpence – coins pre-dating not only decimal currency but also, significantly, 1952. An old shawl and a shovel and hammer were also recovered.

The presence of the shovel and hammer seemed to indicate that the bones belonged to a crime victim who had been buried by her killer.

The body was in a spot about four kilometres from Tullaree where Stanley Livingstone used to graze cattle.

This was significant, in light of the suggestion that Livingstone's wife once blurted to a friend that he had run cattle back and forth over the grave, to hide the freshly-turned earth – an allegation she later refused to repeat to police.

Senior Sergeant Townsend said he believed Livingstone killed the old woman in a fit of rage and then buried the body. 'He had a bad temper. I believe he hit her, and she may have fallen and possibly fractured her skull. He panicked, put the body in the four-wheel-drive and later buried it.'

He said he believed the theory that Livingstone then ran cattle over the grave.

'Everything seemed to point to him as the killer,' he said. Esme Livingstone had told at least four people at separate times over many years that her husband was responsible for Margaret Clement's death.

In 1980, the inquest into Miss Clement's death was told that

Esme Livingstone had confided to a friend that her husband had organised to have Miss Clement killed.

Jean Lesley Sharp gave evidence that Mrs Livingstone said her husband had forced Miss Clement to sign documents at gunpoint, and later organised to have her killed.

Another friend said that Mrs Livingstone had once handed her a letter and told her: 'If I disappear suddenly, hand this to the police.'

The woman said she opened the letter years later and it read: 'He was in a temper as usual. He got rid of the body. The grave is not very far from the house.' Unfortunately, the letter could not be produced for the coroner.

The inquest was also told Mrs Livingstone had told someone else that her husband paid £500 to two notorious Melbourne criminals of the 1950s, Bradley and Bradshaw, to get rid of the body. Mrs Livingstone denied the claims at the inquest.

Stanley Livingstone, who had played sixteen games for Footscray as a ruckman, had been known for feats of strength such as lifting a full 44-gallon drum on to a truck. He was a hard worker and a shrewd farmer.

After selling the Clement property at a massive profit, he bought another property at Yea before selling out and buying the $1.5million, 3240-hectare property on Curtis Island, off the Queensland coast – a long way from South Gippsland and nosy neighbours with long memories.

He was never charged over the Clement murder.

He told the inquest that he had nothing to do with the disappearance.

'I did not do anything to Miss Clement, I'll guarantee that,' he told the coroner in a crowded South Gippsland courtroom. Under the old man's watchful eye, his wife also gave evidence denying any knowledge about the death.

The coroner, Kevin Mason, was unimpressed. He said the evidence of the Livingstones was not truthful. 'I think they were, in their answers, in a number of ways, far from frank with the court,' he noted in his finding.

But he concluded that the bones found near Venus Bay could not be positively identified as those of Margaret Clement.

Among those spoken to by police was a Ren Lanzon from Gladstone in Queensland, who had got to know Stanley Livingstone in his old age.

Lanzon described Livingstone as a man with a strange sense of humour. 'He sometimes joked about killing someone. He said he was going to write a book called *How to Kill Your Wife*.'

CHAPTER 8

Beauty and the Beast

'You've heard the expression 'dead meat' – well, that's what you're going to be.'

VETERAN homicide investigator Charlie Bezzina was on leave and driving towards Gippsland in eastern Victoria when his mobile phone rang.

The man at the other end didn't need to introduce himself. They had known each other for almost ten years, although they would never be friends.

The caller was Vic Ramchen. He had phoned to say that one of his three gifted children had just won an international maths prize in the United States.

Bezzina congratulated the proud father and wished his children well. But as he drove on, he wondered why Ramchen felt compelled to share the news with him.

The detective knew he would soon charge Ramchen with the murder of his missing wife, a crime the suspect had always denied. He believed Ramchen was giving him a message ... but what?

Was Ramchen saying that whatever had happened in April 1992, when Jacqui Ramchen disappeared from her South Yarra mansion, had not harmed the children?

Did he want the detective to know that, despite the police belief he was a murderer, he was still a good father?

Or was he saying that his children were better off without a mother who could have destroyed his family and their financial security? That, in desperate times, the end can justify the means?

It is one small mystery wrapped inside the enigma of a murder investigation that will always remain suspended in time.

WHEN Jacqueline Mertens returned to Melbourne in 1980 after eight years overseas, she was broke – but the flighty former model had a plan to make sure she would always enjoy the lavish lifestyle she had pursued around the world.

The 1970s television game show hostess wanted a husband, children, a mansion and money – lots of it.

To win her version of the jackpot, the 32-year-old planned to use the most ancient method of all. She knew her bankable assets were her stunning looks and smouldering sexuality. The former model on the successful TV quiz show *The Price is Right* no longer strutted the catwalk, but she still turned heads in the street.

After her modest television career, she had gone to Hong Kong and married. When that relationship failed, she moved to London to work in fashion and modelling before returning to Australia.

Her plan to find a rich husband was not an original one, but what made Jacqui Mertens different was she was honest about her intentions and ruthlessly determined in her application.

She would later confide to friends that she was going to marry for money, and that love would come later.

One friend told police: 'She ran out of money and came back to Australia. Jacqui was 32 at the time and she had told her mother that the first man who came along she would marry. She seemed to have set a time limit. She mentioned that the man had to have money.'

But Jacqui was not prepared to trust fate and initiated her own star search. She remembered a stern-faced civil engineer with a business brain she had met by chance at a Melbourne restaurant eight years earlier.

They had gone out once when she was about to leave to be married in Hong Kong. Now she wondered whether he was still available.

She found out within weeks of returning to Melbourne. His name was Slavik Ramchen. He was a hard-working, hard-drinking divorcee, known as Vic or Victor.

Ramchen's younger sister, Erika, was working as his secretary at his Richmond office when an attractive and confident woman walked in.

'I thought she was someone wanting to sell carbon paper or something and I asked her why she wanted to see Vic and she stated she was a friend,' Erika was to recall.

'I don't think Vic recognised her. Jacqui jogged Vic's memory and then we all had a drink in the office.' The two not-so-old friends went out to dinner that night.

'The next morning I learnt that Jacqui had stayed with Vic that night ... I thought that it would be a one-night stand,' Erika said.

She was wrong.

The couple began to date, and about a month later, Erika arrived at the home she shared with Vic in Erin Street, Richmond, to find Jacqui 'sitting out the front of his house on a suitcase'. The next day, she moved in.

Erika did not trust the younger woman. 'During this time I saw a great deal of Jacqui, as we were living in the same house and it was apparent that Jacqui was persistently asking Vic to marry her. She was constantly trying to project herself as being a potential model wife.'

Ramchen's sister was not the only one with doubts. Jacqui's father, Josephus, said: 'I first met Victor about a week before he and Jacqui married. They came to our house in Belgrave. As soon as I met Victor, I did not like him. I thought he was too smooth or devious or something like that.'

In June 1980, they married at the registry office. It was no society wedding but the model and the businessman seemed happy enough. She was obviously a classic beauty but it would be many years before police would allege he was the classic beast.

RAMCHEN had built up a strong civil engineering firm and was expanding into property development with projects in Gisborne and Northcote. His work was professional and thorough. He once promised to build ten shops in twelve weeks for the Gisborne development. He made the deadline.

In 1979 he had bought a 'weekender' – Macedon Grange, a beautiful 100-hectare property near Woodend. In the early 1980s, he built a big bluestone house there. By the late '80s, the property was valued at almost $1.5million.

Property prices were buoyant and life was good. Ramchen was gruff, hard and uncompromising, but according to Erika, he wasn't violent: 'Vic barks, but does not bite'.

BEAUTY AND THE BEAST

Business associates say Ramchen was confident to the point of arrogance and bristled with self-belief. 'Nothing seemed to worry him,' one said.

He would leave his shops empty rather than compromise on rent.

He was rich and getting richer. Jacqui seemed content, but she soon made it clear she wanted more – she wanted to be the model mother as well as a socialite wife. Vic, eight years older, had lingering doubts. 'I did not really want children ... I considered myself too old to be kicking footballs around and other such fatherly activities, but she was young and wanted children.'

Vic warmed to the idea and the couple had two boys and a girl. All were to become gifted students – despite the trauma they were to endure.

Friends said Jacqui was a good mother. 'She and Lev (her eldest) were particularly close. He was very much a mummy's boy. She was protective of him and the other children,' former neighbour Christine Mills told police.

Another neighbour, Elizabeth Farrell, also noticed how close Lev was to his mother 'back then'.

After the birth of their third child in 1989, the Ramchens bought the 100-year-old mansion, Fairbairn, in Domain Road, South Yarra, for almost $3million.

The once-beautiful two-storey home had been renovated in the 1920s, but had been in decline for years. The Ramchens were determined to return it to its prime. It would be the perfect stage for their showcase marriage.

One business contact remembers going to the house soon after the Ramchens moved in. 'There were between 40 and 50 tradesmen swarming around. I said it looked like a great place and Vic said, "It will be when I've finished".'

Jacqui told a friend they were spending 'hundreds of thousands' on the renovations. Then came the crash – financial, emotional and physical.

THE first semi-public fracture in the marriage happened a year after the wedding.

The Ramchens, Erika and her husband Michael were having a drink and a chat. Vic Ramchen was holding court, making the point that education was the cornerstone of success. Michael solemnly agreed. According to Erika: 'With that, Jacqui said that whatever they could get with their education and money she could get "with this" and she pointed to her female part.'

Vic was shocked and angry at this vulgar display. He stormed out and within a few hours Jacqui moved back to her parents' home in Belgrave.

According to Erika, Jacqui was desperate to patch up their problems and went to his office. 'She was begging and pleading for Vic to take her back and she physically dropped to her knees and continued to beg.'

The next day she had moved back. Their problems didn't surface – at least publicly – for another decade.

Some relationships slowly disintegrate; others explode. Few turn into the running, public battle the Ramchens waged with each other. Even Vic would later say to police that his marriage would 'make a bloody good soapie'.

The big gates and tall spiked fence in front of the mansion could not conceal the ongoing war.

Marlene Gould lived next door with her husband Noel, and three adult children. On December 21, 1991, she was cleaning up after her son's 21st birthday when she heard the Ramchens abusing each other. 'He was putting his hands on her and she was saying, "Leave me alone".'

Five days later there was another argument.

'She was saying things like, "I'm sick of you calling me a whore and a prostitute ... If I as much as look sideways you think I'm having an affair with everybody ... I may as well be dead as living the way you treat me".

'I heard Vic say, "Why don't you kill me?" She said, "Stand in front of the car and I'll run you over." Vic stood in front of the car, the BMW. Jacqui got in, turned on the motor, opened the door, yelled out, "Get down the driveway further so that I can run at you." Vic did this, and then Jacqui drove at him quite quickly. When the car got near him Vic jumped out of the way and Jacqui put the brakes on.

'I couldn't say if the car would have hit Vic if he didn't move. I didn't know if Jacqui would have been able to stop. Jacqui screamed out he was a coward. She said, "You won't even stand there and let me kill you, but you'll be happy when you kill me".'

She heard more arguments and saw Vic's mother yelling, 'This wouldn't happen if you were a good wife ... You should be a good wife. You must have sex with your husband.'

'Later that night, I heard them out the back. I heard laughing and I think they were playing with the kids, so everything appeared okay to me.'

It was a pattern that was repeated regularly – moments of insane anger punctuating an apparently normal family life. Jacqui's brother, Jack Mertens, went to the Domain Road house to visit his sister. What followed left the quiet farmer stunned. He later told police that Ramchen 'started saying that Jacqui was a whore and he was making accusations about her ... At one stage, Jacqui started slapping Vic across the face and on the chest.'

Ramchen asked to see Mertens inside and, according to the

brother, said: 'Look, Jack, I don't know what to do, whether to shoot myself or her.'

Later, in the backyard, 'Vic kept calling Jacqui a slut and a whore and Jacqui lost it again and grabbed a ladder and threw it at him. She was calling him a pig. She also threw a glass at Vic, but it missed him and hit the wall beside him.'

Even though her brother suggested she go with him, she remained determined to stay at the mansion. News of the arguments spread. It became the talk of their children's private school, Christ Church Grammar.

In 1992, a group of mothers and a teacher were standing together at pick-up time at the school when Vic Ramchen walked past. According to one of the mothers, Maree Turner, he said, 'How do you do? I'm Vic Ramchen and my wife is a harlot'.

Jacqui was no more interested in keeping matters private, telling Turner that Vic demanded sex 'eight times a day'.

In early 1992, Jacqui saw a woman she knew from when their children had attended the same kindergarten. They went for coffee at the Jam Factory in Prahran.

As the children drank milkshakes, Jacqui Ramchen unburdened herself to the increasingly embarrassed acquaintance. 'I was uncomfortable that her children were present when she talked of Vic and the problems they were experiencing.'

Jacqui talked of their financial problems and said she and her husband began drinking wine and arguing after the morning school run. 'This was said in front of the children.'

Jacqui told another friend, Helen Grant, that Ramchen was 'watching her every move. She said that Victor was smart but she said that she could outsmart him.' Grant described Jacqui Ramchen as a sensitive and loving mother.

Ramchen was known as a quiet and brooding man. As his

marriage began to unravel, so did he. Once, when queried about an overdue account at his local service station, Ramchen showed his increasingly bizarre behaviour. Manager David Sasse told police that in a shop full of people Ramchen yelled out, 'I'm experiencing matrimonial difficulties'.

'Everyone's mouths dropped and (they) looked at him in embarrassment,' Sasse said.

The couple yelled in the streets, argued at parties and involved friends, relatives and strangers in their fights. Some were bemused, others horrified, while most were rivetted by this real-life soap opera.

Once, Ramchen drove to the school to spy on his wife during a fundraising card night. 'I could see Jacqui and this man and he was definitely paying her much more than friendly attention. I went in and told her to come home with me,' Ramchen would later tell police.

On March 20, 1992, police were called to the house for a routine domestic disturbance.

Constable Peter Easton said Jacqui Ramchen claimed she was in the 'process of filing for divorce' and she had moved to the rear of the house.

Jacqui told the police she would leave when she was financially stable. 'She indicated strongly that at this time she would also take the children when she left.'

As police were talking to Jacqui her husband interjected, saying: 'You're nothing but a slut. You're a whore.' When police tried to calm him: 'He then redirected his hostility towards us,' Easton said.

Jacqui started talking to a Catholic nun about her marriage. Victor rang Sister Michele Kennan and asked to see her. The nun was uncomfortable with the meeting, but finally agreed after Ramchen persisted.

He brought two bottles of wine as gifts, and 'evidence' – a love letter and a bag of his wife's lingerie – to prove she was sexually promiscuous.

According to Jacqui's mother, Hennie Mertens, Ramchen beat her daughter. Eight months before she disappeared, Jacqui drove to her parents' Phillip Island home. 'She was all bruised and her hair was all over the place, she had scratches on the face and bruises on her arms.'

Jacqui's father, Josephus Mertens, had not liked Ramchen from their first meeting. His feelings grew to hatred and he refused to visit the Domain Road mansion.

He said he had suspected his daughter was the victim of violence for at least three years, but Jacqui continued to claim she had 'walked into a door or things like that'.

He said she came to their home with bruises on her back and legs, scratches on her face and a 'big bald patch on her head where her hair had been pulled out'. She then finally told her father she had been beaten by her husband.

'We tried to get Jacqui to leave Victor and to come and live at home but she would not leave,' Josephus said.

Ramchen would later admit to police that eight months before she disappeared, 'I grabbed her by the hair ... yes, there could have been some scratches.'

She complained to her doctor that her husband had beaten her but, as a magistrates' court would later hear, there was no independent evidence that Ramchen routinely beat his wife, although there was no argument that she often suffered bruises and scratches.

For months, Ramchen believed his wife was having affairs; it would appear that at times she had baited the older man – first suggesting, then denying that she had a string of mystery lovers.

His fears and anger increased when she had breast enlargement surgery. 'I mean, who are you doing this for? ... Who you gonna show your bloody boobs to?' he reportedly asked her.

He would tell police his suspicions grew when 'she started buying lacy lingerie ... I could not believe she was buying it for my benefit'.

He would later declare: 'She had the morals of an alley cat.'

Ramchen's concerns over his wife's fidelity were justified. She did have a fling with the father of another child at the school – a man she admitted to friends she actively pursued and seduced.

GARY Forrester, a barrister from St Kilda, had separated from his wife and would arrive at school around 3pm to pick up his children. He was one of the only males in the yard.

'Jacqui approached me and asked if I wanted to have a coffee at the school.' He agreed immediately. The former model was used to getting what she wanted.

'Jacqui then asked if I was living by myself and asked if I wanted her to visit me sometimes.'

They had a brief affair, but it was never going to last.

According to Forrester, he started to get threatening phone calls from a male in August 1991. 'I remember on one occasion he stated to me, "You've heard the expression 'dead meat' – well, that's what you're going to be".'

In one call, the man he believed was Victor suggested they meet and talk about it 'man to man' but the barrister declined the offer.

Forrester continued to deny the affair. In one call the man said, 'You're lying to me, you mongrel. I'm going to fix you. You're dead meat. You had better get back to America and stay there, you're finished here. I'll kill you.'

Ramchen drove to Forrester's St Kilda house and took his nine-year-old son Lev with him. The boy was being dragged into the black hole of his parents' mutual hatred.

According to Forrester, the angry husband said in front of Lev, 'What am I going to tell this kid? You've been out f...... his mother'.

Forrester broke off all contact with Jacqui.

At a chance meeting when he saw Ramchen in the schoolyard he tried to engage him in a neutral conversation, but Victor responded: 'You'll pay for this'. Even after Jacqui disappeared in April 1992, the cold war continued. Forrester said that in late July Ramchen said, 'I haven't forgotten'. At another chance meeting he called the barrister 'scum'.

He contacted Forrester's estranged wife, who said later: 'Vic was saying that he had friends in the Mafia and he had plenty of money, but he wouldn't do anything yet and his friends said they could have Gary and Jacqui put in the bottom of the sea.'

What made it even stranger was that the ex-wife was a Melbourne magistrate – not the type of person usually taken into confidence over murder plans.

Late in 1991, Ramchen saw the magistrate again. 'He said that he had forgiven Gary but he had not forgiven Jacqui ... I felt that Victor was a vindictive person.'

Her concerns grew when in February 1992, she saw Ramchen at the school. 'I noticed that Victor was hiding behind a fence ... I saw Jacqui nearby and felt that Victor was watching her.'

Forrester was not the only man to receive threats. Jacqui's dentist, Dr Larry Benge, said he received three phone calls at his Knox surgery accusing him of having an affair with his patient.

He then received four phone calls at home before changing his number to a silent line.

But the tragedy was broader than a betrayed husband and a missing wife. According to Forrester, three months after Jacqui went missing he was confronted by Lev in the school. The boy 'came up to me and said, "Just you wait until I get bigger and I'll fix you up".'

IT was a wet night on April 8, 1992, and only half the women in the adult education class at Prahran TAFE turned up for the three-hour millinery course. It was that night that Jacqui decided to 'hold court'. About six women crowded around in a semi-circle while Jacqui sat in the middle, legs crossed. 'She basically announced that she was going to tell us her life story,' one recalled.

The story was one of show business, fame, glamour, sex, violence, betrayal, adultery, greed and intrigue. They were enthralled.

One of the students, Debra Elliott, told police: 'We all suggested to her that if her husband was that bad she should leave him, but she said no because if she did that she would never see her kids again.

'Jacqui said that she had an affair with one of the fathers from the school where her kids went ... she took a fancy to him.'

Another student, Jane Stevens, said Ramchen told the group her husband beat her and trapped her in the house. 'She wanted to have an affair and she told us that she had one with a lawyer. She admitted that she had instigated it. She told us that she had eyed off this guy whilst collecting the children. She went to bed with him a couple of times, but the affair didn't last long.'

Julie Costello recalls being shocked by the rambling monologue. 'She said, "I don't care what happens to me now ... I don't care if he kills me".'

Two days later she disappeared.

AT 8.30am on April 10, 1992, Jacqui Ramchen drove her children to school in Punt Road, South Yarra, in her blue BMW. The school insisted a parent or carer sign the attendance book on arrival and again when picking up children.

Jacqui signed the book when she dropped them off and was designated to pick them up. Yet it was Vic who collected them at 2.50pm that day – ten minutes early. There was no sign of Jacqui.

The school had not been notified of the change of arrangements as was required. But it was a minor breach of the rules and no-one worried – at the time.

Jacqui's tiny circle of friends revolved around the school. She had become the subject of real concern and idle gossip among many of the mothers in the schoolyard.

But it was the last day of term one and it would be two weeks before anyone at school noticed she was gone – and it would be five weeks before she was reported missing.

Hennie Mertens, who knew the relationship between her daughter and son-in-law was destructive, said she received a phone call at her Phillip Island home on April 5 and could hear Vic in the background being typically abusive.

Jacqui said she would ring back on her mother's birthday on April 12 and would come down to the island with the children in the second week of the holidays.

She was not to hear from her daughter again.

She repeatedly tried to ring Jacqui, but the phone was always engaged. She knew that Vic often took the phone off the hook when he didn't want to be disturbed. So concerned was she about her daughter's state of mind, she started to ring psychiatric hospitals to see if she had been admitted.

Mothers at the school started to talk when Vic took over the duty of dropping his children off in the mornings. One said she was frightened to approach the man with the notorious temper. Finally, two weeks into the second term, one asked about Jacqui and Ramchen responded: 'She's gone and I don't care if I never see her again'.

One mother, Anne Dutton, still remembers her reaction: 'My words were, "Oh my God, I hope he hasn't done away with her".'

On May 11 or 12 Hennie Mertens rang Vic's mother, Anna Ramchen, who told her to go to Jacqui and Vic's house. When she went to Fairbairn, Ramchen said, 'Well, she left me'. Mrs Mertens spoke to Sister Kennan, the nun who reported Jacqui missing to the Prahran police.

When the investigation began, the mother of three had been missing 38 days and the trail was already cold.

On May 18, 1992, Sergeant Elizabeth Batten and Constable Wayne Treloar went to the mansion to make inquiries about Jacqui Ramchen's disappearance.

They found the front gates were chained and padlocked. They had to scale the two-metre fence. They told Ramchen his wife had been reported missing. His response was that she had left him and 'was really just a slut'.

When he was asked why he hadn't bothered to report her disappearance he said: 'I wasn't too concerned because I believe that she has run off with whoever, like some little tramp, and I did not even consider that there was any need to be worried about her safety'.

Police took a statement from nine-year-old Lev Ramchen. It is an extraordinary and tragic document from a gifted boy who lost his childhood due to his parents' obsessions.

'Jacqui is my natural mother. I do not love my mother because I cannot love someone who was destroying the family ... According to her she started the affair in September, 1991.

We believe the affair started earlier. When I say we, I mean my father and I. My father said he would not forget what Gary Forrester had done to the family.

'When we realised she was gone, my father was not really upset. He did not really care. He had started not to care whether she stayed or left about two weeks before she left.'

Ten years later, his father's defence team at the murder committal called Lev, one of the top VCE students in the state and enrolled in law at Melbourne University. He told the court: 'It's not entirely clear, then or now, where she is or what happened to her.'

JUST before Jacqui Ramchen went missing Victor's property empire was beginning to crumble. He was pouring money into his home, which, like his marriage, was just a shell.

When police searched the house in 1992 they found the front entrance area could have been a cover shot from *Vogue*, furnished with exquisite antiques and period pieces. The rest of the ground floor was functional but upstairs was 'very poor' with empty rooms and mattresses strewn on the floor.

His Woodend property, Macedon Grange, with its expensive bluestone homestead, was put on the market in 1988 but no-one would pay the asking price of $1.4million.

The property crash, coupled with high interest rates, left Ramchen dangerously exposed. According to a police financial profile, his gross annual rental income was around $382,000 from shops in Northcote and Gisborne, but his interest bill from the Commonwealth Bank was $416,000.

He bought the Domain Road house in late 1988 at the height of the property peak at around $2.8million, but within four years values in South Yarra and Toorak had been slashed.

According to a police analysis, the value of the house had

dropped at least $1million by 1992. But interest rates were still crippling.

Five weeks before Jacqui disappeared, the Commonwealth Bank had sent Ramchen a letter demanding the repayment of a $3.1million loan. If his wife had divorced him and demanded $1.5million he may have been forced to sell all his property at the bottom of the cycle.

A family law court lawyer said if the Ramchens had become involved in a bitter divorce, legal fees could have been up to $300,000.

Two months before she disappeared, Jacqui told her mother she had started divorce proceedings and would be free in eight months. She had moved into the back of the mansion and, though they lived under the one roof, they were technically separated.

She told friends that Vic would use 'every cent' to fight a custody battle over the children.

Ramchen would later tell police his wife said, 'I want a divorce,' and he responded 'It's not that bloody simple. We've got three kids, you know. We've got a bad economy, you know, there's properties'.

Vic didn't trust his wife and yet when she disappeared he made no efforts to find her. Jacqui married for money, a house and for children, yet she walked out on all three.

According to police, she had access to five family and business accounts and up to $350,000, yet there is no record of her trying to withdraw any money or of her husband bothering to inquire if any of the money was missing.

He either knew she wouldn't move on the cash or he was beyond caring.

Vic Ramchen's finances slowly recovered. By 2002, Fairbairn was estimated to be worth around $4million. Real estate experts say the Woodend homestead's market value was around $1million after four small lots from the property had been sold for about $320,000.

The day Jacqui went missing Vic left his children with his mother and went with a friend to Macedon Grange. The next day he returned and took his children out for a Chinese meal, showing little concern that his wife was gone, even though her BMW was still parked in the drive.

WITHIN a few weeks the mysteries surrounding the Ramchens spread to their country property with reports of two unexplained burglaries.

The first break-in was alleged to have occurred between April 24 and May 1, 1992 – but police found little sense in the crime.

The thieves gained access to the house by jemmying a wooden side door. It was strange because the point of entry was visible from the road, even though there were obvious access points away from public view.

The burglars showed uncharacteristic consideration, choosing the point of entry that caused the least damage to the property.

The thieves also appeared to know what they wanted. There was no ransacking of the house, and no apparent search for valuables. They stole a large woollen rug, three smaller rugs and a small colour television.

The large rug was under a solid coffee table, which would have taken two strong people to move yet the value of the rug was not substantial.

Police at the scene wondered why the thieves would ignore valuables to take the rug. They have concluded the rug must have been important to someone. Or someone wanted it to disappear.

In mid-July, thieves broke into the property again. This time they used bolt cutters to cut a padlock before breaking into a machinery shed.

They took some of Jacqui's perfumes and an antique table that was one of her favourites. Vic said he believed one of Jacqui's lovers was behind the theft, but police say if she had wanted her gear she had a key. Nothing else was taken. The thieves had to walk past valuables to get the smaller items.

POLICE spent years trying to find out what happened to Jacqui Ramchen. They searched Fairbairn, the Woodend property and a bird-watching area near Werribee frequented by the family, but found nothing. They even used radar to check under a concrete floor at Fairbairn.

Few people, no matter how desperate or cunning, can disappear without leaving electronic footprints through interlinked computers.

Police checked credit cards, Medicare, immigration, change of name records, taxation, social security, births, deaths and marriages, and road traffic authorities. They found Jacqui Ramchen's licence had lapsed and she had not tried to get money from any of the family bank accounts.

Police had established motive and opportunity for Jacqui's murder. What they lacked was a body. They would have to prove not only who did it but that it was done at all.

Homicide squad detectives prepared a brief of evidence and lawyers from the Office of Public Prosecutions agreed there was sufficient evidence to justify charging Victor Ramchen with murder.

The OPP's established standard is that the evidence to be presented before a jury would support a 'reasonable prospect of conviction'. But it was always going to a high-risk prosecution. Without a body, murder is notoriously difficult to prove.

On July 27, 2001, Detective Senior Sergeant Bezzina finally arrested Ramchen. The suspect didn't see it coming. 'I'm shocked. I mean I can't see the basis for these charges,' he protested.

Asked if he wanted to say anything he responded: 'Not at this stage, there will be plenty said later, obviously.'

And there was.

The committal hearing took eight expensive days. Ramchen had a top legal team expertly led by Robert Richter QC, the silk department's silk, who includes controversial businessman John Elliott, ATSIC leader Geoff Clark and colourful Melbourne mediator Mick Gatto among his high-profile clients.

Witnesses swore that Jacqui would never leave her children, and always contacted her family on birthdays, anniversaries and special events. They said they were convinced she was dead.

But others said she discussed 'vanishing without trace' into Asia.

One witness, Dr Elizabeth Farrell, said: 'She told me that she was leaving. When she told me that I had the feeling that she was leaving without the children.' Another said Jacqui told her: 'If I had to disappear, I could.'

Richter argued that the Crown could not prove that the missing woman had not deliberately disappeared – or had fled and met her death at the hands of someone other than her husband.

On March 14, 2002, Magistrate Kim Parkinson found there was insufficient evidence to present Ramchen before a Supreme Court jury on the charge of murder. He was released.

Police had to pay his legal costs of almost $180,000. But, after the hearing, Ramchen, then 61, was a much less imposing figure. Soon after he was acquitted, he was diagnosed with terminal cancer.

Ramchen was determined to settle his affairs. He put the mansion on the market – originally for $5.85million, but later dropped the asking price to $3million plus. In July, 2002, it went to auction and was passed in at $3.8million before being sold for an undisclosed price. Macedon Grange was also put on the market for $1.475million.

Charlie Bezzina passed a message to the ill man. He wanted an anonymous letter telling him where Jacqui's body was hidden. 'I would like to be able to find her for the sake of the family.' The letter never arrived.

Ramchen died in October 2002 and his fortune was distributed according to his will. But under the law his wife would have had a legally binding case for a share.

All the former TV glamour-girl, who dreamt of being a millionaire, had to do was come forward like a delirious game show contestant.

But of course she did not. She could not.

IN 1950 Hennie and Josephus Mertens and their three children left Rotterdam in their native Holland for Australia. The young mother couldn't speak English and was left to survive in a house in the bush near Monbulk while her husband worked in the building trade. She later started making sandwiches for a local shop, then serving food in a small local restaurant.

Within ten years Hennie Mertens felt confident enough to start her own business. She took over a local hall used for bush dances and turned it into the Highwood Inn, a restaurant catering for day trippers with home-made soups, old-style roasts, and traditional desserts. 'They loved my jelly wine trifle,' she recalls.

Her daughter Jacqui worked at the restaurant even before she left school.

'She was a popular hostess. She was good with children, everyone liked her.'

Jacqui showed her creative talents while still at school, painting European winter scenes on the wall of the Highwood Inn.

Hennie Mertens said her teenage daughter was a beauty who remained unaffected by her looks.

She tells the story of a friend of the family – a lonely, plain-looking boy – who couldn't get a date for the local social event of the year.

Jacqui offered to go as his partner and the boy was the proudest person at the dance. He died suddenly about a year later.

'She had a very good heart and cared for people.'

Hennie knows her daughter is dead and she knows the murderer will never appear before a jury. 'It is on your mind every day.'

Jacqui would never have just walked away from her family, she said. 'She told me she couldn't leave her children.'

Hennie Mertens went to the magistrates' court to listen to the evidence gathered against Victor. She felt sadness, anger and a strange sense of relief.

The anger was over hearing lies about her daughter and the sadness was finding the case would remain unsolved.

But the feeling of relief came when she saw her three grandchildren outside the court – all seemingly healthy and content.

'I was happy to see that Vic had looked after them. They all look well. He is a good father.'

She remains bitter that Vic had stopped her seeing her grandchildren. 'I hope one day when they are old enough they will come here. They will always be welcome.'

She was moved to see Lev. Mature beyond his years, the gifted student had inherited his mother's fine-boned features. 'He is just like her.'

Footnote. Vic Ramchen didn't want kids – he thought he was too old. But when he became a father he was determined that nothing would stand in the way of his children having every opportunity to excel.

He taught them that discipline, hard work and talent would overcome all obstacles.

He didn't live to see them grow into young adults. Despite the trauma of the parental arguments, the affair, the publicity and the death of both parents, the Ramchen children excelled just as their father had hoped.

In 2005 his youngest, Kim, 17, achieved the perfect VCE ENTER score of 99.95. Lev, five years older, had also achieved the perfect score while sister, Bobbi, produced an outstanding 99 in her year.

Lev told the *Sunday Herald Sun* that he did not believe his father was a murderer. 'Knowing my father, I just don't believe he could hurt anyone. He was quite a gentle person.'

To the children so gifted in mathematics it just didn't add up.

RATS

Margaret Clement ... the lady in the swamp.

RATS

Esme Livingstone ... warm hands, cold heart.

RATS

Esme ... took her secret to the grave.

RATS

Stanley Livingstone ... did he get away with murder?

RATS

Jacqui Ramchen ... the model wife who vanished.

RATS

Jacqui with host Gary Meadows on *The Price is Right*.

RATS

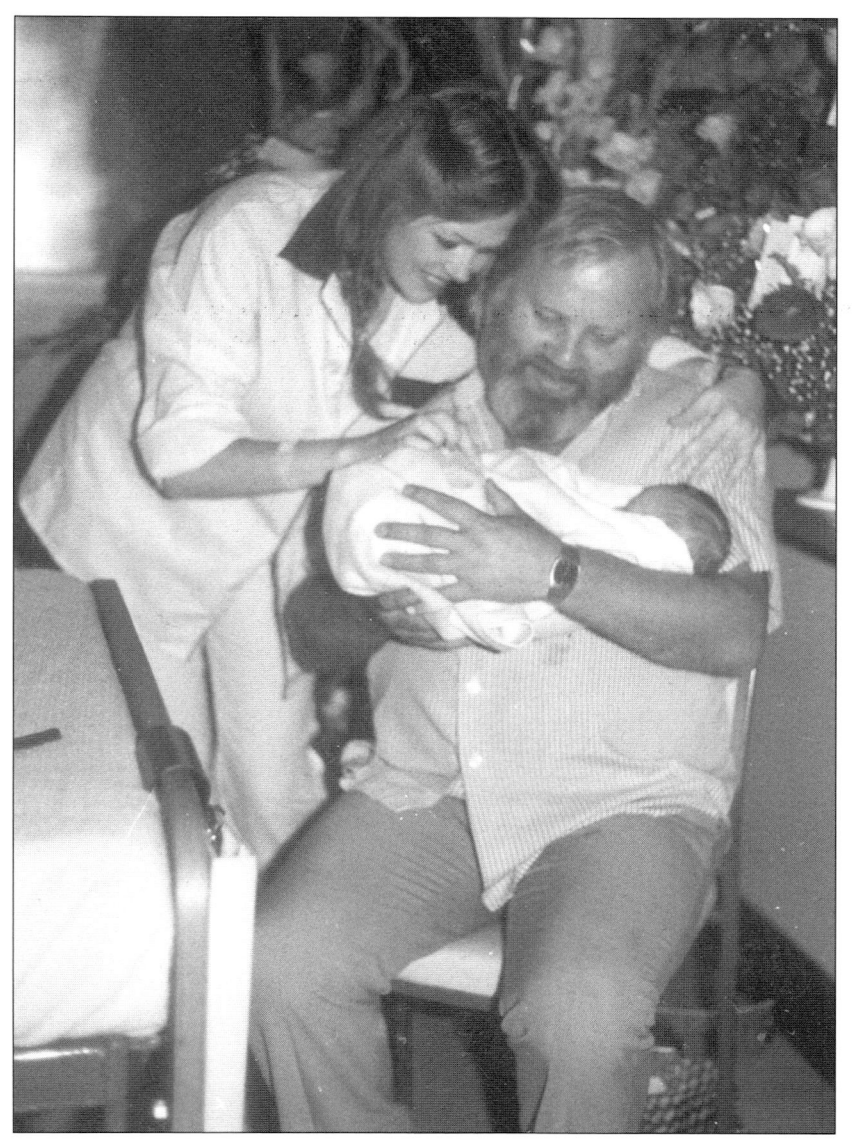

And baby makes three ... millionaire Vic Ramchen with Jacqui and their first born.

— RATS —

The Ramchens' real estate … 'Fairbairn' in South Yarra (above) and an old auction poster for their Woodend property.

RATS

A mother's love ... Jacqui with her oldest son, Lev.

RATS

Bad Company? Wrong band, right idea …

RATS

Jo Jo Zep and the Falcons join a young Victor Peirce (on vocals) and his fellow Pentridge prisoners for some jailhouse rock.

— RATS —

Victor George Peirce ... obviously lost his balance in a police station.

The late Victor Peirce (left) with loving wife Wendy 'The Witch'.

RATS

Russell Morgan Harrod ... did he shoot 'Johnny' Setek? You be the judge.

RATS

'Johnny' Setek ... his body has never been found. His battered panel van (pictured left) was.

─── RATS ───

Detective Senior Sergeant John Morrish ... death was Harrod's only escape.

RATS

His dogs lived well ... but he didn't. Setek's shack and caravan in the bush.

CHAPTER 9

Bad to the Bone

He often got an erection when he charged into a bank. He was just so excited. He planned the jobs and then they did the robberies. He got off on it.

SHE was the ace in the pack – the witness who could prove to a jury of strangers how a gang of Melbourne armed robbers became police killers. Taskforce detectives had worked on her for months, chipping away, hoping they could turn her against the men they were convinced had ambushed and murdered two young police constables in Walsh Street, South Yarra on October 12, 1988.

She knew the rules. To talk to police, let alone give evidence for them, was an act of unforgivable betrayal. In the twisted vernacular of the underworld, to give evidence – to tell the truth – is to 'turn dog'. And they wanted her to become the biggest dog of all. Finally she told them she would cross the line.

Wendy Peirce was to be the 94th, and most important, witness in the 1991 Supreme Court trial of those accused of the killings, not only for what she was going to say under oath, but because of who she was. Experienced defence barristers could easily discredit many of the witnesses in the case – career criminals looking to curry favour, men trying to do deals with authorities over their own criminal activities, or those who could only provide small snippets about events that took years to build, hours to plan and just minutes to execute.

But Peirce was no camp follower, no outsider looking in. She was the wife of the alleged ringleader. Her adult life had been spent in the bloodied world of Australia's most notorious crime cell – the Pettingill–Allen–Peirce clan. Her husband and the father of her children was Victor George Peirce, the leader of a gang of armed robbers hitting targets around Melbourne.

Wendy Peirce was the reason police were confident they could convict the men charged with the murders of the two young policemen, Steven Tynan and Damian Eyre. She was also the reason they failed.

In January, 1991, after having made extensive police statements accusing her husband of organising the shootings, she recanted. The case went to trial in February, 1991, in the Supreme Court without her videotaped testimony. All four accused were acquitted. But, seventeen years after Walsh Street, Wendy Peirce finally admitted what police always knew and no jury would ever hear her say: her husband did it.

IT is an early spring afternoon in Port Melbourne. Wendy Peirce sits at an outside table near Station Pier, ignoring the bite in the wind off the bay. The remaining tables outside are empty. Inside the cafe is warm and busy, but outside no-one minds if you smoke and you can chat without worrying about eavesdroppers.

In front of her is a book, in which there is a photograph of her late husband. A detective is leading him in handcuffs to court. The prisoner's right eye is puffy and closing. 'They bashed him with gun butts,' she says matter-of-factly. 'He needed a few stitches.' She speaks without anger or grief. To her it seems to be just an occupational hazard for the career criminal.

Parked just ten metres away is her husband's 1993 maroon Holden Commodore sedan – the car he was sitting in when he was shot dead in an unsolved gangland killing in Bay Street, Port Melbourne, on May 1, 2002. When police returned the bloodied sedan after completing forensic testing, Wendy Peirce had it cleaned and detailed and decided to keep it 'for sentimental reasons'.

Victor, she explains, had a soft spot for Commodores and nearly always used stolen ones when committing armed robberies.

Wendy Peirce has spent nearly 30 years watching, committing and concealing serious crime. She talks of her history with no obvious signs of guilt or embarrassment.

But she has agreed to talk, she says, to set the record straight. 'I have been an idiot. If I would have me life back, I wouldn't have done this. It has been a total waste.'

She is considering changing her name and trying to bury her past. She says her son Victor is burdened with carrying the name of his father, a brutal gunman, drug dealer, police killer and gangland murder victim. Her daughter is still filled with anguish at losing her father to an underworld ambush. Her youngest son goes to school near where his father was shot dead.

IN the Supreme Court trial that followed the Walsh Street killings, the prosecution case was that Peirce and his crew were driven by a pathological hatred of police, that festered after police killed two of their mates the year before Walsh Street – Mark Militano in March and Frankie Valastro in June. Detectives maintained that both men, who had long histories of violence, were shot when they refused to surrender and threatened police with guns.

Peirce's gang, meanwhile, was convinced the armed robbery squad had become a hit team.

After Militano's death, detectives claim, the gang pledged that if police were to kill more of their mates they would respond in kind. There were rumours and whispers of a two-for-one revenge pact and there was also talk that members of the squad might be ambushed in the driveways of their own homes.

On October 11, 1988, Peirce's best friend and armed robbery partner, Graeme Jensen, was shot dead by police in a botched arrest at Narre Warren after Jensen went to buy a spark plug for his mower.

Early the following morning, the two young policemen, Tynan and Eyre, were killed in Walsh Street, South Yarra.

It didn't take detectives long to work out that this was a cold-blooded ambush with a dumped car used as bait to lure police – any police – into the street. And at the top of a very short list of immediate suspects was the Peirce team.

Within a day Victor Peirce's mother, Kath Pettingill, matriarch of the notorious crime family, was quoted saying she knew her children were the prime suspects but denying they were involved. 'It wasn't us,' she said unblinkingly. 'I hate coppers, but those boys didn't do anything. Our family wouldn't do that. We were not involved. You don't kill two innocent coppers. If you want to get back, you would kill the copper who killed Graeme.'

Police responded immediately by conducting a series of, sometimes brutal, raids. They were sending a clear message to the underworld – all business was off until the police killers were charged and in jail.

At first, Wendy Peirce stood her ground. Apparently loyal to her in-laws, she posed for the media with one of her children in the debris after heavy-handed police raided her house.

Homicide squad detective Jim Conomy formally interviewed her on November 9, 1988. Not only did she refuse to implicate her husband, she gave him an alibi: they were together all night in a Tullamarine motel and he did not leave. It was a lie.

On December 30, 1988, Victor Peirce was formally charged with two counts of murder over Walsh Street. Three other men – Peirce's half-brother Trevor Pettingill, Anthony Farrell and Peter David McEvoy – were charged. Two other suspects, Jedd Houghton and Gary Abdallah, were shot dead by police in separate incidents. Peirce's young nephew, Jason Ryan, was also charged, although he became a protected witness for the prosecution.

With no witnesses, police built a complex case that relied heavily on forensic evidence linking a shotgun used in Walsh Street to an earlier armed robbery allegedly conducted by the suspects. Much of the prosecution testimony was tainted by the fact that it was from career criminals who were never going to be regarded as reliable.

MEANWHILE, members of the Ty-Eyre taskforce set up to investigate the murders continued to visit Wendy Peirce. They didn't use tough-guy tactics, but gently tried to persuade her that this would be the one chance she would ever have to change her life, to leave the underworld and make a fresh start.

In July, 1989, eight months after the murders, Peirce spent three days with Detective Inspector David Sprague and Senior Detective Colin McLaren, of the Ty-Eyre taskforce, making an explosive 31-page statement. On Sunday, July 16, she told the detectives she wished to go into the witness protection scheme.

Two days later, in an interview room in the homicide squad office, she repeated her statement on videotape – a confession the details of which have never previously been made public, and which could have condemned her husband to life in prison.

Wearing heavy make-up, Wendy Peirce appeared remarkably relaxed as she read her statement. Yes, she had been with her husband at the Tullamarine motel on the night that Jensen had been killed, but 'Victor was absent from the motel most of the night until the morning'. In other words, he had plenty of time to drive to Walsh Street and return.

She read her statement in a monotone, stumbling over some of the words. But the message was clear. 'He disliked police so much that he would often say to me, "I'd love to knock them dogs". His hatred of police was so vicious that at times I was scared to be with him.'

She said the whole family hated police, but Victor was the worst. 'On many occasions he would be holding on to a handgun and would say, "I would love to knock Jacks (police)".'

Wendy Peirce said there was one armed robbery squad detective 'he wanted to put off (kill)'.

According to her, after police raided Peirce's family in February, 1988, Victor 'was yelling and screaming and in such a rage from yelling that he started crying from temper'.

Why, then, had she protected him with a false statement to police?

'I have been an alibi witness for Victor many times. I did so out of loyalty to him and also out of fear. I was well aware he would bash me if I didn't ... I was fearful that Victor would kill me if I didn't supply an alibi.'

In this version of events, when he first learned that Jensen had been killed by police, he said, '"Oh Jesus" and had tears in his eyes'.

Wendy Peirce told police that her husband then rang McEvoy and said, 'What can we do mate, Graeme's dead, what can we do?'

She said he told her, 'I'm next, they'll shoot me now; they're dogs, they knocked Graeme for no good reason.'

What she then said was the magic bullet that police believed would blow a hole in Peirce's story that he spent the night with his wife.

She said when they went to bed he had his arm under her head. She heard him get up and get dressed. But she had learned over the previous thirteen years when it was best to mind her own business, and she chose not to move or call out. 'I heard him leave the motel.' She dozed and when he came back, hours later, she could see him in the first light of dawn.

The taskforce was delighted. They had infiltrated the family that lived by the code of silence. Once recruited, Wendy Peirce became an enthusiastic witness. She filled tape after tape with confessions implicating Peirce in murders and unsolved armed robberies.

Peirce, she said, was an expert at hiding guns and she had seen him in their shed sawing off the barrel of a shotgun. She recalled he had said with the pride of a home handyman, 'This will be a beauty, Witch (her nickname).'

She told police that once, while sitting with Graeme Jensen, her husband had become annoyed because they had run out of marijuana. 'He was playing with a revolver and said, "Get up and dance".' When she refused, she said, 'he shot twice between my legs'. The bullets were left implanted in the skirting board.

Police and prosecution lawyers were confident that once a jury heard her version of Walsh Street they would convict the four men in the dock without hesitation. After all, why would a woman lie to help convict the father of her children?

For more than a year Wendy Peirce lived in witness protection, waiting for the day she would be called to help send her husband to jail.

The committal hearing in late 1989 and early 1990 proved to be the perfect dress rehearsal. She answered all questions and made it clear her husband was the key figure in the group that killed the two police as a random payback after their mate Graeme Jensen was shot dead by police during an attempted arrest the previous day.

She was cross-examined ruthlessly but stood up to the test. A court veteran, she had acted as an unofficial legal assistant during many of the family's battles with the law. But the jury would never hear her testimony. In the pre-trial voir dire hearing – to establish admissible evidence without a jury present – at the Supreme Court in January 1991, Wendy Peirce changed her story and effectively sabotaged the police case.

After eighteen months in protection (estimated to have cost $2million) and after swearing to her husband's involvement at the committal hearings, Peirce betrayed her police minders and saved her husband from conviction and a certain life sentence. Not only did she deny that her husband was involved, she declared that she had never seen him with guns in their Richmond home.

In December, 1992, Wendy Peirce was found guilty of perjury and sentenced to eighteen months' jail with a minimum of nine, over the statements she made in the Supreme Court voir dire. In sentencing her, Judge Ross said the perjury was premeditated and she had shown no signs of remorse.

SITTING at the Port Melbourne cafe, Peirce maintains she was never going to give evidence that would incriminate her husband – that her decision to go into witness protection was part of a family plan to sabotage the prosecution from the inside. She now says that although he organised the murders, her husband initially felt there would never be enough evidence to justify his arrest. 'He covered his tracks and he didn't think he'd get pinched.' But when Victor Peirce's sister, Vicki Brooks, and her son Jason Ryan went into witness protection, the police case became stronger.

At first, Wendy Peirce stayed staunch, following the underworld code of refusing to make admissions. 'My first statement was to Jim Conomy (on November 9, 1988), stating that we had nothing to do with it. Noonan wanted to charge me with murder.'

Wendy Peirce claims she knew her alibi was worthless and no-one would believe her. She claims that Peter Allen – Victor's half-brother and the jailhouse lawyer of the family – was the one who decided that she would be more valuable if she appeared to change sides.

'He said, "If you give evidence for Victor he'll go down (be convicted). With your priors (convictions), the jury won't believe you." He said that if I somersaulted them (changed sides) ... I would get no more than eighteen months for perjury and he was spot on.'

She said she never intended to give evidence against Victor and that she stayed in contact with him even when in witness protection. 'I would talk to Mum, and Kath (Pettingill, Victor's mother) was there to pass on messages to Victor. I was posting him letters and photos. I always loved Victor and I was never going to give evidence against him.'

Police claim the suggestion that Wendy was planted as a

witness is a fantasy. One member of the taskforce says she saw the chance to start a new life and grabbed it, but had second thoughts when she realised that she would have to work rather than living off the proceeds of drugs and armed robberies.

Another said she was happy when she was 'duchessed' by the taskforce but felt miffed when moved to Canberra and put in public housing by witness protection.

'She saw that even before the trial she was no longer special. She realised that after she had given evidence she would be left to fend for herself,' one policeman said.

One detective said she was besotted by one of her guards and decided to return to the Peirce camp when the policeman was moved to other duties.

Inspector John Noonan, who was joint head of the taskforce, blames the legal system. It was simply too long from arrest to the trial to hold the unreliable Peirce, he says. 'They (Victor Peirce and his family) kept at her, getting messages to her that everything would be all right and if she changed her story back she would move back with Victor. She was getting messages from Peirce in prison through third parties, that he understood the pressure she was under but they belonged together. They told her they could look after her better than the police.'

He says he has no doubt that if a jury had heard her evidence, all four accused men would have been convicted.

He believes that when she refused to repeat her story on oath she should still have been called as a witness so the interview videos could have been played to the jury. 'They could have seen them for themselves and decided if she was telling the truth.'

The treatment of Wendy Peirce split the taskforce when some members were banned from dealing with her for fear their confrontational style would push her out of the prosecution camp.

Joint taskforce head Commander David Sprague said police lacked the professionalism in witness protection at the time to deal with someone like Wendy Peirce. 'She could not cope with witness protection. I think we had a real chance in the early days, but as the case dragged on, she changed sides again.'

He said she was difficult to control, continuing to shoplift and drive without a licence while under witness protection.

In the early months she was protected by the taskforce and treated as a star. She stayed in hotels – some of them luxurious – and was constantly moved. She was flattered, taken out for meals and her children were entertained, including on sailing trips around Port Phillip Bay.

But as the months dragged on towards the trial, she was put into the much less glamorous witness protection program. Many of her young guards had trouble concealing their contempt for the wife of a police killer. She had lost her friends and her extended family, and the detectives who had persuaded her to become a prosecution witness were no longer there to fortify her resolve.

Senior police say she had a glimpse of her future as a struggling single mother, and she didn't like it.

WENDY Peirce says her husband was a criminal with two great passions – his love of armed robberies and his hatred of police. 'Victor was the planner. He loved doing stick-ups. He was the one who would do all the planning and tell the others what to do.'

Police say the core members in the team, known as the Flemington Crew, were Jedd Houghton, Graeme Jensen, Peter David McEvoy, Paul Prideaux and Lindsay Rountree. The specialist car thief for the gang was Gary Abdallah.

Jedd Houghton would be shot dead by police in a Bendigo caravan park on November 17, 1988. Abdallah was shot dead by police in a Carlton flat in April, 1989.

'He (Abdallah) was always good with Holdens. Victor would tell him to steal two and have one left at a certain spot.' The armed robbery team would do the job in one stolen Holden before switching to the second a few kilometres away.

To Peirce it was a job. Nearly every day he would head off to observe possible targets and plan armed robberies. 'He was an absolute expert,' says Wendy proudly.

But if it was a job, he certainly loved his work. 'He told me he often got an erection when he charged into a bank. He was just so excited. He planned the jobs and then they did the robberies. He got off on it.

'I always got him to ring me straight after a job to make sure he was OK. Then I'd tell him to get home with the money. I loved it.'

The most money she saw was $200,000 after Peirce robbed the ANZ Bank in Ringwood in January 1988. 'He did heaps, he did over twenty armed robberies.'

The money, she now admits, was laundered through lawyer Tom Scriva, but none remains. 'We wasted it all. We wanted to buy a new house near Toolern Vale (near Diggers Rest). We had five acres picked out, but we just spent all the money. We bought kids' clothes, toys and jewellery – anything we wanted. I would go into town and spend $5000 a day shopping. I'd buy things just for the sake of it.'

Gaetano 'Tom' Scriva, 55, died of natural causes in July, 2000, but by then the remainder of the black money he was holding for his gangster clients had disappeared.

According to Wendy Peirce, her husband robbed banks in East Bentleigh, Ringwood and Knox City in 1988. He also hit security guards carrying cash boxes into banks and attacked couriers picking up large amounts of cash. 'He would knock them out and take the money,' she recalls.

She says that when armed robbery squad detectives came to interview him, he told her that if he didn't come back it would mean they had 'loaded' him (fabricated evidence to justify an arrest). 'He came home and said they told him to pull up on the banks or they would load him.'

And Walsh Street?

'It was more Jedd and Macca (McEvoy) than the others. Jedd was the trigger man, he had the shotgun. Macca took (Damian Eyre's) handgun. Victor was pissed off with him for that. Abdallah knocked (stole) the car. I don't think (Anthony) Farrell and Trevor (Pettingill) were even there.'

But she says it was her husband who organised the killings. 'It (Walsh Street) was spur of the moment, we were on the run. Victor was the organiser.'

Wendy Peirce says he was convinced police were going to kill him. 'We went on the run, living in motels with the kids.'

But she says he showed no regrets over what he did. 'He just said, "They deserved their whack. It could have been me".'

According to Wendy, the death of Jensen hit Peirce hard. 'Graeme was his best mate. He idolised him.' But what he didn't know at the time was that his best mate and his wife were having an affair.

'It just happened. Graeme would come over to see Victor to talk about jobs and he would wink at me. Then he came over and Victor wasn't there and it just happened.'

It was the relationship rather than the double murder that led Peirce to his only moment of remorse. He told her, 'If I had known about the affair, I wouldn't have done it (Walsh Street).'

IT HAS taken Wendy Peirce years to agree to tell her story. Her private life is a disaster, her family is collapsing and she is heavily in debt.

She says she hopes her life can show others that there is no glamour in the underworld. She claims that the death of her husband has finally given her the victim's perspective of crime.

She was just a teenager from a law-abiding family when she met Peirce and his mother, Kath Pettingill. She fell in love both with the criminal and his gangster lifestyle.

But in 1983, she says, Victor wanted to leave his criminal past and get a job. He had just been released from Ararat prison after serving two years and they moved into a rented unit in Albert Park, suburbs away from the rest of his family.

But Peirce's half-brother, Dennis Allen, rang and offered to give them a house next to his in Chestnut Street, Richmond.

'Once we moved in, that was the end. Victor was always helping out Dennis. If we hadn't moved there then none of this would have happened – none of the murders, the armed robberies and the drugs. If we hadn't moved there then Victor would be alive today and so would those two police (Tynan and Eyre).'

Allen was a prolific drug dealer in the early 1980s. 'I saw Victor with cash, sometimes $50,000, sometimes $100,000. I saw Dennis with $500,000.' Allen had many bank accounts but also liked to bury cash so it could never be traced. Much of it was never recovered when he died of natural causes in 1987. 'When he got sick, he couldn't remember anything. It must all still be buried around Richmond.'

Police say Allen was responsible for up to eleven murders and Wendy Peirce says she learned from experience to read the signs when her brother-in-law was 'about to go off'.

One day in August, 1984, she saw Allen turn and look coldly at small-time crook Wayne Stanhope, then turn up the volume of the stereo, to drown the shots he was about to fire. 'I told him, "Not in my house".' Allen begrudgingly took Stanhope next door to shoot him, leaving the body in the boot of a car in the street for two days.

Allen was also blamed for the deaths of associates Victor Gouroff and Greg Pasche in 1983, Helga Wagnegg in 1984 and Anton Kenny in 1985.

'Dennis gave Helga Wagnegg pure heroin. They poured buckets of water from the Yarra River down her throat to try and make it look like she drowned. Anton did nothing wrong. There was no reason. Dennis didn't need a reason.

'Victor Gouroff killed Greg Pasche. Dennis killed Gouroff because he didn't get rid of the body properly. Pasche said something out of school and Gouroff stabbed him. He was in the kitchen saying, "Dennis, help me, help me". Dennis picked up a bayonet and stabbed him in the head. They dragged him into the backyard and wrapped him up. There was no need for any of this. It was madness.'

Wendy Peirce is also able to confirm a police theory on a more recent Melbourne killing. In 2000, Peirce's best friend, Frank Benvenuto, was murdered – almost certainly by Andrew 'Benji' Veniamin, who was shot dead in a Carlton restaurant in 2004.

She says Benvenuto was murdered because he had ordered the killing of another underworld identity in the 1990s.

She says that as Benvenuto lay dying he managed to ring Victor on his mobile phone. 'He just groaned.' A few minutes later, the phone rang again. It was a major crime figure informing Peirce that Benvenuto was dead. How he knew so quickly has never been explained.

She says there can be no doubt it was a professional hit rather than a robbery gone wrong. 'There was $64,000 in the boot of Frank's car and they didn't even take it. Benji wanted a meeting with Victor and they met in a Port Melbourne park. He wanted to know if Victor was going to back up for Frank. He was his best mate. Victor took a gun and Benji would have been armed.' They agreed that there would be no payback.

'Frank kept my family going for six years (while Victor was in jail). Frank was a lovely man.'

In police circles there is no name more detested than that of Victor Peirce. Many openly rejoiced when he was finally murdered. They saw it as justice that having been acquitted in the Supreme Court he should ultimately be shot himself, sitting in the same make of car used to ambush Tynan and Eyre in Walsh Street. He even died in the same place, the Alfred Hospital.

Wendy Peirce says she has no regrets about refusing to implicate her husband at the Walsh Street trial, even though it condemned her to bring up her children in the criminal world. 'I loved Victor – I can't change that.'

She used to hate police, but seeing them professionally investigate her husband's death, even though he had killed two of theirs, has made her think again.

She has told her story, she says, to free herself from the past and so that no-one can accuse her of hiding from what she has done. She says her children have suffered because of the choices she made and she now regrets wasting her life in the world of violence, drugs and treachery.

'I can't take back what I have done, but it is all worth nothing. If I say sorry most people won't believe me. I just don't want my children to suffer because of what we did.'

Wendy Peirce has been a central figure in violent crime for nearly 30 years, but she says that only after seeing the long-term anguish of her children following the murder of their father does she finally understand how victims of such crimes suffer.

'I want to keep away from criminals now. I want to bring my

kids up in peace. I am proud of my children. They have not become involved in criminal activities. I wish I could be like them.'

ALL IN THE FAMILY

Kathleen Pettingill – Former barmaid and madam. Heavily connected with the underworld for twenty years. Had one eye shot out in 1978. Had six sons and a daughter, all with criminal records. Three have now died.

Dennis Bruce Allen – Kath's son. Drug dealer, murderer, pimp, police informer, gunman. Allen was investigated over eleven deaths in the 1980s. He was on a murder charge when he died in 1987 from heart disease.

Peter John Allen – Kath's son. Considered one of the best 'jailhouse lawyers' in the state. Ran a heroin empire while in jail. Now serving a sentence for armed robbery.

Lex Peirce – Kath's son. Minor criminal record. Pallbearer, with Trevor Pettingill, at Victor's funeral.

Wendy Margaret Peirce – Victor's wife. Was to give evidence against Victor over the Walsh Street murders but changed her story. Convicted of perjury. Gave birth to her youngest child in jail.

Victor George Peirce – Kath's son. Had a string of convictions. Tried and acquitted of the Walsh Street killings. Served six years for drug trafficking. Released in April, 1998. Murdered on May 1, 2002.

Trevor Pettingill – Kath's son. Tried and acquitted over Walsh Street. History of drugs and burglaries. Has been described as 'an emotional wreck'.

Jamie Pettingill – Kath's son. As a teenager, he was involved in the armed robbery of a Clifton Hill hotel. Died of a drug overdose in 1985.

Jason Ryan – Victor Peirce's nephew. Star prosecution witness who turned against the family and gave evidence over Walsh Street. Has battled drug addiction for years.

Vicki Brooks – Jason's mother and Kath's daughter. Turned against family and gave evidence for the prosecution at the Walsh Street trial. Went into witness protection.

Anthony Leigh Farrell – Friend of Victor Peirce. Acquitted of Walsh Street. Has been battling heroin addiction.

Peter David McEvoy – Part of Victor Peirce's armed robbery gang. Acquitted of Walsh Street. Convicted of armed robbery. Released and believed to be living in country Victoria.

Jedd Houghton – Armed robber and alleged shooter at Walsh Street. Was shot dead by members of the Special Operations Group on November 17, 1988, when police raided a cabin in a Bendigo caravan park where he was hiding.

Andrew 'Benji' Veniamin – Hitman alleged to have killed Victor Peirce's best friend Frank Benvenuto on May 8, 2000. Peirce and Veniamin held peace talks in a suburban park. Veniamin was shot dead in a Carlton restaurant on March 23, 2004.

Graeme Russell Jensen – Career criminal and Victor Peirce's best friend. Shot dead by police as he was intercepted at a Narre Warren shopping strip on October 11, 1988. His death sparked the murder of constables Steven Tynan and Damian Eyre thirteen hours later.

Gary Abdallah – Alleged car thief who provided getaway cars for Peirce's armed robbery gang. Said to have stolen the car used to lure police to Walsh Street. Shot by police inside a Carlton flat on April 9, 1989, and died from his wounds 40 days later.

• It seemed almost inevitable that Victor Peirce would eventually be pulled into Melbourne's underworld war.

Ruthless, deadly and an expert planner, he was cunning enough to survive decades of violence, but too stupid to quit while he had a head.

For four years police pursued different theories on why he was murdered. Then, in 2006, the Purana anti-ganglands taskforce finally made the breakthrough.

Victor Peirce was murdered not because of whom he killed, but whom he wouldn't.

Peirce was ambushed and shot in cold blood because he accepted, and then reneged on, a contract to kill another powerful underworld figure.

Police established that Peirce's killer was prolific hitman Andrew 'Benji' Veniamin, himself later shot dead by industrial mediator Mick Gatto in a self-defence shooting in a Carlton restaurant on March 23, 2004.

So much for the parkland peace talks between Veniamin and Peirce. Sadly, it seems that paid hitmen sometimes tell fibs.

Purana detectives have evidence that Peirce accepted a

$200,000 contract to kill standover man and drug dealer Jason Moran. They also know that a second career criminal was shot as punishment when he also failed to kill Moran.

Peirce was paid $100,000 in advance but then refused to carry out the contract and is believed to have warned Moran his life was in danger.

Moran was a prominent mourner at Peirce's funeral service at St Peter and Paul's Catholic Church in South Melbourne on May 9, 2002.

But Peirce's warning did not save Moran. He and his friend Pasquale Barbaro were shot dead while watching a junior football clinic at Essendon North on June 21, 2003.

Police say Veniamin was involved in at least five Melbourne underworld murders – those of Frank Benvenuto (Beaumaris, May 2000), Dino Dibra (West Sunshine, October 2002), Nik Radev (Coburg, April 2003) and Paul Kallipolitis (Sunshine, October 2003) were shot dead.

Police suspect convicted murderer Mark Anthony Smith also accepted a contract he did not fulfil. But an attempt to kill Smith failed when he was shot in the neck in the driveway of his Keilor home on December 28, 2002. He recovered and fled to Queensland for several months.

There remains a $100,000 reward for information leading to solution of Victor Peirce's murder. Veniamin is dead, but the second member of the hit-team that killed Peirce remains alive. For the moment.

CHAPTER 10

A Dog's Tale

Police had the blood, but where was the body?

'JOHNNY' Setek was not used to winning. His marriage had broken down, he had drifted through a succession of dead-end jobs and his attempts to get rich through gold mining had failed. But there was one thing in his life that showed him he wasn't a loser. And that was Super Dux, Setek's star greyhound.

Setek had been associated with greyhound racing for more than twenty years and he knew all about false promises and shattered dreams. But this time it would be different.

Super Dux was strong, quick and loved to run. And the battling trainer could see something else in that long, lean body – his dog had a giant heart and a winner's spirit.

For six years Setek lived in the bush in his old caravan, parked under a rusted shed of corrugated iron. It was going nowhere and neither was he.

For most of that time, he had used basic machinery to move tonnes of earth and rock at his small mining claim in the Kingower State Forest, near Inglewood, north-west of Bendigo in central Victoria.

It was off the same road that the 27 kilogram Hand of Faith nugget had been found a decade earlier, but all Setek found was that he was in the right place at the wrong time.

Setek, 60, would occasionally find a small nugget that he would swap for groceries at a local store. He kept a small, water-filled jar containing a few specks of gold – as if to remind himself there was still hope of that one big find.

The reality was that he was a pensioner who had lost contact with his wife and children and was just managing to survive on his fortnightly welfare payments. But those who knew him said the one thing he hadn't lost was his passion for life.

And he loved dogs, greyhounds in particular.

He had a doberman, a greyhound bitch called Royal Vintage, and a litter of eight pups. But Super Dux was his favourite.

Super Dux was no canine Phar Lap, but the young dog showed promise. It had finished third in its first start and won its last two races at Horsham and Shepparton.

If Setek had been a cunning punter, he would have tried to talk down his dog to improve the odds. But Johnny was an enthusiast. He told everybody he knew about Super Dux and urged them to back it at its next start at Shepparton on August 19, 1993.

He was so confident that the usually conservative local policeman gave him $5 to bet on the dog at the track that night. A less conservative man might have risked perhaps $25.

ZDENEK Setek had been one of thousands of young men who fled post-war Europe for Australia. He was just seventeen when he arrived in 1949, but he could not settle in his adopted country. In 1965, he returned to Czechoslovakia and two years later married Miladia, who had two children from her previous marriage.

They tried to make a home in Holland, but in 1969 sailed to Melbourne before moving to Bonegilla and, later, Bethanga. They had a daughter, but after four unhappy years of marriage, they separated.

Setek told friends he fought the Nazis when he was fourteen and had been fighting to make a living ever since.

He drifted around Australia, working as a truck driver, crane operator, chef and builder. He was one of thousands of itinerant workers who scrape together a living of sort throughout country Australia.

In 1987, he moved to Inglewood from NSW and squatted in his dilapidated caravan off Ironbark Dam Road. Locals began to call the area Setek's Hut.

Strictly speaking, it was illegal for Setek to live there, but a state mining warden persuaded Goldquest Mining to allow Setek to stay in return for acting as a caretaker on the property.

'Johnny' was cunning and resourceful, supplementing his old-age pension with small amounts of cash from scrap and illegally selling firewood gathered in the state forest.

He spent more money on food for his dogs than for himself. As a pensioner, Setek lived on budget cuts of meat and made his own grappa from local fruit. But Super Dux was fed on a diet of steak.

In 1992, Russell Morgan Harrod, then 66, moved to the area and the two battlers found they shared an interest in greyhounds.

Harrod, a divorced builder from Carlton, and the eccentric European immigrant became close friends. Harrod said he became co-trainer of Super Dux on the promise of half the winnings.

On the morning of August 19, 1993, Harrod drove to Ironbark Dam Road. He said Setek was still asleep so he massaged the star greyhound and fed the dog prime steak. Super Dux was to race at Shepparton that night.

The dog looked fit and ready. He had been trained the bush way – chasing a lure attached to Setek's battered Ford panel van along a rough track.

Johnny, the self-taught handyman, had built an exercise machine for his dogs. It may have been a basic life for a man, but it was Club Med for greyhounds, at least compared with the working dogs around a place like Inglewood, where most dogs spend their lives on short rations and a long chain, with the promise of a bullet if they don't measure up.

That afternoon the greyhound was given another top-class meal while the two pensioners were content with take-away pies.

They put Super Dux in the back of Johnny's old rusted Falcon van and drove into town.

The first stop was the Inglewood butcher. When the optimistic Setek asked the shop manager, Adrian Starr, for $500 to back the dog, Starr knocked him back.

Setek popped in to get his mail, telling the postmistress, Marie Ralph, that Super Dux would win that night. They then stopped at Ray Stagg's garage for $20 worth of fuel for the round trip.

When they got to the races they paid the $2 kennel fee and bought another round of pies for an early dinner while the bookies set up.

The two men walked the dog until the first race but it wasn't to be Super Dux's night. He finished second last.

A DOG'S TALE

It is here that the story of two battlers and a dog takes a turn into lies, mystery, deceit and greed.

According to Harrod, they loaded Super Dux into the van, then Setek saw an old friend – a man known only as 'Maurie' – an Italian-looking gentleman with a large moustache. They talked for 30 minutes before parting. No-one at the track would later be able to recall seeing the mysterious Maurie.

The next day, Setek and Harrod worked for nearly six hours building permanent concrete dog runs at Setek's property. The greyhound owner clearly planned to continue living at his basic squat. According to Harrod, they had dinner together and watched television in the caravan before parting for the night. At 8.15am the next day Harrod went back to the property.

He must have had a remarkable eye for detail. Five months later, he was able to tell the police that Setek had been dressed in a 'brown suit, brown pork-pie hat, brown shoes and blue tie. He had his brown suitcase in his hand'.

'He told me he was going to Tasmania with Maurie for a week's holiday. I almost fell over because this was the first I had heard about it.

'I asked about his dogs and he just said, "I'll be right." By this I thought he meant I was going to look after everything for him.'

Harrod said they then drove Johnny's old van to Bendigo and Johnny got out at the post office and told him Maurie was going to pick him up there. It was 9.15am, he said.

'I haven't seen Johnny since that day.'

And nobody else has, either.

HARROD would later claim his partner first rang to say he was staying another fortnight, then a week later, he rang again. 'He said he had bad news, he was staying in Tassie permanently.

'He got a job training dogs and he was now in Launceston. He told me to sell everything and put the money into building my house. He told me he wanted $1500 for Super Dux, $300 for each pup and $9000 for his Fiat Bulldozer.'

The bulldozer turned out to be owned by someone else. Harrod tried to sell the caravan for $2000. Then he moved it onto his four-hectare property where he was building a house. He took Setek's tools and clothes and began to drive his old van.

He helped strip the corrugated iron from the shed so a friend could use it to build his own.

He sold Super Dux and the pups for less than $2000. Super Dux would never win again.

Within weeks of Setek disappearing, everything he owned had been sold or used. There was little left to indicate he had ever existed.

In November, Harrod said, his mate rang again. Harrod claimed he told him the Inglewood police wanted to talk to him. Despite having dropped into the station for a cup of coffee at least once a week for years, Setek's attitude appeared to have changed.

'He just said "I ain't gotta do nothing".'

'I told him I had sold Super Dux and he said he had heard about it. He didn't ask me for the money at all.' Harrod said the call lasted two minutes.

Soon the locals were talking. They couldn't believe Setek, the friendly bush identity, would leave without saying goodbye and they knew he wouldn't leave his greyhounds.

Local pastor Reverend Donald Ride said, 'I felt that he favoured his dogs in detriment to himself in that he spent a lot of money feeding them and caring for them.'

A mining warden, Kevin Ryan, had known Setek for about

four years. 'His dogs were his life. John had one greyhound, two alsatians, and a doberman to my knowledge and he used to take great care of them.'

Another local, Alan Gardner, said he was a 'bit of a battler, with most of his money being spent on his greyhounds'.

Even Harrod admitted: 'Johnny really loved his dogs'.

Setek was an eccentric but an honest one.

He was given a line of credit at the hardware shop, grocery store, spare parts business, garage and livestock store. He prided himself on always paying his bills but when he left he did not settle his accounts.

Every fortnight $315 would be put into his Commonwealth Bank account and every fortnight he would take it out to pay his bills.

A week before he disappeared he withdrew his pension money, leaving a balance of $5.21.

The pensioner didn't touch the account again despite his fortnightly payments. By February 24, 1994, there was $4496.61 in the account – a fortune for the struggling gold prospector.

It wasn't long before police were told Setek was missing. They went to Harrod, who told the story of his friend walking out and giving up everything he owned.

They didn't believe him. No-one did.

Detectives sent forensic experts to check Setek's old caravan. They may not have found the smoking gun, but they found the next best thing ... a blanket with a bullet hole in it.

Scientific tests showed the muzzle had been against the blanket when the rifle was fired. Whoever pulled the trigger did it at point-blank range. There was also evidence a bullet was fired inside the caravan.

Detectives tracked down Setek's daughter, Alice, and took a

DNA test, which showed the blood found around the bullet hole was a 98 per cent paternal match with her.

Police had the blood, but where was the body?

CAROL LEACH was worried because her horses were getting out of a nearby paddock so she decided to check the gates.

She had to drive past the Loddon Valley Abattoirs and the local offal pits. She knew the area well as her husband ran a backhoe business and sometimes dug trenches in the pits.

As she drove past, she saw Setek's distinctive old Ford, which she had often seen parked opposite her house when he was in town.

She thought idly that Johnny was hunting in the pits for food for his dogs. She gave him a wave, then realised it was the wrong man. 'When I first saw the man he appeared to panic.'

She said the man she saw was well-dressed, which surprised her because of the stench and filth of the pits.

It was, as she would find out much later, one or two days after Setek had gone missing.

About ten weeks later, Carol Leach was operating a cement mixer for her husband near the post office when she looked up and saw the panel van.

There was a man sitting in the driver's seat. He was the one she had seen at the offal pits.

It would be four years from the time Setek disappeared until police were to search the pits. They used earth-moving equipment but, with hundreds of buried animal carcasses, it was a hopeless task.

Detective Senior Sergeant John Morrish had a sign on his desk that read: 'Old age and treachery will overcome youth and talent.'

The veteran investigator was known in police circles as 'The

A DOG'S TALE

Pope' because people were often filled with an overwhelming desire to confess when in his company.

It was Morrish who was to arrest Harrod for murder in August 2000. The suspect was 71 and had moved to Golden Beach in Gippsland, well away from the home he built and the whispers he created.

Harrod had a minor criminal record, beginning when he was convicted of horse stealing in 1944 and ending when, in January 1973, he was found guilty of car theft.

Memories play tricks. When Harrod became a murder suspect, his views on his missing mate seemed to change suddenly.

Setek was no longer the eccentric pensioner with a love of dogs, but a brutal manipulator.

Senior Detective Kate Fairbank said to him: 'Everybody we've spoken to has said how dedicated Johnny was to his dogs. He loved his dogs, he would never leave them like that.'

Harrod: 'That's all bull. Well, I was up there for eighteen months, nearly two years ... and I've seen him kick the dogs, hit his dogs and all and he was a ... the only thing he ... he was worried about was the bloody money for 'em. That's all bull, being dedicated to his dogs. 'Cos he ... I used to feed 'em and look after 'em, wash 'em. Clean out the dog runs for him of a morning, he ... while he's still in bed. He was only using me.'

'But you're good mates?' Fairbank asked.

'Yeah, we're good mates, yeah.'

THE truth of what happened to Johnny Setek was supposed to be decided by a Supreme Court jury in Bendigo in 2002 but the case lapsed when Russell Harrod died in November 2001, from lung cancer. He was 75.

Morrish had earlier approached him and said if he thought he was going to die, he should clear his conscience by confessing where he hid the body.

'I can't do that,' he said. 'I didn't do it.'

── CHAPTER 11 ──

Rats in a Trap

Who pulled the trigger?

IT is human nature to parade our successes while hiding our failures and Archie Butterly was human, though some would say only just.

Butterly was a career criminal with a long record and a big mouth. He liked to brag about how he shot nineteen people, but he didn't talk much about the time he was chased up a tree by a police dog, then fell out and accidentally shot himself in the head.

It was a mishap that would repeat itself. Butterly was to find that he didn't have much luck with police dogs, or police guns for that matter.

To shoot yourself once is clumsy – and in Butterly's case it was also accidental. But twice? That seems unlikely. Butterly was shot a second time – again in the head – but the question that will probably never be answered is this: did he pull the trigger himself, preferring to take his own life rather than to return to police custody, or was he shot at close range by a friend who then got away with murder?

What is beyond dispute is that Butterly was always a good candidate for a bad end. He was violent, ruthless and had a pathological hatred of police.

ARCHIE Ferguson Butterly arrived in Australia from Scotland in the Olympic year of 1956, aged ten. Scotland's gain was Australia's loss. Just four years later young Butterly was to acquire his first criminal conviction, the first of eighteen registered before he was legally an adult.

While still a young man he accidentally shot and killed a Melbourne man during a robbery and was sentenced to ten years for manslaughter. An allegedly cool criminal, he obviously hadn't heard that guns have safety catches to prevent nasty surprises, tragic consequences and long jail terms.

This was the pattern of his adult life – violence with a touch of stupidity. His long stint in an adult prison was a finishing school that turned a mean youth into a dangerous man. He teamed up with criminal associates he would keep during a short, violent and wasted life. One of his closest criminal contacts was the notorious hit man Christopher Dale Flannery, who would later be murdered in Sydney.

During the armed robbery of a Perth department store, Butterly shot and wounded a security guard. As so often happened with Butterly, the crime was violent but fruitless – he was caught in Sydney a week later. No wonder he spent more than 35 years in jail or on the run.

His biggest crime was typical. It was violent, audacious, and breathtaking, but doomed to fail. On March 7, 1993, he was involved in a daring escape with another prisoner, Peter Gibb, and Gibb's lover, a prison officer named Heather Parker.

As the Victorian State Coroner, Graeme Johnstone, later stated, Parker was married to another prison officer and was working at the Melbourne Remand Centre, 'when she became romantically involved and obsessed with Gibb'.

Fellow prison officers were aware of the growing relationship and, while they ostracised her, few did anything to stop or report the affair. They turned the other cheek. So did she.

Both Butterly and Gibb were housed in unit five of the Melbourne Remand Centre, in Spencer Street, Melbourne. This was a new prison, not made out of the traditional bluestone and barbed wire. A squat, red brick block on the outskirts of the central business district, it was thought to be state of the art. There had never been a successful escape from the centre – until Gibb and Butterly blew their way out.

Butterly and Gibb escaped from the Remand Centre using smuggled explosives to blow out one of the strengthened windows.

In something like a scene from a prisoner of war escape movie, the two men used sheets to clamber from the window, but the accident-prone Butterly injured his right foot when he dropped to the concrete footpath below.

The escape was well planned. A getaway car was waiting and the men had at least one handgun. But they had difficulty starting the car and as they finally pulled away, the plan was already beginning to unravel.

A prison officer gave chase in a taxi and Gibb crashed the car into a guardrail on entry to the Westgate Freeway, near Southbank. A motorcyclist stopped to help and the escapees stole the motorbike, Gibb driving and Butterly holding on as pillion passenger. But, again they crashed. It began to appear more like a scene from *Keystone Cops* than *Colditz* – except the escapees had a gun with real bullets.

The prison officer who had followed them flagged down a police divisional van and warned the two police that the men who crashed the motorcycle were escapees and armed.

The coroner later found: 'One of the police officers, Senior Constable Warren Treloar, drew his baton, approached the escapees and was shot twice without warning by Butterly. He was seriously wounded but survived. Treloar recalls a male leaning over him trying to remove his police revolver. Whilst Treloar struggled to resist, a male voice said, "Get back or he's dead". It was a warning to Treloar's partner, Senior Constable Jan Schoenpflug.'

Apparently, Gibb removed the revolver and attempted to empty it. One round remained in the cylinder.

Butterly later took the revolver with him to the police van. That single round was later to kill him.

The policeman Schoenpflug and Butterly had fired at each other at close range but, as often happens in a gun battle, they missed. It was then that Butterly had threatened that if the officer didn't back off, he would kill his injured partner.

The policeman had no choice and the two men stole the police van. They drove to South Melbourne, where Parker was waiting, then to a storage warehouse in Seaford, where they swapped cars and headed to country Victoria.

But the hope of a clean getaway was in tatters. Both men were injured, Gibb with a damaged left arm and Butterly with internal injuries from the crash.

They went to the Latrobe Valley Hospital in Gippsland for treatment and then headed for Woods Point in the hills.

Gibb was sore but mobile. Butterly was bleeding internally and in deep trouble. Nasty when well, he was downright

dangerous when in pain and he began to act in a threatening way to his accomplices. Gibb and Parker knew they were sinking fast; they had a lame partner who had shot and badly wounded a police officer.
Meanwhile, Parker's prison officer husband was shattered – left with two young children and too many unanswered questions, he needed help and turned to a most unlikely source. The children were taken to see the shot policeman, Warren Treloar. He told them their mother wasn't a bad woman but that she had just done a bad thing. Some felt that, in the circumstances, his view was rather generous.

WHILE on the run the frightened couple and their wounded mate stayed at the historic Gaffneys Creek Hotel, in the bush inland from the Latrobe Valley. Gibb and Parker had a meal in the dining room and took food to their room to feed Butterly, who was still losing blood from his injuries.

So much blood, in fact, that they burnt the hotel to the ground so that the bloodied room would not tip off police that the escapees had been there.

But the police were closing in and the escapees were effectively cornered. Experienced police believed that the manhunt would end in a gun battle, but this time not between armed escapees and police ambushed on a Melbourne street. This time the Special Operations Group would be in the police front line.

Coroner Johnstone later found that Parker and Gibb feared not only the police but also their co-offender. 'In view of the recent incident at Southbank where a police officer was shot and (of) Butterly's erratic and dangerous behaviour, it is also likely that Gibb and Parker were in some fear of what would happen in the event they were cornered by police. That fear was born of Butterly's erratic behaviour and hatred of police and the long-term involvement in a violent criminal culture of both men. Gibb apparently believed (in his record of interview) that it was "an unwritten rule if an officer gets shot, that's it", and he was terrified.'

At 10.30am on Friday, March 12, 1993, the Special Operations Group was notified by D24 that there had been a possible sighting of Gibb and Parker at the Gaffneys Creek Hotel. Within 45 minutes a crew was on its way to the scene in a police helicopter and a back-up team was ordered to follow by road.

It was later discovered that the last known sighting was 7.30 the previous night about five kilometres from Gaffneys Creek on the road to Jamieson.

The following day, search and rescue police, dog squad teams, local units and four SOG members in the helicopter searched for the three.

But it was not the police who would provide the breakthrough. It was two bushwalkers who found the fugitives' car, hidden in scrub at a normally peaceful place called Picnic Point.

Police logically thought the three would have to return to their car, so they abandoned the helicopter and vehicles to walk in, believing they had a good chance of surprising their targets. They did not want the noise of the motors to warn the three but no-one told the media and, like buzzards circling a carcass, television network helicopters followed police into the area.

Police began what would turn out to be a deadly game of hide-and-seek.

BUTTERLY was well hidden in a scrub-covered hollow overlooking the river. It was the violent man's idea of a gunman's foxhole and he almost certainly had decided to die in his ditch. But at whose hand?

Close to immobile because of his injuries, he must have known he had no chance to break cover. This would be his final statement.

He was well armed. With him was a sleeping bag, a bag containing spare .223 ammunition for his Colt automatic rifle, a pump action shotgun with cartridges, the .38 Smith & Wesson revolver stolen from the policeman in Melbourne, and clothing, food and beer.

According to a police report on *Operation Santana*, as the search was named: 'When search arrived at front of vehicle the dog immediately started to track strongly.' About twenty metres from the car, although nothing was seen, police dog Shamus paused and sniffed the air. It was enough. At that moment one of the escapees – almost certainly Butterly – opened up, firing about seven shots.

Special Operations Group Senior Constable Damien Hehir was patrolling to give support to the searching dog unit. In the first set of shots fired from the bunker, Hehir was shot in the back of the right leg.

According to a police report: 'Other rounds passed so close to Hehir's head that he could feel them. The offender's weapon was a Colt .223 rifle that fired projectiles travelling at approximately 3000 feet per second.'

Hehir moved about twenty metres backwards and told his team leader that he had been shot.

'Despite having been shot, Hehir then moved forward with his team leader, crawling through the river to the forward position occupied by Senior Constable David Empey,' the report said.

Hehir's wound was checked at this location and found to

comprise a lateral tear across the rear of his thigh. Hehir later moved to a position forward of Empey's location and assisted other SOG members.

Senior Constable Empey fired his weapon and then twice backed into the river to give himself cover while he changed magazines, emerging to fire a total of 45 shots.

'He reloaded under water and continued the exchange of fire with the offender. He made a conscious decision to stand his ground and provide cover for the dog squad and other SOG members.

'His actions demonstrated the highest level of bravery, his coolness, courage and ability to perform under the most extreme conditions.

'Empey's actions in this incident were exceptional. His individual effort in remaining in position and providing covering fire for the dog squad and other SOG members almost certainly prevented further injury or loss of life among police members.'

According to the coroner: 'Empey entered the water firing, reloaded under water, surfaced and fired again. This process was repeated until he had exhausted three twenty-shot magazines. He later gave some covering fire.

'In spite of the rapid nature of the events the response appeared well directed and controlled.'

Eight or nine shots were fired from the escapee's hiding spot, but after Empey fired, there was momentary silence.

According to police, after the shots were fired the gunman could be heard 'moaning and breathing'. Some police said it sounded like snoring.

While snipers kept their guns trained on the spot another group of police grabbed Gibb and Parker less than twenty metres from Butterly's lair. They were found 'fleeing along (the) creek line. They would not state if Butterly was in the vicinity.'

A Special Operations Group member was ordered to push through a thicket of blackberry bushes to get into a position to identify Butterley. A stun grenade was thrown into Butterley's hide-out and there was no movement. He was already dead.

According to evidence at the inquest: 'Shamus was sent in to investigate. Shamus returned with blood on his muzzle.'

Later, Butterly's body was discovered with a gunshot wound to the right side of the head.

He was shot with a police bullet, but it was not fired by a police officer. While SOG police fired 55 shots during the gun battle, they did not kill Butterly.

The coroner found: 'He had been shot with a single round from the police issue .38 calibre revolver previously taken by him from (the police officer at) Southbank.'

But who pulled the trigger?

ONE theory was that Butterly didn't want to go back to jail and so shot himself. The more romantic suggested that he was prepared to give his friends covering fire so they could escape, knowing it would cost him his life.

But this scenario poses more questions than it answers. Why would a man with a hatred of police, or a desire to buy time, not use up all his ammunition firing at police before he killed himself?

Butterly still had seven rounds in his rifle and a bag of spare ammunition when he died.

He had already been wounded before the fatal shot – struck in the head with a small fragment of a police shot that ricocheted off the shotgun in the bag lying in front of him.

The other theory is that either Gibb or Parker, not wanting to be in a shoot-out to the death, placed the police revolver behind Butterly's right ear and squeezed the trigger.

Coroner Johnstone found: 'There are a number of factors that create a difficulty in finally concluding the circumstances surrounding the shooting ... Even though Butterly was erratic and injured it is difficult to reconcile the fact that in a shoot-out with police he did not continue to fire until his supply of .223 ammunition was exhausted.

When it is realised not only did he have a number of full magazines in the kitbag but also the rifle was found with one round in the chamber and six in the magazine it becomes even more puzzling.

His behaviour at Southbank was indicative of a determined pattern to escape at all costs and to deal with police.

'Submissions on behalf of the family suggest that Butterly may have been firing to buy time for Gibb and Parker to escape. Although this could not be ruled out as a possibility it does not explain why he did not gain as much time as possible for their escape and use the large amount of ammunition remaining ... '

Whether Butterly took his own life after firing a limited number of rounds at police or whether Gibb or Parker shot him will remain unanswered.

But it is reasonable to conclude that Butterly was determined to stay and be involved in a shoot-out with police.

Whether he was also determined to keep Gibb and Parker with him is another matter.

The coroner conceded that there were several possible scenarios. 'Each is an alternative but not evidence on which a finding can be made. It is possible that Gibb and Parker were at the river's edge away from the hide when the firing commenced and Butterly for some reason decided to take his own life.

'One theory may be that due to a sense of loyalty between the two men Gibb remained in the hide and was present when he was shot. In this possible scenario the shooting of a determined Butterly may have been the only chance for Gibb's survival.

'Who shot Archie Butterly at this stage remains a mystery.'

IN 1994 the Director of Public Prosecutions was asked for an opinion to see if Gibb, Parker or both could be charged with murder.

The then Director of Public Prosecutions, Bernard Bongiorno, stated: 'There is ample evidence that one or other of them killed Butterly ... ' but he concluded there was 'insufficient evidence to charge Parker and Gibb with Butterly's murder solely because there is insufficient evidence to prove that Butterly's death was brought about by a joint enterprise on their part.'

Bongiorno found there was no evidence that 'would permit a jury to come to the conclusion that Butterly's death was the result of a joint enterprise as that term is understood in the criminal law.

'The construction of a joint enterprise between Gibb and Parker depends on the proposition that one of them shot Butterly because they were both hampered in their overall object by Butterly's disability.

'Whilst this may well be the case, there are other competing hypotheses which, in the absence of evidence, cannot be excluded.

'For example, there is no evidence to exclude a proposition that Butterly requested one of them to shoot him rather than permit his inevitable capture by police. This might even have occurred with the active dissent of the other.'

Forensic examinations found gunshot residue on Parker's right hand. It certainly supported the suggestion that Parker pulled the trigger on Butterly, but it was hardly solid evidence. The coroner found: 'The alleged single particle of .38 revolver gunshot residue on Parker's right hand is not indicative of whether or not she fired a revolver ... It would be dangerous to draw any conclusions on evidence of a single particle.'

In other words, Butterly may have asked to be killed, Gibb and Parker may have decided to kill him to escape, or one of the couple may have just taken it upon themselves to shoot their injured 'mate'.

Too many choices for a jury, it was decided, although some police point to the gunshot residue on Parker's hand as the best clue to what really happened.

Medical evidence submitted in court was that Butterly was alive from 30 minutes to three hours after he was shot in the head.

Forensic examination of the body showed Butterly was shot behind the right ear at such close range that the ear lobe was displaced.

Probably only three people know what happened. One is dead and the other two aren't talking.

The irony was that Gibb escaped to avoid what he expected to be a long jail term for armed robbery. But once he was recaptured, he was ultimately acquitted of the charges at his retrial. If he had sat tight in the Remand Centre, he would have been freed years earlier.

Both Parker and Gibb were jailed over the escape and offences committed on the run. Parker, the fallen prison officer, would learn what it was like to be on the other side of the cell door.

The pair was reunited after both completed their jail terms in 1997. They were to have a child together, and a telemovie was made about their lives.

But it wasn't all living-happily-ever-after for the couple. Gibb would later return to jail after being convicted of stealing a jet ski.

On March 16, 1995, Senior Constables Warren Treloar, Jan Schoenpflug, Trevor Berryman and police dog Shamus received bravery awards for their part in the pursuit and apprehension of the fugitives.

But there were two glaring omissions – Senior Constables Hehir and Empey went unrecognised, even though their courage and their performances were superb.

Hehir had stayed at his post under fire despite being wounded, while Empey reloaded under water and kept Butterly's position under fire to protect searching police in exposed positions.

They went unrewarded because 'Force policy precludes members of the Special Operations Group from receiving formal recognition for exceptional performance'.

In other words, they were expected to do it. Just another day at the office for the men who call themselves 'Sons of God'.

But ten years after the gun battle at Jamieson, a submission was made to Chief Commissioner Christine Nixon that the policy should change. She agreed and six SOG members were presented with the Valour Award. These included Hehir and Empey.

There was one upside to the bizarre escape and Butterly's unexplained death. Several detectives had to return repeatedly to the crime scene for further examination. On each trip, as well as their crime kits, they took their fishing rods and a large ice-filled Esky.

As luck would have it, right near where Archie Butterly made his last stand is a top fishing spot full of wild brown trout.

CHAPTER 12

Inside Job

Everybody knows he is a target. Except, it seems, the police whose job it is to know.

THE man in the dock knows there's a bullet out there somewhere with his name on it. But he doesn't know it's already in the hitman's revolver, and there's an itchy finger on the trigger, counting down the minutes.

His name is Raymond Patrick Bennett, also known as Ray Chuck, and he has just stepped into the old Melbourne Magistrates' Court from the holding cells.

If he's worried, it doesn't show on his boxer's face – almost handsome despite its broken nose sprinkled with freckles and the dark eyes set in a hard gaze. It's a face that doesn't quite match the bold check jacket with the leather elbow patches, which looks like something a jackaroo might buy in a reckless moment on a city holiday.

At 31, Bennett might be the most dashing Australian crook of his generation, but a reputation like that wins enemies, and he has plenty.

So many that, for seven weeks before this day, he has pointedly avoided bail, preferring the predictable discomforts of the Pentridge remand yards to his chances on the outside. He's always been game, but not foolhardy.

Still, he ought to feel safe here, in court, surrounded by dozens of people – including lawyers and policemen – and just across the road from Russell Street police headquarters. But he doesn't.

He has told his lawyer, who waits above, that he wants his wife kept away from the public areas of the court. He has taken out a huge life insurance policy, asking if the company will pay if he's 'shot walking down the street'.

Months earlier, he sent his young son overseas to keep him out of danger.

In one of the court cells reached through the door behind him is a message freshly written on the wall: *RAY CHUCK, YOU WILL GET YOUR'S IN DUE COURSE YOU FUCKEN DOG.*

Everybody knows he is a target. Except, it seems, the police whose job it is to know.

Bennett is in court for committal on armed robbery charges over a $69,000 payroll heist in Yarraville. A magistrate has to weigh the evidence to judge if he should be tried in a higher court.

Like all prisoners in custody who have to front a magistrate, he has been brought in through the Court One dock. Committals are automatically adjourned to one of the two courts upstairs, in a double-storey extension behind the main court.

Depending on who's telling the story, three – or perhaps two – detectives escort Bennett past the crowded bench seats and people standing at the back of the room, and into the open courtyard for the short walk to the stairs leading to courts ten and eleven.

By coincidence, there is a union demonstration at Trades Hall, a block away, and 167 officers have been called out, leaving Russell Street police headquarters short of the uniformed police who usually escort prisoners. Which is why, it is later explained, two consorting squad detectives called Glare and Strang are asked to help an armed robbery detective, John Mugavin, to escort Bennett.

As Bennett and his escort walk past, a young constable waiting to give evidence mistakes the well-dressed robber for another detective.

It's easy to see why. The dashing crook is a cut above the crowd in the courtyard.

The nineteenth century court is Dickensian, and Hogarth could have drawn those waiting their turn in the dock.

There are pimps, prostitutes, thieves, vagrants, drunks, louts and lost souls from the seedy side of a big city – the bad, the sad and the slightly mad, all chain-smoking in the courtyard. Bit players in this depressing daily drama, they watch surreptitiously as Bennett the underworld star is led past, through the doors and upstairs to his fate ...

A minute later, three shots crash through the buzz of muttered conversations. There is a clatter of footsteps in the sudden silence. Someone upstairs yells, 'It's a .38. Get a gun!' Then the screaming starts.

A young *Age* newspaper reporter in the main court looks at his watch and scrawls down the time. It is 10.17 on that Monday morning, six days after the 1979 Melbourne Cup.

WHEN he heard the shots, Constable Chris Carnie jumped up from his bench in the courtyard. So did Constable Alan Hill, who'd been waiting nervously to give evidence in the first case of his new career.

The two uniformed officers ran to the door leading to the stairs. Later, they gave slightly different accounts of where Bennett was standing, but it was probably on the landing between the first and second flight of steps.

What neither has ever forgotten is that he had his arms crossed over his chest, and was bleeding from wounds in both hands.

He said, 'I've been shot in the heart.'

Carnie caught Bennett as his legs buckled. He and Hill carried him through the courtyard and into the tiled vestibule outside the clerk's office near the Russell Street doorway.

Hill, a former Navy medic, tried mouth-to-mouth and heart massage. He knew it was no use. A bullet had burst the pulmonary artery; Bennett was drowning in his own blood.

Bennett's lawyer, Joe Gullaci, who would later become a no-nonsense County Court judge, rushed downstairs with the dying man's wife, Gail.

He pushed the stricken woman (he described her years later as 'incredibly brave') into the clerk's office so she couldn't see the wounds.

An ambulance came, but police stopped the pair getting in it to go to St Vincent's Hospital. They jumped in a police car, but the driver took them in exactly the opposite direction from the hospital – towards Elizabeth Street.

It was symbolic, perhaps, of the way the whole affair was handled. Except by the gunman, whose timing and preparation seemed almost too good to be true.

A court reporter for *The Sun* newspaper, Julie Herd, had sat briefly on a bench beside the man before going into court ten to wait for the case to begin. She assumed he was a lawyer. He had gold-rimmed glasses, a full head of hair and a beard. He appeared calm and was dressed, she thought, in a dark blue suit.

One of the two consorting squad detectives with Bennett, Phil Glare, also took the man to be a solicitor. Glare said the man walked towards Bennett, looked at him and said, 'Cop this, you mother-fucker' as he drew a snub-nosed revolver from inside his coat and fired three shots.

Bennett turned and ran down the stairs. Glare yelled, 'He's off. Grab him!'

Mugavin chased Bennett, assuming the shots were blanks and that it was an escape attempt, he later said.

Glare moved towards the gunman, who pointed the pistol at him and warned, 'Don't make me do it'.

According to later coronial evidence, Glare's colleague Paul Strang was inside the courtroom, where he helped Detective Sergeant Noel Anderson remove a pistol – allegedly used in Bennett's armed robbery – from an exhibit bag.

Meanwhile, the gunman had threatened a civilian witness, Raymond Aarons, – 'Move and I'll blow your fucking head off' – then waited to see if anyone was going to follow him and slipped through a side door leading down a maze of back stairs and passages to a tin shed behind the police garage.

An inspector, Bill Horman, later to be promoted to Deputy Commissioner and appointed as Tasmanian Police Commissioner, held the door shut, fearing the gunman was trapped and would try to come out.

When Anderson produced the exhibit pistol, Horman opened the door and Anderson rushed through.

But by then, the gunman was long gone – through a hole already carefully prepared in the corrugated iron shed wall. The hole opened into a car park at the neighbouring Royal Melbourne Institute of Technology. It was the perfect escape route – and it reeked of an inside job. Whoever did it had an expert knowledge of the court and the police car park, or easy access to people who did have such knowledge.

By the time Bennett was pronounced dead an hour later, the rumour mill was humming.

Frantic reporters with deadlines for the year's biggest crime story quoted unnamed police sources suggesting an 'outside' hit man was paid big money – the mooted sum was $50,000 – to do the killing. But before the last edition of the now defunct afternoon daily, *The Herald*, had hit the streets a different story was circulating inside Russell Street.

At 2pm the head of the consorting squad, Angus Ritchie, took a call from an informer claiming the hit had been organised inside Ritchie's own squad.

Some squad members jokingly encouraged the rumours in the police club that night. 'We couldn't buy a drink for a week,' recalls a retired detective who still doesn't fancy being named over the incident. 'Half the force thought we did it.'

Within days, the squad members would regret feeding the rumours because one detective was told there was a contract on his life to avenge Bennett's death. He carried a gun for two years.

Detectives, unable to protect Bennett when he was alive, were given orders to guard his corpse. They were instructed to go to the North Melbourne funeral home where the body was lying after police heard his enemies planned to break in, cut his hands off and send them to his wife.

Meanwhile, the public was still being fed the company line of a contract killer.

Details of the more sinister theory, involving police, were not made public until the inquest finally began in March 1981. But that was later.

INSIDE JOB

TO his friends, Ray Bennett was tough, loyal, and good company. His lawyer, Joe Gullaci, liked him – though he admits Bennett and his mates were 'big kids with guns', professional armed robbers who terrified people and wouldn't hesitate to shoot rivals.

'These blokes were pretty good at their trade – in and out quickly (on robberies) and no shots fired and no drugs – unlike the current crop running around using their own product. It seemed to me they were thieves with some honour,' the hard-bitten Gullaci recalls.

It was this 'honour' that eventually got Bennett killed. There were other reasons, too.

One was the 'Great Bookie Robbery' of April 21, 1976, which later became the subject of a television mini-series.

It became well-known that Bennett planned the robbery, flying secretly to Australia for a few days while on pre-release leave from a prison on the Isle of Wight. He and his friend, Brian O'Callaghan, had led the 'Kangaroo Gang', robbing jewellery shops all over Europe.

In what became known as the Great Bookie Robbery, six of Bennett's team robbed bookmakers on settling day at the Victorian Club, then in Queen Street.

A seventh man, in Pentridge at the time, received his share of a haul that was somewhat greater than the official figure of $1.4million, because of undeclared cash bets.

The robbery earned Bennett and his crew the unwanted attention of people who wanted to redistribute their wealth, some of them willing to use bolt cutters and blowtorches. There was even a plot by former friends to sell out the gang to the insurance underwriters saddled with the massive loss.

Police, bookmakers, and other criminals suddenly had several million reasons to resent Bennett. Tension rose between

Bennett's crew and a group of painters and dockers led by the Kane brothers, Brian, Les and Ray.

Certain members of the consorting squad backed the Kanes, standover men who had controlled 'ghosting' rackets on the wharves for years.

Those who took part deny this was the corrupt alliance it appears.

As one long-time underworld observer notes, 'The square-head world sees only the blue water on top, not the sharks underneath'.

From the viewpoint of some consorting squad detectives, whose job was to swim with the sharks, it was necessary to keep one group of man-eaters where they could see them.

THE 'consorters' were feared in the 1970s. Squad members called themselves the 'Fletcher Jones' boys – because, the joke went, like the clothing store of that name, they could 'fit anybody'. Before DNA testing, target profiling and flow charts, they gathered intelligence in pubs, nightclubs and race tracks.

Their brief was to know what heavy criminals were up to, and to act first to prevent crimes.

Their tool of trade – apart from sledgehammers, planted 'throwaway' guns, unsigned statements and illegal telephone taps – was the draconian consorting law (now no longer regularly used) that meant that if a known criminal was caught consorting with another known criminal both could be charged and jailed.

Squad members worked unsupervised, in small groups. Many socialised with criminals and had their own favourites. They were used as trouble-shooters by some senior police who turned a blind eye to methods used.

Some found the people they thought were the villains and

then either massaged or fabricated evidence to suit their conclusions. Sometimes they were right.

One offender who'd been shot while being arrested – the kidnapper Edwin John Eastwood – had his wounded leg stretched in hospital to force him to talk.

It was an era when some of the heavy squads made their own rules and exacted severe punishment on any outsider who broke them.

When one of the Kane brothers pulled up at traffic lights and noticed an off-duty detective with his heavily pregnant wife in the car next to him, he made a mistake that was to cost him several months in jail.

Kane wound his window down and threatened the policeman, using a string of profanities. The detective quietly told him he was going too far, but the hyped-up Kane did not see the danger signs.

It was late December when the detective's squad mates caught up with Kane. They presented the career criminal with several sticks of gelignite, neatly wrapped in Christmas paper. As soon as he saw the gift he knew the evidence against him would be overwhelming.

He didn't need a forensic report to know his fingerprints would be all over the package ... they had taken the paper from a drawer in Kane's flat and gift-wrapped it in front of him.

After he was charged he told a senior policeman, 'I knew I shouldn't have shot my mouth off.'

The policeman responded, 'You take one of this squad on, you take all of us on.'

It was around the same time that a known hit man accepted a contract, which police were aware of, but they didn't know who the target was or when the murder would take place.

To stop the shooting, a detective simply walked up to the hit man, gave him an unloaded gun and said, 'This is yours, Ron'. The contract killer was charged with being a felon in possession of a firearm. The hit was never carried out.

In the interview room, a suspect who answered a question with 'no comment' could soon find that it was more an opening statement in protracted negotiations than a concluding remark.

One detective, annoyed that his suspect refused to make a statement, removed his size fourteen boot, claiming it was his 'shoe phone'.

He put it to his ear, then turned to the suspect and said, 'It's for you', before beating the man around the head with the boot. The suspect then began to answer questions.

Every time the answers weren't correct the detective would again remove his boot, claiming he was taking another call. The suspect would then begin to answer questions again.

In another interview, an armed robber refused to talk. Finally, a naked detective ran into the room and hit him around the head. The suspect, possibly more frightened of being confronted by a naked, overweight detective than the beating, confessed readily.

While most squads at the time bent the rules to suit themselves, the consorting squad had made it an art form. Consorters, whose job it was to go to places where criminals hung out, combined business and pleasure for fun and profit. Some race clubs were so grateful to have them on course that they slung them payments in plain envelopes ... written off as security payments, which, of course, they were.

The money was put in a slush fund largely used to entertain interstate detectives who would always arrive thirsty and hungry.

The consorters didn't like critics. A retired detective told the authors that when a former criminal and prison activist, Joey

Hamilton, publicly complained about some of the squad's methods, two squad members went to his house in Carlton and blew it up with explosives. When Hamilton said he believed the police were responsible for the attack, few believed him – but he was right.

'It was a different time,' the retired detective says nostalgically, before offering the opinion that the Walsh Street murders – and the consequent mayhem – would have been prevented if consorters had still been working.

This was the consorting squad before the police hierarchy decided that its dogs of war were out of control and disbanded it.

Some consorters acted as judge and jury. The question is: were they also prepared to be executioners?

The circumstantial evidence is intriguing rather than damning.

One grievance the consorters had against Ray Bennett came from the fact that they provided unofficial security for bookmakers on settling days at the Victorian Club. But, on the day the Bennett gang struck, the usual crew of armed detectives was not there – they had been sent at the last minute on an errand to Frankston, a coincidence that led some to suspect Bennett had connived with a corrupt senior officer to set up the robbery.

One slip during the robbery probably sowed the seeds of the gang's destruction.

When the masked men ordered all present to lie face down, one said to the then well-known boxing trainer Ambrose Palmer, 'You too, Ambrose'.

The robber instantly regretted his half-friendly warning. He had once trained at Palmer's gymnasium and knew the old man would recognise his voice. Palmer naturally forgot to mention this to police, the story goes, but accidentally let slip the robber's identity to people connected with the Kane brothers. Word got around, and members of Bennett's gang became targets for opportunists who wanted a share of the bookies' cash.

It was an ideal scenario for gang warfare. War was declared in a Richmond hotel in mid-1978, when Vincent Mikkelsen – a friend of Bennett's – refused a drink from Brian Kane. Mikkelsen committed an even graver social indiscretion by winning the resulting fight – and biting off part of Kane's ear in the process.

Musing much later about Kane's reaction to this humiliating disfigurement, Joe Gullaci said, 'It's hard to be the number one standover man in town when you've got a piece bitten out of your ear'. (It was this sort of earthy wisdom that later led Gullaci to become a respected County Court judge.)

That mouthful of ear was eventually to give Melbourne's underworld heartburn and put the wind up the police force. But all Brian Kane knew then was that it was bad for his reputation – and that wasn't good for business.

Mikkelsen came to expect massive retaliation. Bennett suggested Mikkelsen's life be spared, and was warned, 'If you stick your head in, it will be blown off'.

From there, the story unfolded with brutal inevitability. Fearing a pre-emptive strike, Brian Kane's brother Les – regarded as the most dangerous brother – moved his second wife, Judy, and their family from the western suburbs to a unit in Wantirna, in the far outer-eastern suburbs.

It was a long way from their normal stamping grounds, but not far enough.

On October 19, 1978, a Thursday night, Les and Judy Kane got home to find three masked men waiting. They shoved Judy

Kane into a bedroom and her husband into the bathroom, where they shot him with silenced 'machine guns' that, the story goes, were .22 calibre rifles originally specially modified for the dreaded 'toecutter' Linus Driscoll, who called the weapons 'the silent one'.

This was ironic, considering persistent unsourced suggestions later that Driscoll took the contract to kill Bennett.

The killers threw Kane's body in the boot of his distinctive pink Ford Futura sedan and drove off. Neither the body nor the car was ever found.

They had a head start because Judy Kane observed painter and docker protocol by not speaking to police until they heard about her husband's 'disappearance' and contacted her first. Bennett told police, straight-faced, that he'd taken a call on the night of Les Kane's death to say that Kane had 'gone off' and he'd immediately gone into hiding, fearing reprisals.

He wasn't the only one to fear reprisals. When the murder case arising from Kane's disappearance went to trial at the Supreme Court in September 1979, court security measures were extraordinary.

There were armed police, marksmen posted outside, and stringent identity and weapon checks on everyone who entered court. Even a prison chaplain, Peter Alexander, was not allowed to visit Bennett.

Bennett, Mikkelsen and their presumed partner-in-crime, Lawrie Prendergast, were acquitted of Kane's death, mainly because of the absence of a body. Though pleased with the result, the three suspected not everyone was convinced of their innocence.

Mikkelsen and Prendergast left Melbourne immediately for distant parts. Prendergast was later to make the mistake of returning. He drove a Volvo, but apparently it didn't keep him safe. His body, like Les Kane's, was never found. (Interestingly, disgraced Sydney detective Roger Rogerson suggested that it was Prendergast and not Roger's drinking buddy Christopher Dale Flannery who shot undercover policeman Michael Drury in 1981, but that is another story.) Bennett, still to face charges on the payroll robbery, chose to stay in custody.

Seven weeks later, he was sent to the Magistrates' Court for committal. This time, oddly enough, there was no security at all.

SO who killed Bennett? And how did he get away with it so easily?

When it finally sat, the brief inquest that was theoretically supposed to investigate the murder raised more questions than answers.

Despite the public interest, and the time available to prepare the brief, the inquest report was a slight document – barely a morsel for the eminent legal talent gathered around the bar table.

Joe Gullaci could not represent Gail Bennett and her family because he had been called as a witness. Instead, she hired a prominent criminal barrister, Jack Lazarus.

Lazarus was aggressive but, on instructions, was not out to lay blame in ways that might fan hostilities and make life hard for the widow and her schoolboy son, Danny.

Peter Alexander, the knockabout priest who buried Bennett, told the authors that Lazarus's brief was to defend Bennett's reputation for the sake of his son – not to lead a murder investigation.

While Lazarus chose his punches carefully, no-one else was swinging wildly, either. The result was a predictably thin account of facts already run in the media – except for one thing.

INSIDE JOB

The brilliant advocate representing the police – John Phillips QC, later to become Chief Justice of Victoria – was forced to air rumours claiming that two detectives were implicated in the murder. Given that Lazarus didn't directly accuse anyone, it was the only way that Phillips could try to put such rumours to rest.

The men Phillips named, albeit gently, were Paul John Strang and Brian Francis Murphy.

Strang, a popular consorting squad detective later dismissed over a minor matter, was one of the three detectives supposed to be escorting Bennett, but happened not to be standing near him when the shots were fired.

Murphy, then with the new metropolitan regional crime squad – nicknamed 'Murphy's Marauders' – had no official reason to be at the Magistrates' Court the day Bennett was killed.

He arrived from his North Fitzroy office after the shooting, and said later he'd thought the activity outside the court was a demonstration.

Extraordinarily, although named at the inquest as a rumoured suspect, Murphy was never interviewed or called to give evidence.

It was that sort of inquiry. Underworld murders are rarely solved, and this never looked like being the exception.

Even the counsel assisting the coroner submitted there was no evidence the police knew of threats to Bennett beforehand, and blamed the media for airing matters 'improperly put in court and never substantiated'.

So solicitous was he about the perception of unfairness to the police involved that the police's own QC was scarcely able to lay it on any thicker.

He claimed it had been a bumper week for rubbishing the police, and called on the media to give full coverage if the coroner found that Murphy and Strang were not involved in the shooting.

Which, of course, is what the coroner did. But not even he, a policeman's son, could swallow his own assisting counsel's preposterous suggestions that the police didn't know beforehand of any threats to Bennett's safety.

While the coroner found who didn't do it, he didn't get close to naming who did.

But time has loosened tongues.

Several detectives involved in the case suggest independently that they've always believed the gunman was Brian Kane, who killed not for money but to avenge the death of his brother, Les. But, they say, it would be extremely unlikely that a criminal as well-known as Kane, could prowl the court precinct to set up his escape route.

One former detective says matter-of-factly that two former colleagues removed four roofing nails and levered open the tin fence escape route days earlier.

Interestingly, an RMIT gardener recalled seeing a man dressed in new overalls and digging with a new garden trowel next to the fence at 6.45am the week before the murder – possibly on the morning of the Melbourne Cup public holiday, when the area would have been almost deserted.

The truth, perhaps, went to the grave with Brian Kane, who was shot dead in the Quarry Hotel in Brunswick in November 1982, almost three years to the day after Bennett's death.

Twenty years on, Brian Murphy was on a short motoring holiday with his wife in Tasmania when contacted by the authors. He said he remembered distinctly the events of late 1979.

So who was the bearded hit man?

'It was Brian,' he said. 'But not this one.'

INSIDE JOB

The strange thing, he added, was that he'd seen a man who looked very like Brian Kane in Lygon Street the night before, and noticed he had grown a beard.

• A generation of the Kane family was destroyed by crime. Two brothers, Les and Brian, were shot dead, while the third, Ray 'Muscles' Kane, was convicted of murder.

Yet twenty years later, the Kanes were again linked to a violent underworld feud.

Les Kane had been married twice. His daughter from his first marriage, Trish, went on to marry an ambitious and ruthless young criminal called Jason Moran.

When Brian Kane was murdered young, Jason placed a death notice in *The Sun* to 'Uncle Brian' from 'Your Little Mate'.

On June 15, 2001, Jason's half-brother Mark was shot dead outside his $1.3million luxury home in the Melbourne suburb of Aberfeldie.

On June 21, 2003, Jason was shot dead, along with his friend Pasquale Barbaro while watching a children's football clinic and on March 31, 2004 Jason's father Lewis was shot while having a cool beer at the Brunswick Club.

Clearly the Kanes and Morans did not subscribe to the often quoted truism: 'Those who do not learn the lessons of history are doomed to repeat them'.

CHAPTER 13

The Silk Worm

'He was black to the core. The most corrupt barrister I've ever known.'

BOB Vernon was 42 and a prominent criminal barrister. Barbara Biggs was fourteen, a troubled runaway with nowhere to go. He had paid her grandmother to allow her to work for him as a live-in babysitter.

She had been sold.

The first day, he picked her up from her grandmother's Melbourne flat.

As they drove to his house, he told her about the job, minding his two small daughters while his wife was a long-term patient in hospital. He turned and looked her up and down.

She felt uneasy. 'You know what else you'll be expected to do,' he said.

She soon found out. That night he seduced her, beginning an illicit sexual relationship that was to last nine months. It ended when he ordered her to leave because he feared she might upset his young daughters by attempting suicide.

The lonely, disturbed girl was desperate for this man – more than old enough to be her father – to love her. The realisation that he regarded her as disposable cut deep.

So begins a dark tale at the heart of an autobiography that has sent a ripple of embarrassment through Australia's legal establishment.

In Moral Danger is a survivor's story of a life salvaged from the wreckage of a dysfunctional family on society's margins. Part *Lolita*, part *The Getting of Wisdom*, part *Jerry Springer* grotesque, it is a gritty real-life soap opera told with brutal candour and black humour.

There is more to this turbulent life story than the sordid secret relationship between a manipulative middle-aged man and a vulnerable schoolgirl, though that is the scandal likely to catch attention.

It exposes the dark side of a gifted man, and suggests that the legal profession, so skilled at rooting out wrongdoers in other fields, is not always sure how to handle its own.

BARBARA Biggs is now in her 40s. She is a fit, healthy, articulate, intelligent woman – but there are hints that she comes from a harder place and does not want to go back there.

The potent story she has written about her life explains why.

Biggs was one of six children with five fathers, four of whom had disappeared, including hers.

Her mother and grandmother brought up the fatherless brood in sordid semi-poverty, skating perilously across the thin ice of the permissive age – the 1960s and '70s – from rented house to rented house, shoplifting, pulling petty frauds and, as the cliché goes, looking for love in all the wrong places.

Biggs's mother, a cheerful, obese woman who attracted men, many of them predatory and worthless, worked as a telephonist but prostituted herself to make extra money. The children gradually realised their grandmother had probably done the same.

Biggs wrote: 'The year before I was born, Ma took to street-walking in Queens Road at Christmas time – to buy presents, she told us later. "They don't grow on trees, you know." My father was her first client, or so she said.

'He told her he was married with three children and worked at a garage. He was short, with olive skin and dark eyes, like me. He had an Australian accent but maybe European heritage. One hand was withered and permanently bent at the wrist: a birth defect, Ma thought.

'Five years later, she met him on the street again and invited him home. "I've got something to show you," she'd told him. She did ... a photo of her six kids on the mantelpiece. She asked him to guess which was his. He picked me straight away. Then she took him into my room and showed me to him while I was sleeping.

'I still imagine him standing there watching me. That's all I know about my father ...'

Missing a father figure and craving attention, the children were vulnerable to the sort of men their mother brought home. One of them was the man Biggs later called 'the Chief'.

The Chief's real name was Robert Vernon. He was one of the best criminal barristers in Australia – and a sexual predator.

Barbara Biggs was still at primary school when Vernon came calling. He was an occasional client of her mother's and would appear sometimes, turning up to whichever shabby rented house they lived in at the time and disappearing into a bedroom with 'Ma', as Biggs called her mother.

As far as she could remember later, the first time Biggs met Vernon she was in third grade, in 1965.

She remembered clearly that he arrived just as she and her older sister, Linda, had finished a bath and were still naked. Embarrassed, they hid behind a couch, but he asked them to dance for him.

He offered them money – 'two bob' each. Barbara wanted to take it, but her sister held her back. They stayed behind the couch until he went into their mother's bedroom.

Another evening, when Barbara was in fifth grade, they caught Vernon looking through the window before he came to the door.

He offered to buy them an ice-cream each – on condition that Barbara go to the shop with him. Their grandmother was looking after them. She urged Barbara to go but, again, her sister Linda grabbed her and whispered: 'Don't go, Barb. He's creepy.'

Vernon conferred with their grandmother, then tried again. 'I only want to take one little girl,' he said. 'I don't know how to look after two little girls.'

Linda held onto Barbara's arm. 'She's not going unless I go, too,' she said, staring at their grandmother defiantly. Four years later, when Biggs was living with Vernon, he told her he had paid the old woman to let her go with him that day – and to work for him later.

Another time, he told her if she ever told the police what was happening, they wouldn't believe her 'because he was a barrister and I was nothing – the daughter of a prostitute'.

No wonder, 25 years on, she finally decided to get even.

ROBERT Roy Vernon was no sad suburban hack with a guilty secret. Around the Victorian Bar – and bars where lawyers drank – they called him 'Rolls-Royce'. It was half-admiring but, like the best nicknames, it carried a subtle connotation, an edge beyond the play on his double-barrelled initials.

In the 1970s, Vernon was one of the best-known criminal barristers in Australia but, like English luxury cars of the era, he was expensive to run and didn't always start on time.

'Rolls-Royce' was no name for an honest plodder or a high-minded lawyer who would take silk (become a Queen's Counsel) and then a place on the bench.

Instead, it hinted at the venality of a big spender with bad habits, a man who got so close to his criminal clients that boundaries blurred.

Many of Vernon's contemporaries regarded him as mysterious, some saw him as sinister and secretive, and few knew him intimately.

On the record, most praise his ability. Off it, few are surprised he stands accused of misconduct, sexual or otherwise.

Some also suggest delicately that he was not just an advocate for his criminal clients in court but an adviser outside it. He crossed the ethical line that separates a clear conscience from easy money.

Brian Bourke, a hard-bitten veteran of criminal defence work who shared big cases and great wins with Vernon, admired his ability more than his character.

'He was fearless of judges ... capable and flamboyant,' Bourke told the authors.

'Bob was an unbridled larrikin. He had charisma the way a lot of crims have it – always money in their pocket and don't care if the sun doesn't rise tomorrow. There were a lot of shades to his life. He knew a lot of crims. All criminal barristers do. You don't cultivate them – but Bob would have.'

On his good days, Vernon was a brilliant defence advocate, a bruising cross-examiner who could destroy witnesses then turn to a jury and use a flair for drama, sentiment and humour to coax an acquittal.

He rarely took notes in court, relying instead on memory and reflexes to conjure a bravura performance. More diligent lawyers wondered at his cavalier attitude but, mostly, he got away with it.

Justice John Starke (the judge forced to sentence Ronald Ryan to hang) once sent a note to Vernon saying he had made the finest address to a jury he had seen in decades.

The praise was genuine. One of the accused in a big armed robbery case, a gunman called Danny Corsetti, also received a message from Starke.

'Don't worry about getting a QC – Bob Vernon will do the job just as well' is the way one of Corsetti's associates remembers it.

'And Bob did do a great job,' adds the source, a convicted murderer and robber. 'He had a very good name among the underworld. He wasn't a bloke who would knock you back.'

Law students and budding barristers were told to watch Vernon cross-examine witnesses and address juries. Charismatic and charming, he dressed sharply and cultivated an air of mystery.

Part of the mystique was that for several years he lived in the gatehouse of the historic Ripponlea mansion, a National Trust property set in vast grounds in a bayside Melbourne suburb.

He wore long leather coats and once effected a pencil-thin moustache and slicked-back hair like the sex symbol film star Errol Flynn – and that was not the only similarity to the hard-living actor, who was famously prosecuted for seducing an under-age girl.

Men found Vernon good company and many women fell for

him. He married three times, and there were other women in between.

Vernon's secretive nature means that few people still living know details of his background, and they aren't talking. He arrived in Melbourne from Sydney in his late twenties and enrolled at the Victorian Bar in 1960.

He hadn't done law at Sydney University, but had been articled to a solicitor and studied in his own time for the NSW Solicitors Admission Board examination, which admitted him in 1957, when he was 27.

He had spent several years in the air force, according to one source, although he told Barbara Biggs he'd been an army officer.

Despite his background – or perhaps because of it – Vernon stood out at the Victorian Bar. His buccaneering style was more in keeping with his hometown: Sydney's legal scene was more raffish and knockabout than the southern city's.

Whereas Melbourne barristers tended to treat each other and the bench politely in court, their Sydney counterparts were more earthy and robust.

The Bar that Vernon joined after he came to Melbourne was a conservative enclave, where those who were not members of the Establishment by birth and education tended to conform with those who were.

Criminal work still tended to be frowned on. But that didn't stop criminal barristers – like that other, even older profession – from flourishing.

There was too much money to be made. And Vernon was one of those who made it – and spent it.

He was not the only colourful and charismatic defence lawyer in Melbourne's courts but, for more than twenty years, he was one of the best. Perhaps only the legendary Frank Galbally was a better advocate, able to rattle witnesses and charm juries. Vernon was not necessarily less brilliant than Galbally – but he was unreliable.

Like many brilliant men, he was easily distracted because he had a lot of interests. Such as military history and tennis. And sex.

Vernon jokingly described himself as looking like 'a broken-down pug', as in a former boxer. The square jaw, broad face, strong cheekbones, bull neck and broad shoulders gave an impression of a hard man, for all the well-cut suits and soft hands. It was an image he fancied.

When Vernon went to Europe with George Hampel – later a judge, now a professor of advocacy – to research a forgery case in the 1970s, he delighted in introducing Hampel as 'El Cordobes', the famous bullfighter – and himself as the great man's bodyguard.

At least, that's the story Vernon liked to tell later. When the authors contacted Hampel recently he did not tell the El Cordobes story, instead recalling Vernon's visits to museums to indulge his passion for military history.

His former travelling companion was, concluded Hampel judiciously, 'a man's man'. It's a phrase, often used in obituaries, that covers a lot of ground.

Other barristers made a living representing career criminals and knew them well enough – but still kept them at a distance. Frank Galbally, for instance, warned his lawyer sons not to drink with their clients.

He knew that to cross the line and fraternise with criminals could be dangerous. But Vernon liked to live dangerously – as one younger barrister found out first-hand.

The younger man – now a senior counsel who insists on anonymity – once went with Vernon to a nightclub used by underworld figures. There they met several armed robbers, clients of Vernon, and were drinking with them when two consorting squad detectives arrived.

Two of the criminals were carrying handguns. Vernon knew this and told them to pass the weapons to him under the table. He hid the pistols in the pockets of his leather overcoat and, when the detectives approached, said he was conferring with his clients.

The detectives searched the criminals, saying they had information the men were armed. They found nothing. After the disgruntled detectives left, Vernon handed the pistols back underneath the table.

The young barrister admired Vernon as a dashing figure, but decided not to go drinking with him and armed robbers again. It didn't stop him taking a case, at Vernon's suggestion, that older, wiser heads had refused.

It was a racing scandal. A shady racehorse owner – now dead, but then suspected of crime connections – and a former jockey were accused of fixing a race in which all but a couple of jockeys had been promised cash if a certain horse won.

It did win and the jockeys were paid. But after the fixers were overheard boasting in a pub, they were charged with fraud.

Vernon represented the horse owner – but not his underling and co-conspirator, the former jockey.

Vernon secretly approached several senior barristers to represent the jockey at three times the normal daily fee – a premium that would, it was obvious, be paid by Vernon's rich and powerful client.

But the lucrative brief had a proviso that spooked seasoned barristers ... whoever took it was expected to tell Vernon if the former jockey (or any of the others) planned to give evidence against the owner.

The unspoken suggestion was that any witness willing to implicate the race-fixer would be intimidated, bashed or even killed.

One barrister who refused the brief told the authors: 'Bob was offering $150 a day at a time when we got $50 a day for murder trials. The deal was we would meet them in motel rooms and that I would have to let them know if my bloke was getting into the witness box. I said "No thank you". It was highly unethical. Years later, I found out that a barrister, now a Supreme Court judge, was also offered that brief and knocked it back. And so was another barrister, now a QC. There was a clear implication the witness would be heavied. Otherwise why would Bob make an issue of it?'

Eventually, the young barrister referred to above agreed to represent the former jockey, though he did not make any deals with Vernon. He was intrigued by the way the prosecution case collapsed.

One reason for this, he knew, was that Vernon had managed to obtain parts of the police brief in advance.

After the committal hearing, the young barrister privately mentioned his misgivings to the prosecutor, who was shocked at the suggestion Vernon had connived to nobble the case. Naively, the young barrister did not think the prosecutor would report the conversation to anyone else. He was wrong.

Within hours, Vernon accused him of telling the prosecutor too much.

Vernon said the outraged prosecutor had contacted a senior officer in the police hierarchy, 'but luckily he's one of ours' – meaning the policeman was friendly with Vernon and had tipped him off.

The nervous young barrister admitted speaking to the prosecutor, but denied passing on any damaging information.

He claimed that the prosecutor, angry at being beaten in court, must have guessed someone had 'got at' the police brief. Vernon didn't believe him – and warned that the race-fixer, a violent man, was angry enough to have the barrister killed.

The barrister called his wife and told her to go to her mother's house. She told him two men had followed her when she picked up their children from school.

Vernon, meanwhile, arranged a meeting with the race-fixer at 6.30 the next morning.

Vernon told the young barrister he should turn up and would 'probably get a flogging' – and warned him that if he didn't turn up. his life could be in danger.

The barrister did not fancy the choice. At dawn the next day, he and his family flew to London. They didn't return for 18 months.

He has never forgotten the incident. Neither has the older barrister who refused the job in the first place.

'A lot of people would think Bob Vernon was a beacon of the criminal bar – a fearless advocate with tons of ability,' he says. 'He had no need to be corrupt ... but he was black to the core. The most corrupt barrister I've ever known.'

None of which comes as any surprise to Barbara Biggs. By the time she was sixteen, she had survived moving to Sydney, several suicide attempts and three months in a psychiatric hospital.

She had also taken an intelligence test that showed she had an IQ of 142. Teachers convinced her she should go back to school and try for university.

She started studying, but was still torn between self-improvement and self-destruction. She worked hard – but couldn't stop herself going to Kings Cross on weekends and bingeing on sex and drugs.

At seventeen, she bought a motorcycle and was involved in a bad crash, but still passed her final exams.

Meanwhile, she had gone from heartbroken to suicidal to realising she had been damaged by Vernon's treatment, but did not yet know how to deal with the knowledge.

'If he told me once that sex was all that mattered, he told me 100 times,' she was to say later. 'He left me with a self-image as a sex toy and I played out that self-image without knowing why. Again and again.'

She was restless and reckless. At eighteen, she went to Thailand, crossed the Cambodian border and persuaded mercenary pilots to fly her into Phnom Penh, then under siege by the Khmer Rouge.

She escaped the city just before it fell. She could easily have died there.

At nineteen, she went to Japan, hoping to get work teaching English, but could not get a work permit.

An Australian girl she met introduced her to a brothel keeper. She became a prostitute, telling herself that it was to pay for university back home. In fact, as she later admitted to herself, she was still playing out the role.

Step by step, she shed her old life and built a new one, though there were hiccups along the way.

In 1978, she worked as a tram conductor – and won national notoriety when she refused to join the union, a stand that halted Melbourne's public transport system.

At 23, she had a baby and, in him, found new hope. She had a series of steadily more respectable jobs. She bought property and renovated houses and prospered.

And all the time she thought about what Vernon had done. But it wasn't until she was 37 that she did something about it.

In 1993, a friend who knew the truth suggested Biggs go to

the police. The sexual offences squad was sympathetic, but there was no chance of prosecution.

The next possibility was a civil action – to sue him for damages. But a lawyer checked and found Vernon was a serial bankrupt.

Like many of his criminal clients, he'd mostly dealt in cash and didn't own assets or pay tax. A civil lawsuit was useless.

The only option was Victoria's Crimes Compensation Tribunal, which was technically not punitive, and did not demand payment from 'guilty' parties.

If it were proved on the balance of probability that someone had suffered from a criminal act, they were awarded money from a central fund.

The hearing was set for December 1996. Considering that a well-known former member of the bar was accused of sexually abusing an under-age girl, it was a scandal waiting to break. But it didn't, despite a few whispers.

Vernon was represented by a former Victorian Solicitor General, Hartog Berkley, but it did him no good.

The magistrate found in favour of Biggs, awarding the maximum compensation of $20,000. Vernon died four months later.

• Barbara Biggs' book *In Moral Danger* became a best-seller as did her second volume, *The Road Home*. She moved to Paris and bought an apartment. It was to be the subject of her third book, *The Accidental Renovator*.

CHAPTER 14

Fishy Business

He was an honest bloke – he just had this thing about banks.

THE eastern snake-necked turtle likes to creep along the muddy bottoms of lakes and dams, eating insects, small fish, tadpoles and even the occasional frog.

It gets its unusual name because its hunting method involves holding its long neck sideways before striking out at its prey, like a snake. And, of course, it comes from the eastern states.

It is not endangered – there is an estimated population of one million – and it is not unique, as there are at least five similar breeds in Australia.

But the habits of the eastern snake-necked turtle have become the subject of scrutiny by police, pathologists and a coroner in an effort to discover how Australia's oldest armed robber died.

The humble eastern snake-necked turtle is not fussy about what it eats. In fact, it is an indiscriminate eater – which means it is quite prepared to feed on just about any unfortunate fish, bird or animal it finds dead in the water.

When the 25-centimetre turtle finds a carcass of any description, it uses its front claws to shred the flesh to scavenge a meal. Which is why the small amphibian has become an unwitting bit player in the bizarre and still unexplained death of Aubrey Maurice Broughill.

It was around 1.20pm on February 17, 1999, when a Wodonga quarry manager called Reg Golding noticed what he thought was a dead sheep floating about a metre from the shore of the eight-hectare flooded quarry.

It was about 30 metres from where workers were repairing a fence and restoring the bank of the quarry at the rear of the CSR Readymix plant on the Lincoln Causeway.

'I walked over to the bank and saw a body floating face down in the water,' Golding was to explain. 'I immediately rang the police via 000 and waited for their arrival.'

One of the first police there was Detective Sergeant Peter Revell, of Wodonga: 'I observed what appeared to be the necks of some form of tortoise or similar bobbing up and down around the body of the deceased.'

When the body was taken from the water, Revell could see the man had not died in a simple swimming accident. He was wearing a striped shirt and his blue denim jeans were caught around his left foot, although the belt was still fastened.

Revell also saw that the man was not wearing underpants and was barefoot.

Police searched his jeans and found spectacles in a case and a brown wallet. In the wallet was $208.90 as well as Medicare, pension and senior cards. There was also a driver's licence for Aubrey Maurice Broughill.

To the trained detective, there was a series of clues that

suggested Broughill was the victim of foul play. He had no car – yet there was no indication he had taken public transport to Wodonga and extensive checks of hotels, motels and refuges showed no signs of him staying in the area. A small, old campfire was found about 400 metres north on the bank. Police found a pile of cold ashes, an upturned empty baked-beans tin and a partially melted plastic wrapper, but no sign that Broughill had used the camp. There were no sleeping bags, tents or items to indicate it had been used as a shelter.

There was no apparent reason to draw Broughill to the region.

The water-filled quarry was hardly a tourist magnet, although the Mitta Mitta Canoe Club, the Albury/Wodonga Ski Club and the Twin City Model Aero Club used it regularly.

There was another reason Detective Sergeant Peter Revell would have suspected that the death of the old man might not have been an accident.

When search and rescue police finally recovered the body seven hours later, they would have noticed a disturbing fact.

Aubrey Maurice Broughill had no testicles.

One theory over the death was that he drowned in the quarry and the turtles chose to eat only his testicles, declining to touch any other part his body.

Another is that he was tortured and dumped in the quarry.

Yet, despite a strong circumstantial case suggesting murder, Aubrey Broughill's death was never treated as a priority homicide squad investigation.

IT was September, 1938 – a year before World War II – when Broughill was first arrested for house-breaking and larceny. He was twelve.

For the next two decades, he committed petty crimes such as stealing a bike, driving without a licence and escaping from custody. Always restless, when he wasn't in jail he would move around the country, working in Victoria, NSW and Queensland. His police record described him as a diesel fitter, but he also worked as an outback boundary rider, a clothes presser, a meat lumper and as a cook at an exclusive Sydney girls' school.

But, in 1961, he became more ambitious – or more desperate. Armed with a gun, he stole a £4000 payroll from the Camberwell Town Hall.

He was soon arrested and sentenced to eight years' hard labour. On his release, he became an unsuccessful burglar and, in the 1970s, at an age when most criminals are looking to retire, he went back to armed robberies.

Aged in his early 50s, he robbed seven banks and became known as the Beanie Bandit, because he always wore a green beanie as a poor form of disguise.

Despite police having security pictures of the Beanie Bandit, they could not identify the middle-aged offender. The detectives who arrested him for his first robbery 20 years earlier had retired.

But when he robbed a State Bank in North Blackburn on March 8, 1979, an off-duty constable saw him drive off and took down the registration number.

The car was registered to Broughill and gave his Corio home address. Members of the armed robbery squad were waiting when the Beanie Bandit got home.

As was his style, once caught Broughill chatted cheerfully with police and took them to a woodpile where he had hidden some of the money.

He was sentenced to fifteen years with a minimum of twelve for seven counts of armed robbery. As an experienced prisoner he did his jail term easily and was released in November, 1986, after serving seven years.

Aged 60, it took Broughill only two weeks to raise the $1000 he needed to buy a .44 magnum pistol and rob the Wantirna National Bank of $11,000. 'I couldn't find work. I kept getting knocked back, so I decided to get a gun and do a stick-up,' he confessed.

He flew to Brisbane for one armed robbery job, but found the pickings better in the south, robbing seven banks and two building societies in Melbourne over the next three months, escaping with a total of more than $50,000.

Security pictures at the first bank job showed the bandit was Broughill, who was this time nicknamed 'Grandpa Harry' because the elderly robber was using the same sort of gun as the Clint Eastwood character Dirty Harry.

This time police had no doubt who they were after. The security picture at the first bank clearly identified the gunman as Broughill and detectives believed he would hide out around Geelong.

At least Aubrey had learned one trick. He operated from Traralgon, 200 kilometres east of where police were looking for him. He was smart enough to rent a flat, but enough of a realist not to bother with a long lease.

Armed robbery squad detectives finally caught him in the flat on February 10, 1987.

Broughill, as always, was a relaxed prisoner. 'Geeze, you gave me a scare before. I was expecting you sooner or later, I knew that I had to be caught ... Yeah mate, I'll come quiet, I'll be no trouble,' he told the arresting officers.

This time he was sentenced to sixteen years' jail with a minimum of twelve.

Detectives wrote on his file, 'will probably re-offend if he is ever released'.

Tragically, they were right.

BROUGHILL was released from prison on November 27, 1995. He moved in with a younger sister in an outer Melbourne suburb. His parole officer reported that Broughill was making an effort to stay out of jail and was working two nights a week at the Victoria Market, unloading trucks.

He did some voluntary work at a nursing home, but spent most of his time fishing and gold prospecting.

His mother had left him $10,000 and he had saved $1400 while in prison. It was not a fortune, but the old wanderer was used to making do.

He built a duck pond for his sister and his case officer noted that Broughill was trying to avoid contact with criminal associates. 'Stated things very stable at present. Really enjoying his freedom ... still has not made any contact with ex-friends from the other side of town.'

He might have had good intentions, but eventually Broughill reverted to type. As a career criminal, he tended to work alone but now, aged in his 70s and with diabetes, high blood pressure and a bad heart, Broughill decided to team up with a gang from South Australia.

According to police, the gang was led by father and son Geoffrey James Stanley and Rodney James Stanley, alias James Weston.

The team, including Broughill, was involved in a series of indiscriminate crimes throughout country Victoria and South Australia that included stealing cars and computer equipment from six grain silos from Ouyen to the South Australian border.

Some of the gang were suspects for a series of crimes committed over thirteen years, including thefts of explosives.

Many of the crimes were opportunistic and others were just plain stupid.

It was January 12, 1999, when thirteen Victorian police

arrested Broughill and four other men, including the Stanleys, as part of an investigation codenamed Heather.

It was Broughill's 73rd birthday. The bandit who had once made headlines had sunk to petty thieving. In the back of the van was a ride-on motor mower stolen from South Australia. Broughill was charged with nineteen offences, including burglary, car theft, stealing from cars and wilful damage. He was released the following day at 4am.

Six days later, a pensioner's ticket under the name A Broughill was purchased for a bus trip from Brisbane to Sydney.

On February 1, he withdrew $200 from his Bendigo Bank account in Williamson Street, Bendigo, and the following day went to his doctor in Croydon and was prescribed Arthrexan for gout.

On February 3, Geoffrey Stanley's de facto wife, Carol Rudd, rang Renmark police asking if Broughill could pick up his Ford utility, which had been seized from the Stanley property as part of Operation Heather.

Senior Detective Lincoln Gore told her to advise Broughill to phone direct.

At 2.35pm that day, Gore received a phone call at the Renmark police station: 'An elderly male voice identified himself as Aubrey Broughill. He stated that he was broke and did not want to come up to Renmark unless he could collect his vehicle.'

His body was found two weeks later.

On February 22, 1999 – five days after the body was discovered – Victorian investigators Senior Detective David Magher and Senior Detective John McIllree went to Geoffrey Stanley's property near Renmark.

Magher asked Stanley about Broughill. 'Stanley appeared nervous in our presence but agreed to answer any questions. We had a casual chat about Broughill in the front yard of his property.'

Stanley told the two detectives an elaborate story of how when they were released from the St Kilda Road police station on January 13, they had breakfast and then walked to Spencer Street to take a train to Adelaide. He said the train was booked out, so they took a train to Swan Hill, then a bus to Mildura, where Geoffrey's son Scott drove them to the Renmark property.

Broughill then tried to get his ute from the police but was unable to do so. Stanley said he drove Broughill more than 200 kilometres to Adelaide so he could catch a bus to Melbourne. He said they went to Franklin Street, where Broughill bought a bus ticket and then booked in to a hotel.

He said he had known him only a few months and Broughill had spent Christmas with Stanley's family. Stanley said Broughill had told him it was the best Christmas he had had.

He volunteered that Broughill was unsteady on his feet and often tripped when walking. Just the sort, perhaps, who could fall into a flooded quarry.

But Broughill's younger sister, Beverley, has a different story. 'He was very fit for his age. He didn't drink or smoke and was a very strong man. He was still very agile.'

What's more, she says, he was 'the strongest swimmer I have ever seen'.

Beverley remembers the family going eeling in the Yarra and her big brother diving in the current. 'He would glide through the water like Johnny Weissmuller.'

McIllree and Magher investigated Stanley's story and were not convinced. After Broughill's release, he had reported on bail at the Boronia police station at 9.50am on January 13. Broughill had not booked a bus ticket in Franklin Street in his own name. He had not booked into a hotel or accommodation house under his name.

But he had been in Adelaide on January 14. He had forgotten his blood pressure medication and went to Dr Karen Woo in Gouger Street for a new prescription. He told her he was from Melbourne and had caught the bus to South Australia. She prescribed him 100 Aldomet tablets, which he bought at a nearby chemist.

Stanley's son, Scott James Stanley, refused to answer any questions police asked about Broughill.

Magher was adamant. In his statement to the inquest he said: 'In my opinion Stanley is not telling the truth about Broughill. The way he spoke to us in Renmark and his demeanour, I believe he is lying.'

On March 5, 1999, Senior Detective Lincoln Gore spoke to Stanley's partner, Carol. He asked her when she had last seen Broughill. She said he had not come back with Stanley on January 13 and she had not seen him since Christmas.

Police might have believed that Geoffrey James Stanley was lying, but if so, what was he trying to conceal?

WHILE Victorian and South Australian police were investigating the Stanley gang for thefts, a second, more serious investigation into their activities, code-named Operation Jarrah, was underway.

Police believed that four men connected with a 30-strong Adelaide-based drug ring had been murdered over seven years.

The four men were drifters without strong family connections – just like Aubrey Broughill.

In a statement tendered in the inquest into Broughill's death, Detective Sergeant John Woite, of the Adelaide Major Crime Investigation Section, said police were investigating the suspected murders of four men – Juan Phillip Morgan, who was seventeen when he went missing in 1992; Leo Joseph Daly, 33, who disappeared in 1998; David Michael McWilliams, 40, who disappeared in 1998; and Robert Stanley Prendergast, 32 when he went missing in 1999.

According to Woite: 'Inquiries revealed that Rodney James Stanley, alias James Weston, born July 19, 1967, and his father, Geoffrey James Stanley, born November 28, 1944, are the common denominator in all of the disappearances.'

None of the bodies was ever recovered.

The police theory was that Juan Phillip Morgan had a minor dispute with one of the gang members and was murdered. Morgan was allegedly buried in a national park near the Victorian border.

Police believe Daly owed the syndicate money and was dragging the chain on paying. He was taken out to sea in a seven-metre boat, shot and dumped overboard in April, 1998. One of those present was McWilliams, who started to worry about what he had done. Seen as a possible weak link, he was allegedly shot and buried in South Australia three months later.

The next was Prendergast, a known drug courier alleged to have been owed money by the syndicate.

Lacking the muscle to physically threaten them, he warned the syndicate heads that he would turn and inform to the National Crime Authority (now replaced by the Australian Crime Commission) that they were trafficking amphetamines and pseudo ecstasy.

They called his bluff and he was never seen again. His body was allegedly buried near Adelaide.

Operation Jarrah detectives arrested Geoffrey Stanley and 'James Weston' for the murder of Leo Daly but the charges were withdrawn in July 1999. A spokesman for the South

Australian DPP said the case was abandoned because the key prosecution witnesses refused to give evidence against them.

According to the head of Operation Jarrah, Detective Senior Sergeant Mick Johnson, the syndicate leaders were 'vicious men who would do anything to protect themselves'. He added: 'We believe that four men were killed over drug debts and to ensure others remained silent.' None of the missing men was seen again and the cases remain open.

But Weston was later implicated in another murder – that of David Kovacic who was stabbed to death in his Kidman Park home in October, 1999.

Telephone intercepts picked up Weston urging two men to rob Kovacic over a drug debt. In the attack, the victim was stabbed in the back. Weston was later sentenced to seven years for assisting the man who stabbed Kovacic and over possessing a trafficable quantity of drugs.

Geoffrey Stanley now lives quietly on a ramshackle fruit block at Renmark, which police believe was used as the centre of the group's car re-birthing operations.

In the raids early in 1999, police seized stolen goods valued at $500,000 from the block. They also seized 202 detonators, ammunition, a Luger pistol, a panel van, four cars, a motorbike and electronic equipment during raids on Stanley's Kulkyne Street home.

On March 5, 2002, he received a 15-month suspended sentence in the Berri court on unlawful possession charges.

EITHER no-one really knows what happened to Aubrey Broughill or, if they do, they aren't saying.

In a report lodged at the inquest, senior pathologist Michael Burke explained the bizarre injuries to the body: 'A longitudinal defect with the scrotum with a well-defined incised-like edge measuring seven centimetres and extending to a more irregular ragged tear at the upper anterior aspect of the scrotum ... The testes are not present ... Examination of the edges of the injury showed no hesitation marks and no serrations or other defects.' In lay terms, he had been castrated. But by whom ... or what?

Burke said: 'It is my understanding that turtles were associated with the deceased's body when the remains were recovered by police. I have had a discussion with veterinary experts regarding the structure of freshwater-turtle mouth parts. I have been informed that the mouth parts have a scissors-like action. The incised-like injury to the scrotum could be explained by post-mortem activity by turtles.'

But he added a proviso. 'It is unusual that no other such injuries were seen on any other part of the deceased's body.'

Police sought an opinion from John Coventry, former president of the Australian Society of Herpetologists – an expert who worked for Museum Victoria's herpetology section for 45 years.

He gave qualified support to the theory that the eastern snake-necked turtle could damage a body.

He said it was 'possible' for the species, 'to feed on a partially submerged human body'.

He said it would be more likely that flesh would be taken from soft tissue areas rather than bony areas such as fingers.

But no-one has been able to explain why the turtles would attack only the testicles and ignore other soft areas of the body such as thighs, cheeks and abdomen.

Michael Swan, the reptile keeper at the Melbourne Zoo, told the authors the snake-necked turtle can break down carrion using a ripping action with front claws just a few millimetres long. He said the turtle would leave shredding marks.

When given the details of Broughill's injuries he said he doubted that turtles were the culprits. 'I have never heard of them being involved in something like that'.

He said the American alligator snapping turtle had been found to feed on human remains in Florida, but he knew of no similar cases in Australia.

He said he couldn't understand why a turtle would concentrate on the testicles. 'I'm no expert on murders, but it sounds to me as if there must have been some form of human intervention.'

John Coventry has now retired but he recalls the Broughill case and is far from convinced about testicle-eating turtles.

He said he had often watched turtles feed by coming off the bottom and snapping at their prospective prey. But he said he was concerned that the wound was reported to be an incised cut and there were no signs of claw marks. He also was surprised to learn that Broughill's pants were caught on one leg.

He said there was insufficient evidence to come to a conclusion. 'I don't really know.'

In July 2001, Coroner John Martin Murphy found: 'Due to the decomposed condition of the body, the cause of death was unascertained.

'However, the deceased suffered an unusual injury to the scrotum with absent testes. The scrotal injuries had a distinct incised-like injury. There were turtles in the water at the quarry and the incised-like injury to the scrotum would be explained by post-mortem activity by turtles.

'It is, however, unusual that no other injuries were seen to any part of the deceased's body.

'I am unable to say if any person or persons contributed to the death of the deceased or if his death was caused by natural causes.'

There could be no real conclusions. No-one could establish why Broughill was in the area, how he entered the water or even a cause of death.

Detective Sergeant Revell said that despite his investigation he was no closer to knowing the truth. 'The body was badly decomposed. He had no reason to be in the district. It remains a mystery.'

There are plenty of theories. One is that Broughill was in the area because he believed the quarry plant contained explosives that he could steal.

But if that were the case, he almost certainly would not have been acting alone. And why was there no sign of his sleeping bag or knapsack? And why was he not wearing shoes?

A stronger theory, perhaps, is that Broughill was killed because someone feared the old man might be prepared to implicate others in a series of crimes.

But detectives who knew Broughill say he always refused to inform.

Armed Robbery Detective Senior Sergeant Ray Watson, who arrested Broughill in 1987, said: 'He was polite and of the old school – prepared to talk about his involvement without ever talking about any criminal associates.'

When asked by Watson's arrest team to identify his armed robbery getaway driver he responded: 'You're not going to ask me to give somebody up, are you?'

Geoff Stanley, the man who police believe was less than forthright over Broughill, has now become a touch more outspoken.

When approached by the authors he was absolute in his view that his old mate was murdered. 'You couldn't wish to meet a better bloke. He was a real gentleman.'

Stanley said he had befriended Broughill six months before

his death when the old man arrived in the district to pick apricots. 'He was an honest bloke – he just had this thing about banks.'

He repeated his version of events saying he had taken him to Adelaide so he could return to Melbourne.

'He said he felt too poorly to drive his ute, so I drove him to Adelaide and put him on a bus to go home.'

But Stanley is prepared to speculate further. 'I reckon the Victoria police done him. I reckon it was murder. I reckon the police picked him up when he got back to Melbourne, did him over and then thought, "Look, the poor bastard's dead, we better get rid of him".'

He said he didn't accept that turtles had eaten Broughill's testicles. 'I won't wear that. Lips, eyes, earlobes, maybe, but not that.'

He said he believed police had a habit of killing criminals they disliked. 'How many have they bumped off?'

Broughill's family insist that if he travelled to Renmark to recover his Ford utility, they cannot understand why he would leave Geoff Stanley's without it.

Years later, Stanley says the ute remains on his property, 'rusted out down the back'.

Aubrey Broughill's niece, Frankie Puccini, delivered a touching eulogy at his funeral. She said in part, 'Your life ended so tragically, leaving us asking why.'

Now, she says, the question remains unanswered. 'It makes you so angry not knowing what happened. We still don't even have a cause of death. But looking at what we know now, we believe Aubrey was murdered.'

CHAPTER 15

Who Killed Jenny Tanner?

He didn't notice the bullet holes through both hands, but they were there: the sort experts call 'classic defence wounds'.

FOR anyone callous enough to pull the trigger, shooting Jennifer Tanner wasn't the problem. Making it look like suicide was, and that's where her killer got it wrong.

Faking suicide meant using the only firearm available to the victim: her husband's bolt-action .22 rifle. When the first shot didn't kill the terrified woman instantly, the self-appointed executioner had to fire another shot into her forehead as her body twitched and thrashed.

In fact, the killer almost certainly fired even more shots on that Wednesday night in November, 1984. If he did, they missed. At least, they missed her head. When Laurie Tanner came home and found his wife's body he didn't notice the bullet holes through both hands, but they were there: the sort experts call 'classic defence wounds'.

All of which, you'd think, would make it likely that someone might consider foul play ...

Even if the pair of country policemen first called to the Tanners' house at Bonnie Doon were fooled by the fact Jennifer's body was slumped on a couch with the rifle between her knees, the muzzle pointing towards her still-bleeding head.

Even if a local doctor dragged from a dinner party agreed it looked like suicide, pronounced life extinct and left, pointing out later it was his job to verify death, not to investigate its causes.

And even if the detective sergeant on call that night ignored alarm signals when the uneasy constables telephoned him again after finding a second bullet shell near the body. Detective Sergeant Ian Welch, known locally as 'Columbo', stuck to his original decision not to make the long drive to attend, nor to bother with fingerprinting or forensic tests.

Even photographs were ruled out, which was lucky for the accredited police photographer on duty that night, a Sergeant Neil Phipps. Despite being rostered on, Phipps had vanished from Mansfield police station to attend to private affairs.

And so the die was cast. The word 'suicide' – repeated to each new person introduced to the case – settled over the tragedy, shrouding the truth.

Bill Kerr, older of the two uniformed policemen at the scene, knew more about traffic fines than shootings. But some things niggled him. Such as the half-drunk cup of coffee and plate of biscuits near Jennifer Tanner's body. And the fact she had asked her husband to bring home a local paper, milk, bread and a 'surprise' – a chocolate bar. It hardly seemed the behavior of a suicidal woman.

There was, too, the fact her 21-month-old son was alone in the house. What mother, if not actually deranged, would commit suicide without making sure her baby was taken care of first? There was no evidence Jenny was deranged. And she hadn't left a suicide note. It didn't gel.

Past midnight, after the ambulance had taken the body to the local hospital, Kerr and his partner, Don Frazer, drove through the lonely countryside. It was time to face the job for which no constable's salary is enough – breaking the news every parent dreads. Along the way, they heard a radio message that Footscray police had gone to Denis Tanner's house in Melbourne, three hours' drive away, but that he wasn't home.

Kerr knew Denis Tanner was the dead woman's brother-in-law, younger brother of Laurie, the shy farmer and shearer who'd married Jenny a few years before, after his first wife had left him. Denis was a tough detective who'd worked much of his time in Melbourne's inner suburbs; he would soon loom large in Kerr's mind.

But, as they turned into the neatly-kept riverside property where Jenny had grown up, the policemen decided to keep any twinges of doubt to themselves. In a few hours, a fatal shooting had become just another sad domestic incident, to be settled as tactfully as possible.

And, despite an inquest twelve months later, that's the way it would stay for another eleven years.

THE second part of the story starts high on a granite-scarred ridge in the windswept hills of Bonnie Doon, in the high country of north-eastern Victoria. On the afternoon of July 20, 1995, a Thursday, two young men with a long rope, a torch and strong nerves lower themselves into an old mineshaft known only to a few locals and shooters.

The two mates find more than they bargain for: a human skeleton, clothed in faded and rotting feminine things. Next day, a homicide crew arrives with forensic experts and the police search and rescue team, equipped with a tripod, pulleys, ropes and harnesses. Among the bones and remnants of clothes they find a metal bracelet, a boot heel, a wristwatch, a ring, a cigarette lighter, a pocket mirror, a knife, keys, lead shot, a .22 cartridge case and shotgun wads.

But the most interesting and unexpected find is a pair of silicone breast implants that have met their manufacturer's claims by standing up to age, gravity and the elements. And it is these that lead later, with some luck, good detective work and a trip to New Zealand, to identifying the skeleton as the remains of Adele Bailey, a transsexual prostitute who had vanished from St Kilda seventeen years before, in the spring of 1978.

Fate deals a card here. By chance, one of the detectives sent to the mineshaft knows the district and some of the people in it. In fact, he knew someone who used to live in a farmhouse in the valley below the ridge.

It is the house where his first cousin, a farmer's wife called Jennifer Tanner, was shot dead eleven years earlier ... a death he knows her parents and friends never accepted as suicide, despite a puzzling insistence by police that it was, unlikely as that seemed to those who knew her.

Two violent deaths ... in a sleepy country district that hadn't seen much crime since the Kelly Gang shot three policemen at Stringybark Creek more than a century before. The coincidence gnaws at the detective and some of his colleagues. They don't believe the two deaths are connected in the sense that one caused another – but they can't help suspecting that whoever had the local knowledge to put the body in the mineshaft might also have had the nerve to kill Jenny Tanner, and set it up to look like a suicide.

The public doesn't know it yet, but there are rumors and

rumblings inside the police force, and speculation of an inside investigation of one of their own – Jenny Tanner's brother-in-law, Denis Tanner, a detective sergeant who'd grown up on the old family property near the mineshaft. Already under suspicion by senior officers over allegations that he corruptly 'sold out' a drug investigation, there is another interesting thing about Sergeant Tanner's past ... he was stationed at St Kilda in 1978, the year Adele Bailey disappeared. The circumstantial evidence about the two deaths has the tang of corruption, cronyism and cover-up, but there is little forensic or eyewitness evidence to back it up. And, it seems, someone wants to keep it that way ...

Two months after the mineshaft gives up its grisly secret, there is another 'coincidence'. The old Tanner homestead, 'Springfield', burns to the ground late on a cool September night, destroying any chance of forensic examination.

The empty house, sold by Denis Tanner's brother Laurie – husband of Jennifer – soon after her death, is owned by an absentee owner who is overseas at the time of the fire. There are no gas or electric appliances being used in the house, which cuts out the most common cause of house fires. And the fire is unusually hot, as if fuelled with paper or other combustibles. It starts inside and burns so fiercely it destroys the building before the local Country Fire Authority brigade gets there.

It is the beginning of a chain of events that leads – after a slow start, and probing of the mystery by *The Sunday Age* newspaper – to an exhaustive police investigation, the quashing of the original inquest into Jennifer Tanner's death, and a new inquiry by Victoria's State Coroner, Graeme Johnstone.

The new inquest starts in early October, 1997, and runs for 23 sitting days scattered over more than a year. It is the system's chance to set the record straight for Jennifer Tanner's family and friends.

On December 10, 1998, the Coroner brings down his finding.

Sergeant Denis Tanner, he tells a packed court room, killed his sister-in-law, shooting her at least three times, and probably four or more, with her husband's bolt-action .22 rifle.

It is fourteen years since Jenny Tanner's body was found slumped on a couch with the rifle propped between her legs – and thirteen years since an inquest hamstrung by the sloppiness of the original police investigation, and haunted by persistent suggestions of a cover-up reaching high into the police force. For the dead woman's blood relatives, justice has not only been agonisingly slow. It seems to them that, for too many painful years, it was denied.

THE Coroner's finding was a damning indictment both of Denis Tanner and the 1985 police investigation.

But despite the public outrage about the case – and the notoriety of the surly, silent man at its centre – one fact had been obvious to police and lawyers from the start: much of the evidence weighed by the Coroner would be inadmissable in a criminal trial, and therefore it would be no use charging Tanner with murder because there was no chance of a conviction.

Without forensic proof or eye witnesses the web of circumstantial evidence was not enough to put before a jury. In essence, all Tanner's highly-skilled defence counsel, Joe Gullaci, would have to do is shrug and say that while his client hadn't been particularly fond of his sister-in-law, there was no law against that. And that his instructions were that his client hadn't been anywhere near Bonnie Doon on the night she died. There was no known witness to testify otherwise. Case closed.

Based on the evidence allowed before the court, a judge would be forced to agree, and instruct a jury accordingly.

The result was a faintly bizarre legal stalemate. A bewildered public, having seen and heard headlines saying the Coroner had named Dennis Tanner as a killer, could not understand why nothing was being done. The consensus among those outside legal, police and media circles was that 'he'd got away with it.' This sense of outrage was aggravated by the fact that Tanner stayed on the police payroll, a situation that could only change if he resigned – or if the department found a way to dismiss him.

Meanwhile, in early 1999, there was another inquest – the one into the death of transsexual Adele Bailey. The State Coroner, Graeme Johnstone, properly ensured there would be no suggestion of prejudice by standing down so that another coroner, Jacinta Heffey, would run the Bailey inquiry.

Compared with the Jennifer Tanner inquest, it was a relatively quick affair, although not without interest to an onlooker. The search for the truth about what happened to a New Zealand-born Pitcairn Islander who had a sex change operation in Cairo before returning to St Kilda to work as a prostitute was bound to attract some interesting witnesses. It did, but in the end it proved only that some very colorful people had managed to survive a quarter century of sex, drugs, crime and law enforcement by failing to recall, at least in the witness stand, details of those incidents that might get other people charged.

Common sense says that Adele Bailey was deliberately abducted and killed. Or that she died in a way that would acutely embarrass a policeman (or policemen) with a sex or drug scandal gone wrong, potentially implicating him (or them) in offences ranging from criminal negligence to corruption to manslaughter.

But there was little chance that street people left over from the 1970s would be supplying the heavy-calibre evidence needed for the coroner to make any other finding than the one she swiftly made: an open finding. In the absence of willing and truthful witnesses, no-one can prove how Adele Bailey died, nor how her body came to be in the mineshaft.

The only chance of the truth about Adele Bailey's last hours on earth becoming public is if someone, somewhere, makes a deathbed confession with their last breath. Meanwhile, don't hold yours.

One thing is certain. It won't be Denis Tanner who does the talking. After the Bailey inquest – for which his legal costs were paid by the Police Association, because his connection with her involved his work – he continued his courtroom policy of silence. Presumably on the same grounds: that is, that to answer questions 'might tend to incriminate' him. As controversy swirled around him for three years he maintained, publicly, a face like a well-kept grave. Even when the State Government specifically amended legislation to give the Chief Commissioner of Police wider powers to dismiss officers – dubbed the 'Tanner clause'– he said little in public.

Instead, poker-faced, he stuck doggedly to his cards and upped the ante. His reputation might have been in tatters, and his family in distress, but he was determined to salvage as much money from the wreckage of his career as he could, in the form of superannuation and leave entitlements. Money, say those who know the man, has always motivated him.

Tanner had an ace up his sleeve when it came to dealing with both police command and with his own union, the Police Association. This was, ironically, his pariah status in the public eye. He was an embarrassment to both sides and, despite any public posture, privately they wanted him to disappear quietly. That gave him the leverage to cut a deal.

It was true that the Chief Commissioner, Neil Comrie, had the power to sack – but it was also true that the Police Association would be forced to fight such a move because of the wider implications for its members. However, this would be expensive, and it would be unpopular with the public and a lot of police, and erode the political clout the association was building. It was a million-dollar battle neither side really wanted, if face could be saved with some diplomatic manoeuvres.

And another, unspoken, suggestion lingered over the case. Tanner had kept silent not only about himself – but about the possible involvement of other police in various matters that, if revealed, would blow up into scandals calculated to wreck reputations, or worse.

Anybody who, like him, had worked 'hot' at inner-suburban police stations like St Kilda and South Melbourne in the 1970s knew where the bodies were buried, metaphorically speaking. There would be those still in the force, some of them in senior positions, who would be happier for him not to be tempted to remember too much.

A bitter, talkative Tanner with nothing to lose and bent on revenge had the potential to embarrass the entire force as well as, perhaps, ruining a few careers. The association knew this as well as senior police did. So there were probably muffled sighs of relief in several quarters when, on July 28, 1999, he beat a very slow-moving axe by resigning. It was no surprise to find out his representatives had been bickering behind the scenes for some time with police command.

The wisdom of Tanner's policy of stony silence was proved as soon as he opened his mouth. Deprived of rank and badge at the age of 45, for the first time in more than 25 years, his public stand-off ended with a whimper rather than a bang.

First, he tried clumsily to quarantine the story of his resignation to two media outlets. This attempt to stare down three years of bad publicity by orchestrating news of his own exit fizzled into farce when heavyweight commercial radio station 3AW neatly scooped him at his own game merely by following up an early-morning 'promo' on the ABC station 3LO, plugging his upcoming live appearance with 3LO morning announcer Jon Faine.

Tanner's pig-headedness – and his parlous position – was proved by the fact that he was reduced to choosing the Faine programme in tandem with an obscure publication called the *High Country Times*, a giveaway local tabloid dropped into the letterboxes in his parents' hometown of Mansfield every Wednesday morning. Its editor and co-proprietor, with whom Tanner had tried to curry favor, happily told 3AW listeners all about the policeman's 'shock' resignation – ten minutes before Tanner himself spoke on ABC radio. This prompted Tanner to complain on air that it was another example of the 'carnivorous' media that, he claimed, had hounded him for three years.

Out of his depth, and struggling under the weight of his own notoriety, Tanner didn't do himself – or the ABC's reputation – any favors.

A distinguishing characteristic of Tanner's progress has been the collateral damage he's inflicted on those around him. It was no different with his resignation.

He conned the earnest and well-meaning ABC producers and presenter with the promise of an 'exclusive' that was in reality a thinly-veiled, self-serving attempt to manipulate the media.

It didn't work well for Tanner – he sounded nervous, defensive and unconvincing trying to answer the few gentle questions put to him. But it also hurt ABC radio's credibility, already tattered by the fact the station had previously made the mistake of using a self-described 'author' of slight credibility – whose actions had been roundly criticised by the Coroner – to comment on the Tanner case during the inquest.

Tanner didn't say much, but each word proved the old saying that it's better to shut up and be thought a fool than to speak up and prove it.

He said hesitantly that he had refused to testify at the inquests on the 'best legal advice' of his lawyers. On the question of his guilt, he said cautiously in his high, whining voice: 'Everybody's entitled to an opinion. So be it.' He claimed he had 'plenty' of friends and supporters, but said 'the general public got its mind made up from a media campaign. I can't help it now. It's been done'.

In short, his 'answers' were the farrago of vague generalities, omissions, half-truths and specific truths that unreliable witnesses almost always use. The host thanked the disgraced detective and accused killer for talking on his programme. He even offered the self-congratulatory rider that this was because 'we' (the ABC) handled such stories more fairly than others. What he didn't know then, of course, was that he was second choice in a field of two.

The truth was, Tanner had offered his 'exclusive' to senior *Herald Sun* reporter Geoff Wilkinson some weeks before ... on condition the reporter reveal who'd given his newspaper a copy of Tanner's wedding photograph a few days earlier. Wilkinson refused point blank, forcing Tanner to slink off to look for a softer target.

The moral of the story is that if you play with snakes, you get bitten. Of course, plenty of other people have come to grief because of Denis Tanner, including his own family. Anybody who saw the inquests unfold over almost two years felt the power of one to cause pain for many.

IT'S a long way from a dusty church hall in Mansfield in 1985 to the new Melbourne Coroner's Court in 1997. The main players in the drama were the same, if older, but there were a few new faces.

Some were witnesses who probably should have been called in 1985. Others could shed light on certain events since then. Then there were the watchers, drawn to the latest episode of a tragedy that has changed many lives.

Those who attended the inquest, in court one, instinctively divided themselves. This subtle segregation was curiously one-sided.

Both Jennifer Tanner and her husband, Laurence James Tanner, belonged to large families.

Jennifer was the eldest of four daughters of Les and Kath Blake, who have lived in the Mansfield district for 30 years, moving there when Jenny was ten.

Laurie Tanner is the oldest of four sons and one daughter of Fred and June Tanner. Tanners have farmed in the district for generations.

For most of the hearing days, the Blakes were accompanied by their surviving daughters, Kris, Clare and Miriam. For the first eight days, Les Blake's two sisters, Val and Joy, also attended. All except two had to travel from the country and stay in Melbourne at their own expense; none wanted to miss a word of evidence.

The Blakes and their relatives and friends crowded into the right side of the chamber, behind the counsel assisting the coroner, Jeremy Rapke, and the senior taskforce members given the job of gathering evidence on Jenny Tanner's death. They were Inspector Paul Newman, Detective Inspector Jeff Calderbank and Detective Sergeant Marty Allison.

By contrast, the other side of the courtroom was deserted. Although Laurie Tanner was one of five children of parents who are still alive, and although he was secretary of the

Mansfield agricultural society at the time his wife was killed, no-one came with him and his brother, Denis, then still a detective sergeant in the Victorian police force. Unlike the Blakes and their relatives and friends, the extended Tanner family evidently did not feel compelled to hear evidence about what might really have happened in the old farmhouse on the night of November 14, 1984. Denis Tanner told a co-author of this book in 1996 'as far as I am concerned it was a thorough investigation' and that he was satisfied with the assumption Jennifer's death was suicide.

On the second and last day of the inquest, a policewoman sat behind Denis Tanner and spoke to him. The only other person to sit voluntarily near the Tanner brothers, and on speaking terms with them, was a retired nurse attempting to finish her first book, which centres on the case. She is middle-aged, tanned, wears much heavy jewellery, and darts from one group to the next before and after each session, speaking loudly and often. The would-be author's financial interest, though keen, would have paled beside that of the defence counsel engaged by the Tanners.

Denis Tanner, formally named as 'a person of interest' in the proceedings, retained Gullaci, a criminal barrister reputed to charge more than $2000 a day, a fee in keeping with a reputation that prompted one policeman outside the court to describe him 'as the best advocate going around'.

Such admiration of Gullaci's pugnacious cross-examination has won him regular work representing police brought before the courts, in between representing alleged Italian organised crime figures who can afford the best. Interestingly, he also represented Denis Tanner at the first inquest into his sister-in-law's death, in 1985.

The thirteen years between inquests evidently did not ease

Laurie Tanner's concerns. Whereas he shared Gullaci's services with his younger brother in 1985, this time he retained a barrister called Tony Hargreaves, an advocate the Police Association recommends to members in trouble.

Gullaci is short, thickset, bald, with a heavy beard, swarthy looks, a gravel voice and a tough turn of phrase that could earn him a bit part in a Mafia movie.

His learned friend, Hargreaves, is taller, younger and less forbidding – more private school than private eye. The pair worked closely together, arriving early at court each day in a sleek, late model Jaguar with the Tanner brothers in the back seat, taking the most expensive limousine ride of their lives.

At the other end of the horseshoe-shaped bar table, bristling with nine black microphones, was Jeremy Rapke, the counsel assisting the Coroner. He is a courteous and formal prosecutor whose gentle air masks a steely logic that rattles more than one experienced witness neatly trapped into contradicting their own evidence. The Tanner brothers sat close together, heightening the contrast between them.

Laurie, then about 50, was tall, thin, wrinkled and worried-looking, with curling hair and a droopy moustache under a long, aquiline nose supporting a pair of metal-rimmed glasses.

Every day he wore the same grey pinstriped suit. A farmer, truck driver and onetime shearer, he looked uncomfortable in business clothes. Long, bony wrists and calloused hands stuck out a long way from his cuffs, and for days he fidgeted continually, looking vaguely into space, rubbing his fingers together or stroking his chin in a nervous mannerism that borders on the compulsive. He has not married again since Jennifer's death, and lives with his parents and motherless son in Mansfield. It's not hard to see why.

The only resemblance between the oldest and the youngest of

the Tanners is the hawk-like nose. Where Laurie is scrawny and weathered, worn with manual work, Denis is beefy and broad-shouldered, with the hard look and soft hands of the pub bouncer he has been in the past, a strong man carrying enough weight to give the impression he'd rather risk a little physical danger than the sort of physical labor his brother Laurie does daily.

Despite suggestions raised in court that he had the motive and the opportunity to kill his sister-in-law, the big detective in the well-tailored navy suit sat quietly, his close-set eyes and stony face for the most part elaborately neutral – as if he were a bored bystander, not someone spending tens of thousands of dollars in legal fees to defend his reputation and his career. He rarely moved except to make notes, looking coolest when the evidence seemed most damaging.

From the outset the Coroner, Graeme Johnstone, made it clear that it is his investigation, run his way. He was patient, measured, polite, but unflinching. He didn't indulge in the clubby legal humor that often flows between bench and bar table in other courts.

He quietly interrupted testimony and cross-examination with shrewd questions aimed at baring facts hidden by legal persiflage, or by the nervousness or reluctance of witnesses. He was quick to probe examples of the disgraceful police work that clearly frustrated Hugh Adams, the Coroner in 1985, who wouldn't buy the suicide scenario and made an open finding after criticising an investigation he found was 'slanted towards a situation of self-inflicted injuries'.

Jeremy Rapke's opening address flagged some of the drama ahead. For the first time, Sergeant Helen Golding's name was made public. This could prove a good thing for Sergeant Golding, godmother to Denis Tanner's children, and formerly his wife's best friend, but unlikely to be on speaking terms with the Tanners again.

Rapke revealed that Sergeant Golding had received a series of death threats, but this dramatic revelation paled beside the appearance of the woman herself a week later, an event marked by everyone entering court being checked for weapons by armed police equipped with metal-detecting wands.

Visibly shaken, but determined, Sergeant Golding told the court she contacted the taskforce after reading an account of Jenny Tanner's death in *The Sunday Age* in June, 1996. She said she was 'terrified', and had not slept properly, walked her dog or ridden her horse since making a statement to investigators about Denis Tanner last October.

Her story was chilling, even in a warm court room full of polite people. She was sent a dagger, covered in fake blood, leaflets from funeral directors thanking her for inquiries that she had not made, a sympathy card with the words 'you're dead' written on it, and a .22 calibre bullet in an envelope. What worried her most, perhaps more than the dagger, was a wreath left on her doorstep with the message 'Time runs out'. There was something more sinister in the symbolism of that, somehow, than in the cruder threats of bullets and fake blood.

On July 8, 1997, she received a letter containing her current work roster, a card with the words 'I miss you' and a letter that read: 'Helen, Are you ignoring the warnings you have received. Do you think they are idle – not so. You're (sic) movements are known – as you can see by the attached roster and you have a new car. How nice. Do not follow through with this – "Life" is not worth it and it won't be worth it. You should have the message by now and if not you soon will. That prick in Melbourne, f...... c... that he is, will soon get his too. If this goes ahead "Your Dead" but not without pain, or alone. You won't get another warning, the moment you make a move to Melbourne start watching your back. Nobody wants to do you any harm but everyone has there (sic) limits and you have pushed yours far enough.'

This campaign of terror prompted an extraordinary statement by the Coroner. After leaving the bench for half an hour, he halted cross-examination to say that although he had sat on many inquests, 'at no stage has a witness been subject to the number of threats as in this'. He said he was troubled by the 'serious nature' of the threats, and called on 'the highest level' of Victoria Police command to guarantee security of Sergeant Golding and her family.

Sergeant Golding's brave evidence was a dramatic postscript to the mystery. But that of former policeman Bill Kerr went to its heart.

Kerr, an amiable man who plays bowls and wryly calls himself 'a dumb country cop', has quietly believed Jennifer Tanner was murdered since an autopsy two days after her death showed she had two bullets in her skull, and bullet wounds in each hand.

Ironically, it was Kerr, called first to the death scene with another policeman, Don Frazer, who began the chain of events that let the death be treated as suicide by others. When he telephoned the nearest Criminal Investigation Branch, at Alexandra, on the night of Jennifer Tanner's death he told Detective Sergeant Ian Welch the scene 'looked like' a suicide. Welch had said not to bother about photographs, forensic tests or fingerprinting.

Kerr stated he called Welch a second time because he grew suspicious after finding a second empty rifle shell at the scene. Welch doggedly denied this, although his memory failed him on several other points when he was cross-examined. Patchy memories were to affect several witnesses, particularly ex-police. Kerr spent hours in the stand under withering cross-examination calculated to discredit him, and although he was often tripped up on details of what happened that night, one thing survived his ordeal by lawyer: proof of his suspicion that Jennifer Tanner was murdered.

He said he was puzzled that two hours after the body was found, he heard a police radio message saying attempts to contact Denis Tanner at his (then) Melbourne home had failed. (Golding later gave evidence that Tanner's wife Lynne told her Denis did not get home until 5am on the night of Jenny Tanner's death.)

Kerr said he was frustrated by 'superiors', who repeatedly denied his requests for forensic tests on the rifle, which he insisted on keeping in his locker at Mansfield police station. His request for a list of questions to be put to Denis Tanner by senior police was also denied.

Months later, Denis Tanner had made a statement to a homicide detective, Senior Sergeant Albert 'Jimmy' Fry, in which he gave a different alibi from the one he'd given Kerr the day after the shooting. But it was not a record of interview, he was not cautioned, and no meaningful questions were put to him.

Fry, also retired, was called to explain this to the Coroner. A dapper, friendly man with a suntan, slip-on shoes, a big dress ring, and a good line in jokes outside court, Fry could pass for a Sydney car salesman. Questioned by Rapke, he rapidly lost his sense of fun.

He at first claimed it wasn't his 'function' to judge whether the shooting should be investigated as a possible murder, and that in any case there was not enough information to form an opinion. But, a few minutes later, he admitted writing a seven-point statement that strongly supported the suicide theory and that dismissed Kerr's request that Denis Tanner be questioned, on grounds that Kerr's suggested questions were 'based on rumour and conjecture.' Fry also swore on oath he hardly knew Denis Tanner at the time, and had not spoken to him since, but he admitted calling Tanner in 1996 to urge him to sue *The Sunday Age* because he thought an article published about Jenny Tanner's death was 'unfair' to Tanner.

Fry said he couldn't explain why he didn't realise, after reading the file provided by Kerr, that Tanner had contradicted his original alibi that he was 'at the trots' on the night of the murder. In the statement Tanner made to Fry, he stated he was providing security at a bingo night at Middle Park.

Superintendent Peter Fleming, later of the anti-corruption unit, was assisting the coroner in 1985. He looks like a bank manager who could be trusted not to cook the books. His memory seemed much sharper than that of some other witnesses, particularly Fry and Welch.

Fleming testified bluntly that the investigation of Jenny Tanner's death was 'grossly inadequate' at every level, and that he was concerned that nothing was done to correct it. He recalled an angry meeting at the homicide offices where, he said, Fry 'was adamant it was suicide,' refused to investigate it, and was supported by his superiors.

Fleming said he had also approached the internal investigations division, but was told the matter was beyond its jurisdiction. He had then done the best he could, in limited time, to investigate it himself, despite being warned it wasn't his job.

'There were rumors this particular matter was not being handled correctly,' he said carefully, adding that a decision was made to start the 1985 inquest because of the long delay already endured.

There were several poignant moments in the first week of the hearing. Bill Kerr, asked why he had made and kept tape recordings of conversations with several key people, and why he had taken his file on the case when he retired in 1993, said: 'Because I probably didn't trust them.'

Coroner: 'Why did you answer like that?'

Kerr: 'When I joined the police force in 1970, it had a squeaky clean reputation. I don't believe it has now. That's probably one of the reasons I got out.'

After giving his evidence, Frazer, by now a sergeant, quietly told the Coroner he regretted the way things were handled on the night Jenny Tanner was shot, and volunteered a defence of Kerr's role in having the case re-opened.

'I know the media has jumped on Bill Kerr's comment that he was just 'a dumb country cop', but he was far from that, Your Worship. I just wish I'd given him more support – as perhaps others should have,' he said.

Ian Welch, the former detective sergeant who became a carpet cleaner, was asked after a bruising exchange with Rapke how he later thought the case should have been handled.

'The scene should have been preserved, and there should have been a full and proper homicide investigation,' he muttered after an awkward pause.

Asked which people a homicide investigation should have interviewed, he said: 'I believe Denis Tanner should have been interviewed.'

'Anybody else?' asked Rapke softly.

'No-one else springs to mind,' replied Welch.

BLOOD'S thicker than water. That's one reason it's so hard to wash away, a point Bruce Tanner could have pondered on the morning of November 15, 1984, when he drove to the old farmhouse where he'd grown up to do something so unpleasant he still resents talking about it.

The job was this: to scrub blood from the couch where his sister-in-law, Jennifer Tanner, had been found shot dead the night before in circumstances that have come back to haunt the family these past years.

It is unclear exactly why the then school principal interrupted his rushed trip – from Girgarre, near Kyabram, to his parents' house at Mansfield – to spend time cleaning the scene of his sister-in-law's alleged suicide. It's also unclear why two of his brothers, then both policemen, did not later comment on his destroying a possible crime scene. All of which is, or was, a touchy subject with Bruce Tanner, judging by his performance in the witness box at the second inquest into Jennifer's death.

Bruce Frederick Tanner was one of four family members unexpectedly subpoenaed to testify in December 1997. The others were his brother Frank, sister-in-law Lynne and mother June, all called from the country at short notice.

None seemed to enjoy the experience any more than the sorry collection of present and past police facing the humiliation of admitting their parts in a 1984 'investigation' they insist was merely 'inept', but over which lingers the whiff of cover-up, cronyism, collusion and corruption. The death scene was not secured, photographs were not taken, forensic tests not done, and a pathologist's suspicions were dismissed. From the first hour the death was treated as a suicide, for reasons that clearly perplexed the coroner, whose task was to unravel the mystery of how – if she didn't suicide, as was painfully obvious – she did die. It's a mystery that drew a lot of people to court, many of them blood relatives of Jennifer's, there to support her parents.

They watched, with the awful fascination of onlookers at a car crash, the spectacle of the Tanner family being torn apart.

Mostly, the Tanners were notable by their absence, except for the pair deemed 'persons of interest', the brothers Laurie and Denis. But when his family was called, Laurie wasn't in court. His barrister handed a doctor's certificate to the coroner to explain that his client was too ill to attend.

He stressed the certificate was 'confidential', but promptly revealed its thrust: that the visibly nervous Laurie was distressed by intense media coverage of the case. The coroner ordered that the Tanner brothers not be filmed or photographed outside the court until they were actually called as witnesses. This order, however, did not extend to the rest of the family, which was to lead to an extraordinary scene outside court. But that came after four Tanners gave evidence.

BRUCE Tanner cut a neat figure in a conservative dark suit, metal-rimmed glasses and moustache. At fifty, the second of the Tanner brothers could pass for a solicitor, accountant or businessman. That is, until he answered the first question put by Jeremy Rapke, counsel assisting the coroner.

The quietly-spoken Rapke, whose courtesy a witness should not mistake for weakness, asked Bruce Tanner his occupation. 'Depends what time of year you're talking about,' came the tart retort. 'Currently I'm a company director.'

The exchange set the tone for the next half hour. Swallowing hard, but defiant, Tanner gritted his way through cross-examination about the intriguing events of the day after Jennifer's death.

His version of those events was that his mother telephoned him about 6am on November 15, 1984, with bad news: his older brother Laurie had returned home from Mansfield the night before to find his wife dead on the couch with his .22 rifle between her knees.

After arranging for staff to fill in for him at his school, Bruce set out for Mansfield to comfort his parents and Laurie. But instead of driving past the farmhouse, which is next to the highway at Bonnie Doon, he stopped and went in.

Asked why he did this instead of going straight to his grieving relatives, Tanner retorted: 'Because the police had informed my mother she was expected to clean up, and there was no way she was going to do that'. Unfortunately, he didn't know the answer to a crucial question: which policeman allegedly gave his mother this peculiar direction.

Asked how he cleaned the blood from the sofa, he snapped, 'How do you usually clean blood off?'

Rapke: 'I don't know, Mr Tanner. Tell me.'

Tanner: 'Cold water. That's what you use to clean blood off.'

Asked why he hadn't inquired about the circumstances surrounding the death, he said he had gone overseas a few weeks later, and hadn't returned for more than a year.

He conceded 'probably' discussing Jennifer's death with his brother, Denis, but said he didn't know two bullets had been found in Jennifer's skull until after he returned from overseas. He also claimed not to have known she had bullet wounds in both hands until he 'read it in the papers' during the current investigation.

'You read all this crap in the papers. Who knows if it's true?' he snapped, scowling. Rapke: 'Do you resent being here?' Tanner: 'I'm losing a day's pay. I have been unemployed for seven months. I just got a job and just when I start I am being dragged here.'

But fears for his reputation didn't curb his temper after that day's hearing. Nor brother Denis's. At a time when it might be prudent not to show a propensity for violence, the two Tanner brothers blew it.

As the family group walked to the court car park, Denis hit a *Herald Sun* photographer in the groin with a brief case. Then Bruce cut loose, throwing open his car door as he accelerated away, knocking the same photographer to the ground. In the car, Denis's wife Lynne, a former policewoman, looked as shattered as she'd looked in court a few hours earlier ...

LYNNE Maree Tanner was a police officer for twelve years, and must have seen plenty of courts, but the blonde, pleasant-looking mother of four looked as bewildered in the witness box as any first-timer.

Her voice was faint, and quavered. If she expected a tough time from Rapke, she was right. He fired questions like punches, aimed at a sore spot: the fact her husband Denis had given two alibis for where he was on the night of Jennifer's death. One, that he was 'at the trots' was demonstrably false, given that there had been no trots meeting closer than Bendigo (in distant central Victoria) on the night in question. Which might be why he came up with the other alibi – claiming he had been doing security at a bingo hall in Middle Park, which was vague and hard to substantiate or disprove.

She said Denis told her he was going to the bingo, but can't recall what night it was, when he left or when he got home to their house in Spotswood. In a curiously roundabout answer, she said she doesn't remember him arriving, but that she 'would have remembered' if he hadn't been home when she got up to feed their baby at 1am.

She shook when Rapke referred to the covert police recording of conversations she had with the godmother of her children, Sergeant Helen Golding. She sobbed when reminded that Golding, her closest friend for years, had given evidence that Lynne told her privately Denis arrived home on the night of the shooting just before Footscray police came to the door around 5am. The court adjourned for 15 minutes while she rushed to the women's toilets in tears, to be comforted by her mother-in-law, the flint-faced June Tanner. Meanwhile, her husband stayed in court, chewing gum and chatting nonchalantly to his barrister, who didn't look happy.

Rapke resumed the attack: 'Helen Golding told this court you told her he (Denis) came home just before the police called.'

Lynne Tanner: 'I don't recall saying it ... to my knowledge he was home.'

There were many other questions, some put by the Coroner. At face value, the answers revealed a woman with astonishingly little knowledge both of her husband of 15 years and of her sister-in-law's death.

No, she didn't know Denis belonged to a pistol club, and couldn't recall him criticising Jennifer the way some other people do. No, she didn't take any interest in the evidence at the first inquest in 1985. No, she didn't know there were two bullets in Jennifer's skull until the first inquest, and that fact didn't arouse her curiosity or suspicions. No, she didn't know about the bullet holes in the hands 'until the last couple of years'.

She said she had never heard rumors of her husband's possible involvement in the shooting. And she didn't know if Denis had driven to Bonnie Doon a few weeks before Jennifer's death to warn her to 'treat Laurie properly'.

FRANK Tanner and his mother, June, got their turn in the box three days later. Frank, who gave his occupation as farm hand, had his sleeves rolled up and chewed gum as he gave evidence. Not as aggressive as Bruce, not as nervous as Lynne, he was offhand and taciturn.

He told the court that when Jennifer was killed, he was a police constable at Hamilton. That 'as far as I know' Laurie and Jennifer were happily married. That it never crossed his mind 'other things' but suicide might have caused Jennifer's death, that he had 'nothing to do with Denis', and had never discussed the case with him.

'I had no idea until the publicity recently that she was shot twice,' he said, which prompted the Coroner to quiz him from the bench, a touch sceptically.

Coroner: 'But Jennifer Tanner is family, is she not? And you didn't inquire as to why it was an open finding (in 1985). You would be more aware than most (as a policeman) about the meaning of an open finding. And that finding was critical of the investigation.'

Frank Tanner: 'What's it to do with me?'

Coroner: 'Did you seek out your brother and ask what was happening?'

Frank Tanner: 'No.'

Coroner: 'You are disinterested?'

He hesitated, then answered slowly: 'Oh ... I've thought about it a bit the past twelve or eighteen months or so. I don't talk to my family about it.'

He confirmed he accompanied Laurie to inspect Jennifer's skull at the Mansfield undertaker after the body was exhumed the previous year in July 1996. But he said he no longer read the papers or watched television news, and didn't discuss 'certain things' with his family.

Coroner: 'Tell me, Mr Tanner, does this current investigation raise doubts in your mind as to the way Jennifer died?'

Tanner: 'It probably has. I still believe she committed suicide – but obviously I would be a fool if I didn't think about it.' He'd been 'a bit sad' when the Springfield farmhouse mysteriously burned to the ground in late 1995, after the discovery of Adele Bailey's skeleton in the mineshaft that the Tanner brothers knew well as children growing up in the district. He said he assumed the house burned because of 'an electrical fault'.

This despite evidence given earlier that a car and a person had been seen near the house when the fire started.

He said he had been 'out fencing' when he got a call 18 months before from Laurie to say there was going to be 'an article in the paper on the Sunday'.

'I think he (Laurie) might have been a bit upset that they were going to point the bone at him.'

Rapke: 'Has the bone been pointed at any other brother?'

Tanner (laughing): 'I think so, don't you? It's been pointed at Denis.'

Rapke: 'You can't believe that any member of your family could stoop to murder?'

Tanner: 'I wouldn't think they could ... anyone that takes a mother away from her little baby is pretty ordinary.'

JUNE Tanner, a thin woman in her seventies, gave her sons the characteristic aquiline nose and a hardy attitude. She dropped her tan handbag on the seat provided in the witness box and stood, ready for action.

Questioned by Rapke, she fiercely denied that Denis ever had a share of the family farm, Springfield, which Laurie had taken over when he married his first wife, Suzanne, in the early 1970s.

She said she knew nothing of the divorce settlement Laurie reached with Suzanne. Other evidence had been led that Laurie Tanner paid $20,000 to Suzanne when she left him, and that Denis later told a Benalla motel broker that he (Denis) had made sure 'the second slut' wouldn't get the lot. But June Tanner would have none of it. She said she knew nothing of

Laurie agreeing to join Denis in a motel venture in the late 1980s. She said none of her sons had any interest in guns, and that she was sure Denis was never a member of a pistol club.

She said she 'got on very well with Jenny, as a matter of fact' and 'popped in and saw her a lot', but that she knew nothing about the state of Jennifer and Laurie's marriage.

She said Jennifer was 'very moody' but she didn't know whether she was contemplating leaving Laurie.

She snapped 'I wouldn't have a clue' three times in answer to questions about Jennifer's avowed dislike of guns.

Rapke: 'Are you close to your sons?'

June Tanner: 'Yes, we are a normal happy family.'

A few seconds later, she added: 'It's thirteen years. It's a long time. A lot of people have got exalted ideas about what happened.' She denied cleaning the house, and didn't give a direct answer when asked if any policeman had told her to clean it. 'That Bill Kerr, I don't know what he told anybody,' she said darkly – and meaninglessly.

Asked if she had any suspicions about the death, she said: 'I am not interested. I'm just interested in bringing my grandson up. You just have to get on with life.

'If it was murder, that would be shocking. I don't follow these things. I don't read the papers.' But a few seconds later, asked how and when she learned Jennifer had two bullet wounds to the head, she answered: 'It was in the paper.'

As she leaves the witness box she snapped, 'Excuse me!' at an investigator as she stepped over his feet. Then she smiled across the room at Denis. He smiled back.

MUCH more evidence was given over eight days. It was divided into two broad categories: police and former police attempting to explain their actions during what is loosely termed 'the first investigation', and expert witnesses demonstrating how unlikely it was that Jennifer Tanner shot herself. The testimony of Dr Norman Sonenberg came in between.

Sonenberg had the misfortune to help the late Dr Peter Dyte perform an autopsy on Jennifer Tanner's body two days after her death. Because Dyte was terminally ill at the time of the first inquest (later quashed) in 1985, Sonenberg was obliged to give evidence on which he had to be re-examined.

It wasn't pleasant for him. Faced with expert opinion from a professor of neurosurgery and a professor of pathology, he elected to fall on his scalpel. He admitted he and Dyte – a polite and deferential man – tried in 1984 to make the two head wounds and two hand wounds fit the police's dogged insistence that it was a suicide. Sonenberg admitted his evidence at the 1985 inquest was unreliable, as was a statement to police last year. 'We were trying to make a round peg fit a square hole,' he said. 'We were trying to make the wounds and the scenario fit a suicide. We spent some time trying to make it fit.'

Sonenberg blamed police for dismissing any possibility of suicide. He didn't name Neil Phipps, then a sergeant at Mansfield, but the since-retired policeman himself admitted being wrong. Phipps, later a chief inspector, and a former homicide detective, told the inquest he'd suddenly changed his mind. He no longer believed Jennifer Tanner could have twice shot herself in the skull.

'What I am saying is that there is a strong possibility that the firearm was operated by someone other than Jennifer Tanner,' he admitted in the witness stand.

Evidence was given earlier by Bill Kerr, the more senior of the two police called to the scene, that Phipps did not attend that night because he was 'working a phantom' night shift, and wasn't at the police station when the first call came. An uncomfortable Phipps denied working the 'phantom' shift, but said he 'blanked out' some details about the case after transferring from Mansfield a few days after Jennifer Tanner's death.

Duncan MacLennan is another former policeman with a problem. MacLennan, who in 1984 was the district inspector, admitted there was a 'general consensus' around the station a few days after the shooting that Denis Tanner might have been involved. But he said he couldn't explain why Kerr had given evidence that his brief to the first inquest was doctored to remove material implicating Tanner.

MacLennan was caught. He could choose to praise Kerr as a diligent and honest senior constable, thus drawing criticism because Kerr's recommendations that Denis Tanner be questioned were ignored. Or he could try to dismiss Kerr as an eccentric dreamer with little experience, as some others had tried to do, leaving himself open to the accusation he left a possible murder investigation in the hands of someone clearly incapable of investigating it.

In the event, he chose to praise Kerr and risk the consequences. And to make the lame claim it wasn't his responsibility to supervise the investigation 'because I was an administrator, not an investigator'.

Pushed by the Coroner to explain why it wasn't a cover-up, he first said it was 'obviously a case of inept police work'. But, asked to explain why Kerr's statement was edited before reaching the Coroner in 1985, he changed tune. 'It implies a cover-up or attempted cover-up. It is not acceptable.'

The Coroner asked if the death was not properly investigated because a serving policeman was involved. MacLennan replied: 'As far as I am concerned, Your Worship, no. I can't speak for others.' Before the inquest the biggest of many questions facing the Coroner was how Jennifer Tanner could shoot herself twice in the brain and through the hands with a bolt-action rifle. That would have appeared to have been put beyond doubt: She couldn't and didn't. Someone else shot her three or four times. Which left some other unanswered questions.

One was this. Even if the investigation was botched from the start by 'inept' police, why did they keep secret – especially from her parents – for almost a year the fact there were two bullet wounds to both the skull and one in each hand?

There were many other questions – about false alibis, inexplicably poor investigation, cronyism, collusion and intimidation. But one that should have been asked the night Jenny Tanner died still stands out.

How could she shoot herself twice in the head, and through both hands, with a bolt-action rifle, and still be found with one hand curled around the barrel?

TEN years after the circumstances surrounding the deaths of Jennifer Tanner and Adele Bailey were exposed as being suspicious, Denis Tanner was still fighting to clear his name.

Having lost his career and his reputation following the coroner's finding that he had shot his sister-in-law, Tanner seemed to take the view he had nothing to lose by running a guerrilla campaign against his accusers. He has been especially critical of members of the police taskforce that gathered evidence for the inquests into the deaths of Jennifer Tanner and Adele Bailey.

Tanner has ingeniously used the police, the judicial system and the media ... in order to agitate about his treatment by the police, the judicial system and the media. In doing so, he might well have succeeded in confusing and obscuring the facts of the case enough to create niggling doubts in the minds of some gullible members of the public.

Counting the original task force, set up in 1996, there have been (at the time of writing) a total of six police investigations into aspects of the case, most of them prompted by the complaints of Tanner or his former police associates, one of whom is threatening civil action against the police force because of a grievance over the way investigators allegedly treated him. The one thing police hate is to be investigated by other police. They see it as treachery – a breach of the unwritten code of 'the brotherhood'.

Despite Tanner's calls for a 'third inquest' into his sister-in-law's death – something that he knows is unlikely to happen – nothing alters a fact that should have been obvious in 1984, and which was made painfully obvious at the second inquest in 1998: that is, Jennifer Tanner did not shoot herself.

The case has been raked over in the media several times – a reflection of the story's potential to sell newspapers and attract viewers and listeners rather than the actual newsworthiness of any so-called developments. Since 1999 Tanner has even called media conferences himself to highlight his grievances, but has not produced any fresh evidence of value. Nor has he ever been able to give a plausible explanation for not giving evidence at the second inquest on grounds that he could incriminate himself.

Because of the case's notoriety – something similar to the Wales-King 'society murders' later – it has been easy for Tanner and others to create headlines on flimsy pretexts to throw up spurious doubts about what really happened to the two victims.

In October, 2005, the Victorian Government announced total rewards of $2million – $1million each – for information leading to conviction of the killer or killers of Jennifer Tanner and Adele Bailey. This was a huge jump from the $50,000 rewards posted in 1999 and indicated the State Government's respect for ongoing public interest in a case that raised the spectres of police cronyism, corruption and cover-ups.

Announcing the rewards, the Chief Commissioner Christine Nixon said it was not an 'issue about Denis Tanner'. But, apparently hinting at a possible conspiracy among former or serving police, she said investigators believed that more than one person had been involved in Adele Bailey's death in 1978. She also said it was 'quite possible' that more than one person had been involved in Jennifer Tanner's death.

'We need to find a way forward for the family,' the commissioner said. 'This issue is not about Denis Tanner. This issue is about anybody in the community being able to come forward. If Mr Tanner has information, the detectives involved are very happy to take a statement from him.'

Detective Senior Sergeant Bill Nash, who led a fresh taskforce to re-investigate and review the work of the first taskforce led by Inspector Paul Newman, confirmed that many months and thousands of man-hours had produced no new evidence to warrant a third inquest.

One of Dennis Tanner's many complaints was that he wanted access to X-rays of Jennifer Tanner's skull found at a Shepparton hospital after the 1998 inquest. But Tanner would have done better not to draw the public's attention to the X-rays because Australian and overseas experts that examined them ruled out the possibility of suicide, supporting the coroner's finding in 1998.

Experts maintain that the first bullet in Jennifer Tanner's brain would have disabled or killed her, and that it was ridiculous to theorise that she would be able to reverse the rifle, work the bolt to eject the empty shell and lever in a fresh one, and then point it at her head and fire it again, presumably with her foot. And shoot herself through the hands in the process. Not even a Hollywood scriptwriter would try to sell such a far-fetched scenario. When the rewards were announced, Dennis Tanner told ABC radio: 'I think Jennifer Tanner killed Jennifer Tanner. I'm not sure about Adele Bailey. I know I didn't.'

Tanner also maintains he knows nothing about the bizarre wool shed incident in 1998 in which his brother Laurie – Jennifer's husband – was allegedly attacked by an unknown man or men at night when he went to his farm wool shed to check on a pump.

Laurie Tanner was to claim later he became unconscious in the attack and when he came to, found a boning knife stuck in his heel and a sharp wire wool clip jammed through his nose like a bull ring.

The Tanner brothers were later to claim that police 'technicians' had carried out the attack when Laurie had accidentally turned up while they were 'bugging' the shearing shed with listening devices. Senior police dismissed the claim as ridiculous. Other unsubstantiated theories include one that the wool shed attackers could have been serving or former police implicated in Adele Bailey's death – and that they were warning the obviously nervous Laurie Tanner not to 'crack' by telling anything he knew to investigators or to the coroner.

Of course, the attack might have been carried out by a borderline psychopath acting alone. Statistics prove that many serious assaults are carried out by people known to the victim.

In another sinister postscript to the case, a bullet hole was found in a window in a St Kilda Road building normally used by the Victorian fraud squad. There are many windows on the eastern side of the building but the one in question happened to open into an office being used by Detective Sergeant Nash's taskforce while it worked on the Tanner case. It seemed it had been fired from a nearby park. It seems that someone, somewhere, had inside information.

CHAPTER 16

Out of His Depth

It's a tip-off — allegedly anonymous — that gets Rocky killed.

ROCKY Iaria's mamma believes in miracles. Long after giving up hope her boy will turn up alive, she prays his body will be found so she can lay him to rest properly, with tears and wreaths, a headstone of Italian marble and all the rites of her religion.

She waits more than six years from the night Rocky disappears, never losing faith. Then, on February 19, 1998, Mrs Iaria gets her miracle.

IT'S a Thursday morning, cloudless and still, another in the endless succession of fine days in the drought-stricken countryside, but perfect for weddings and funerals.

The gravedigger at Pine Lodge lawn cemetery, a peaceful spot on the Benalla road in the flat country east of Shepparton, trundles through the cemetery gate in a tip truck. There's a funeral later that day; he has to open a grave so that the recently deceased Derwent Phillip Pearson – known all his life as Jim – can be buried with his wife Dulcie, who left him behind in early August 1991.

The gravedigger reverses the truck to the Pearson grave, which is near a tree at the rear of the cemetery, well away from the road. Then he starts the yellow Massey Ferguson tractor with its front-end bucket and backhoe, and begins work, the rattle and hum of the diesel motor echoing across the flat paddocks.

The soil has settled a little in the six and a half years since Dulcie Pearson left her Jim, but it's easy digging with the backhoe.

The operator knows from practice just how deep to go without hitting the coffin below. It's all worked out – the first coffin into a double grave is buried two metres deep, leaving plenty of room for the second to sit above, with a few centimetres of earth sandwiched between the two.

That's the way it's supposed to be, anyway. Which is why the gravedigger is surprised, he later tells police, when the jaws of the backhoe strike something odd only 'a couple of feet down'. He gets off the tractor and peers into the hole.

He works the levers, then stares and feels a flutter of apprehension. Poking through the loose earth is something swaddled in black plastic. The steel jaws have torn the plastic, and stinking slime oozes from the tear. For a moment, he thinks there's been some ghastly mistake; perhaps someone has buried a baby in the wrong grave.

It's the wrong grave, all right. Whoever buried the thing wrapped in plastic made a mistake. They picked a fresh grave where the ground was already disturbed, but they didn't realise – or didn't care – that one day it would be reopened. Otherwise, it could have been the perfect crime.

OUT OF HIS DEPTH

The gravedigger doesn't know any of that yet. He calls a supervisor, who tells him to proceed carefully. He does. He jiggles the foul-smelling thing into the bucket of the front-end loader and places it gently on the truck.

As he does, the plastic tears some more, and he sees the leg of a pair of beige-coloured jeans. It's then he knows it's a job for the police. He kills the motor and reaches for his mobile telephone again.

ROCKY Andrew Iaria would have turned 27 in 1998, as his father, Antonio, recalls sadly when asked about the fourth of his six children. Iaria senior is a leathery little man with the marks of many seasons on his face.

He speaks fractured English, learnt after arriving from Calabria at age fourteen, and doesn't say much. His wife, Raffaela, says little more, but her eyes glisten with tears as she spreads on the table a handful of photographs marking milestones of her boy's short life.

Here's Rocky the toddler. Then the cheeky schoolboy, the cocky teenager, and the sharply dressed best man at a cousin's wedding, his curly hair short at the sides, shoulder length at the back, tumbling over the rented tuxedo as he looks at the camera with a faint smile on his angular young face.

The wedding picture is the one his mother chooses for the memorial cards given to mourners at the requiem Mass when they re-bury Rocky – in his own grave, this time – at Myrtleford on March 3, 1998.

In another snap, taken when Rocky is about seventeen, he sports a windcheater with the words 'Already A Legend' on it, a gold ring on his index finger, a cigarette, and a nonchalant look. He looks like a kid who wants to be a tough guy.

That impression is reinforced in another picture, released by police. Eyes narrowed, he's blowing out a plume of smoke and wearing a sharp, checked bomber jacket – the same one he wears the night he goes missing in September, 1991.

By that time Rocky's twenty, and in big trouble, just like a real tough guy. But he isn't that tough, he isn't that smart, and he doesn't realise the trouble is big enough to get his head blown off with a shotgun. How can he? He's only a kid.

Rocky Iaria was born and bred in Shepparton, where his mother moved from Myrtleford after she married Antonio in 1966. Raffaela Iaria will never forget the day she bought her bridesmaids' dresses for the wedding. It was the day Shepparton closed down for the funerals of two local teenagers, Garry Heywood and Abina Madill, abducted on February 10, 1966, and found murdered sixteen days later.

It's a crime that shocked Australia, and was to echo down the years until the killer, the man they call 'Mr Stinky', was caught almost two decades later.

The young bride could hardly guess that she, like the dead teenagers' parents she pitied that afternoon, will later also suffer the agony of not knowing a child's fate.

Not just for sixteen days, but for more than six years. In the 1990s, however, neither her son's disappearance nor the discovery of his body is to rate much more than local headlines.

One reason for this is that as violent death becomes more common, reaction to it wanes. Another is that for a long time Rocky Iaria's disappearance is only that – any public interest in the mystery fades with time and the lingering suggestion that he might have run away.

Thirdly, the taint of a criminal connection hangs over the case. And, finally, the missing man belongs to people who tend to keep their tragedies private – and to settle grievances their own way.

OUT OF HIS DEPTH

THE Iarias live, for a while, on a small orchard at Shepparton East before moving into the town when the children are small. They work hard but keep, in many ways, the peasant mindset of their forebears. They belong to a tight-knit local Calabrian community, which, by the 1960s, dominated the Melbourne wholesale fruit and vegetable market.

Some families flourish more than the Iarias, such as the Latorres, who work hard and become well-known and relatively prosperous figures in the market scene.

By the late 1980s, Mario Latorre, born in 1942, has a fruit business at Epsom, near Bendigo. His brother John Latorre, born in 1959, is a stallholder at the wholesale market in Melbourne.

Their younger brother, Vincent Paul Latorre (not to be confused with an influential relative, also Vincent Latorre, now of Werribee) stays on the farm at Shepparton.

Vince Latorre loves fast cars and he finds the money to buy them. In the late 1980s he owns, according to local police, two customised 'Brock' Commodores, instantly recognisable to anyone interested in cars. It's hardly surprising that Rocky Iaria – ten years younger, also car crazy, and a seasonal farm worker – gravitates towards Latorre, a fellow Calabrian who hires farm workers he can trust in a business where edible fruit and vegetables aren't the only produce.

Rocky not only works for Latorre. He hangs around with him and another colourful Shepparton East identity, Danny Murtagh, who has married into a local Italian family.

Keeping such company isn't wise for young Rocky, according to police intelligence, which in 1989 puts some of the locals high on a list of suspects for a series of burglaries and robberies of wealthy Italians.

They don't come much wealthier than Stephen Monti, a

millionaire tomato grower from Bendigo, who returns to his home in Napier Street, White Hills, on the evening of May 16, 1989, to find his back door blocked, his front door open and the house ransacked.

Gone are a clock radio, a camera, a video recorder, watches and leather jackets. But what really hurts is that Monti's open fireplace is smashed and the safe that had been bricked into it is gone. Few people know the safe exists, let alone what's inside, but Monti tells police there was about $300,000 cash, 110 ounces of gold and expensive jewellery. Estimates of the total value of the haul range from $500,000 to $700,000.

For several reasons, the best being a tip-off, police suspect the Shepparton crew for the Monti heist. One reason for this is that Vince Latorre's distinctive Brock special is seen near Monti's house. In fact, a truck driver with a keen eye for cars notices it four times on the day of the robbery.

The truckie, one Stuart Andrew Young, is later to testify in court to seeing the car at Goornong, between Shepparton and Bendigo, early that morning, then at a McEwans hardware store about 11.30am where he sees two men in the car and a third getting into it after buying some 'jemmy' bars, the housebreaker's tool of choice.

Later, Young sees the car in a side street near Monti's home. And, about 3.30pm, he sees it turn into the Epsom Fruit Works, owned by Mario Latorre.

Young isn't the only witness. It seems to others that Rocky Iaria, or someone very like him, is keeping lookout in Napier Street around the time of the burglary. Unfortunately, he tries hiding behind a post that's thinner than he is, which makes him look both ridiculous and suspect. If it is Iaria dodging guiltily behind the road sign – as the Crown later claims – then as a crook the boy makes a good fruit picker.

OUT OF HIS DEPTH

THE execution of the Bendigo burglary might be amateurish, but there's nothing amateur about the information that prompts it, nor the size of the prize. It is deemed a major crime and therefore a job for the major crime squad, a group later disbanded amid official misgivings about the activities of a few of its members.

The official line on what happens next is, in the words of one policeman, that the squad 'commenced an investigation that identified two suspects at Shepparton'. Meaning that at dawn one day soon after the Monti job, a crew of major crime detectives uses a sledgehammer to open the door of the unit Latorre then lives in with his wife, Angela Robinson, and their small son.

It's a heavy-handed affair, and Latorre later complains about the detectives frightening his family. Meanwhile, at the Iarias' house in Orchard Court, Rocky also cops a rude awakening.

The pair are questioned in separate rooms at Shepparton police station. Latorre is 29, heavily built and quiet. He agrees he was in Bendigo on the day of the burglary, but says he was visiting his brother.

In the next interview room, his employee and alleged accomplice, barely nineteen, has a little more explaining to do. The police have found goods that look suspiciously like Monti's at his house. Rocky claims he bought them from a stranger selling 'hot' stuff.

Despite the denials, the detectives put together what they judge is a strong case, which is set to go to court in early 1991. But a funny thing happens on the way to trial. The police, it seems, aren't the only ones doing their homework; someone else believes, or is told, that Vince Latorre might know where the Monti loot is.

This is why – about 1.30am on Thursday, July 20, 1989 –

Latorre is abducted from his flat by two men wearing masks, caps and overalls. They tie and gag his wife and leave her in the flat, bundle him into a car, bound and blindfolded, and drive into the bush. There they bash and interrogate him for more than an hour.

Latorre doesn't talk. Either he is brave, or it's true he doesn't know what's happened to the loot because he didn't do the burglary, or he's even more frightened of someone else than he is of the thugs working him over. Whatever the reason, the abductors get nothing from him.

Bleeding and battered, he's driven back to Shepparton and shoved out the door near his unit, still tied and blindfolded. He has to be taken to hospital.

Local police soon hear of two men who'd been staying at a Shepparton motel the night before.

An alert receptionist tells them she assumed the pair were police special operations group members because they were dressed in dark blue overalls and baseball caps, and acting as if they were planning some sort of raid.

Local police trace calls the men made from the motel room. Curiously, some of the calls are to detectives – one in Melbourne and one in Bendigo. The local police aren't sure if this is linked with Latorre's suspicion that a third person was lurking in the background where he was bashed. Latorre thinks his assailants stopped working him over to consult someone else, but he can't be sure.

Like the mysterious telephone calls, Latorre's suspicions of a third person being involved in his abduction come to nothing. What does happen is that two standover men, Chris Dudkowski and Robert Punicki, are arrested, charged and convicted of the abduction and assault of Latorre, among other offences.

The pair, who have been well-known bouncers at Shepparton

hotels, are described by police as 'opportunists' acting independently to find the Monti money.

Dudkowski and Punicki go along with this. They are especially discreet after one is warned in jail he'll be 'knocked' (killed) and an inquisitive lawyer is warned that he'll be 'loaded up' with bogus drug charges if there is any loose talk about anybody else being involved.

Allegations of such activities have no bearing, of course, on the subsequent disbanding of the major crime squad, despite speculation to the contrary. If there is any background involvement by rogue cops in the abduction and bashing of Latorre, it is unclear who they are.

Not all police work is as surefooted as the Dudkowski–Punicki arrests. Surveillance police working for the major crime squad waste several days watching the wrong Vince Latorre, an uncle of the wanted man who then lived in Doyle's Road, Shepparton, some distance from his nephew.

Despite such bumbling, the major crime squad is confident when Latorre and Iaria finally face the Bendigo County Court on February 11, 1991. But not all jury members, after a hearing that stretches into early March, are so sure of the police case. The result is a hung jury, meaning a retrial.

At the time, Rocky Iaria is happy enough to avoid a conviction, even if it means facing another trial later that year. But the truth is, if he'd been found guilty and gone to jail he'd probably be alive today.

It's a tip-off – allegedly anonymous – that gets Rocky killed.

The official version of events is that someone telephones Bendigo police to say a relative of Iaria's, a tobacco farmer near Myrtleford, has a video recorder stolen in the Monti burglary.

A detective goes to the farm and identifies the machine as Monti's. The relative says he bought it for $150, while Rocky was present. It's the link the prosecution needs to tie Rocky to the burglary. Which it does – on September 6, 1991, just seventeen days before the second trial is set to start.

ROCKY is driving around that Friday afternoon in his white XW Falcon. About 3pm, he ferries cold drinks to his older brothers, who are pruning fruit trees, then comes home to the house in Orchard Court his parents have put up as surety for the $50,000 bail to guarantee he will front at the new trial.

In the lull before the evening meal, he kicks a football around the backyard with two of his brothers, Nick and Fiore, still schoolboys.

His mother calls out to ask him if he will be home to eat with the family.

He asks his brothers to tell her he'll be home 'about eight or nine o'clock'. Then he gets into the Falcon and drives off. They don't see him again. Ever.

He doesn't meet his brother, Paddy, at a parking spot near the lake where young bucks gather on Friday nights. It's not the first time Rocky has stayed out all night. But it is the first time he doesn't phone early next morning to tell his parents he's all right.

They're worried. On Sunday, they visit a local detective at home ... accompanied by Vince Latorre. The detective is wary as he suspects they are trying to use him to make it look as if Rocky's disappearance is not just jumping bail. He soon changes his mind.

He talks to Latorre and the Iarias separately. Latorre, he is to recall, shrugs off Rocky's disappearance, saying he doesn't know where he is, and suspects Rocky has 'pissed off because he's shit-frightened of the second trial coming up'.

But Antonio Iaria is ashen with fear for his son. He thinks the boy is dead, that he would never run away without telling the family, and in any case he wouldn't jump bail because it would cost the family their house. The father's distress is convincing.

The detective sends the family to the police station to file a missing persons report. Iaria's disappearance isn't made public until two days later, when the *Shepparton News* runs a small story saying police 'fear for the safety' of a local man after the discovery of his car the day before in the car park at Benalla railway station.

There's speculation Rocky has fled the district on the train, but his family knows it's not true, as much as they would like it to be.

Two weeks later, on September 23, the new trial begins at Bendigo. Latorre, facing the jury alone, is quickly acquitted. Evidence involving Iaria is inadmissible, and so the case against Latorre doesn't stand up, just as predicted.

Latorre returns to the vast, white ranch-style house built on the orchard he has bought in Central Avenue, Shepparton East, near the old place where he and his brothers grew up. Close, too, to his friend Danny Murtagh, who has come under police notice for stealing farm machinery and other offences.

For the Iarias, there is an appalling silence that is to last more than six years. Grieving for their boy, but not knowing what has happened, they hire a lawyer for court hearings to lift the $50,000 bail surety on their house. Eventually, they sell out and move to Myrtleford, away from cruel rumours in Shepparton that they have hidden Rocky interstate or overseas.

Finally, at least, they have a grave to tend. But will it end there?

SUSPICIONS lingered in Shepparton about who killed Rocky Iaria. When the autopsy showed he died of a shotgun blast, it made some people think hard about a gun handed anonymously to police in 1993.

It was a sawn-off, single-barrel shotgun, found in an irrigation channel at Shepparton East. It was identified as a Stirling ... registered to Danny Murtagh. Questioned, Murtagh asserted the gun had been damaged in a fire, then given to an unknown person, who might well have sawn it off and thrown it in the channel. Police have not proved the gun is linked to Iaria's murder, but believe it could be a vital clue in any future trial. Unfortunately, they don't know who handed in the weapon – and it has since reportedly been destroyed in a clean-up of Shepparton police station.

Chances of finding who handed in the shotgun faded when the officer in charge of Shepparton CIB, a Detective Sergeant Barry Stevens, made a public appeal on local television in which, inexplicably, he described the weapon as a 'long-barrelled firearm' handed in during a gun amnesty.

Meanwhile, strange things happened in the orchards and farms around Shepparton. Police were set to move against a local gang suspected of stealing irrigation equipment from an Italian farming family at Tatura in 1997, when a neighbour talked of giving evidence.

Days later the neighbour's entire tomato crop – a year's work worth tens of thousands of dollars – withered and died. It had been poisoned. The theft case collapsed through a lack of evidence. 'I don't want a bullet in the back of my head,' a potential witness told police.

The thieves are feared, but they have their own fears, too. Especially one – a man many in the district believe was behind the Monti burglary and, consequently, the murder of Rocky Iaria.

The old Calabrian way of seeking revenge, says a man who knows the main players, would not simply be to kill the person suspected of murdering Rocky Iaria. It would be to kill that person's son, when the boy turns the same age Rocky was when he died. He says it has already been decided.

CHAPTER 17

The Highway Predator

'We are focusing on the one suspect.'

EXPERIENCE told Graeme Brenchley that dumping unwanted remains in the scrub at Tynong North would go unnoticed. He knew the local foxes and wild dogs on the eastern outskirts of Melbourne would make short work of the bloody load sitting in the back of his ute.

Brenchley, a local garage owner, and mates, Tom Looby and Len Trewin, spent that early summer's Saturday morning slaughtering nine lambs at the shed of his Garfield property and they now needed somewhere to dump the offal.

While Trewin went to the cool room to store the carcasses, Brenchley and Looby hopped into the ute and headed to a familiar patch of bush at Tynong North.

Too close to Melbourne to be a getaway and too far to be an outlying suburb, the area attracts few bushwalkers and sightseers. A small island of scrub surrounded by farmland, there are no streams or mountains, no scenic spots, no points of great historical importance and no major attractions, except for the nearby Gumbuya Leisure Park. Millions of people choose to drive past the park's giant golden neck pheasant statue every year on their way to more popular bush locations. But to Brenchley, it was the ideal spot to let the wildlife clean up his morning's work.

Exactly 1865 metres along Brew Road, north from the Princes Highway, a dead-end dirt track meanders 205 metres to a forked tree. To the left runs a maze of wallaby tracks that lead into the tussock grass and scrubland near a disused sand quarry – now filled with water.

Brenchley reversed the ute between two trees near the sand quarry and was about to dump the lamb remains. 'We knew that there were foxes in that area so it was our intention to spread the offal in the bush area to feed them, as Tom and I shoot them in the winter time.'

But the amateur slaughtermen and keen hunters weren't the first to discover that the bush of Tynong North can hide a multitude of sins.

Someone else had been up that track to dump remains – at least three times – a few months earlier.

Brenchley walked about fifteen metres along a wallaby track. 'I looked to my right and saw what appeared to be a body. I called out to Tom, "Christ, there's a body over here." Then, when I had a good look, I saw a second body. I called out, "No, there are two of them".'

It was about 2pm on December 6, 1980. Police were to discover the bodies of three women – Catherine Headland, 14, Ann-Marie Sargent, 18, and Bertha Miller, 73.

It would take a further two years to find a fourth body on the other side of Brew Road – that of Narumol Stephenson, a woman abducted from Northcote in November, 1980. It is possible that one serial killer abducted and murdered the four women and may be responsible for up to seven unsolved murders in Melbourne.

Several generations of detectives have examined and re-examined the case. Some claim they know the identity of the man who killed all seven victims. Others suggest that while there can be no doubt that Headland, Sargent and Miller were killed by the one person, coincidence alone links the remaining four unsolved murders.

More than two thousand people were interviewed in the original investigation and 11,400 pages of notes taken but, nearly twenty years on, the files were again taken from storage, largely due to the lobbying of the man who was Chief Commissioner at the time of the murders, Sinclair Imrie 'Mick' Miller.

DURING five decades of policing, Mick Miller was never one to tolerate loose ends. A stickler for protocol, procedure and probity, he would not intrude on an investigation, as he knew it should remain in the hands of his detectives.

In 1980, he was determined not to interfere with the Tynong North case, even though the former homicide detective, lecturer at the detective training school and crime commissioner must have been sorely tempted.

His interest in the case was more than just professional. It was deeply personal – one of the victims was Bertha Miller, his spinster aunt.

The idea that Mick Miller would use his influence to upgrade an investigation because he was a relative of a victim would be an insult. Miller didn't just play by the rules, he wrote most of them. Personal interests were set aside; he had a police force to run. But after his 1987 retirement from the force, the frustration he felt over the case became greater when he began to research his family tree. Next to his aunt's name he was forced to write that her murder remained unsolved.

He felt he owed her another effort to solve the crime. Aged in his 70s, and despite open-heart surgery, Miller maintained his powerful sense of purpose and his unshakeable view that all crimes are solvable.

But he offered the next generation of investigators more than encouragement – he gave them a fresh lead. He believed that one of the original suspects had been written out of the case too quickly and concluded that a crucial alibi – accepted at the time of the original investigation – may have been false.

The alibi was that the suspect was at work at the time of two of the murders and the handwritten worksheets proved that he could not be the killer. But Miller believed factory work practices at the time opened the possibility that the sheets could have been faked or the suspect could have left his job for hours without being noticed.

The original investigators worked on the basis that the killer selected his victims at random, picking up women hitchhiking or waiting for public transport.

Miller believed the three women whose remains were found in a cluster in Tynong North may not have been grabbed by an opportunistic killer, but carefully selected by a man they all knew.

If the Miller theory was right, the two younger women were abducted, molested and murdered, while the elder woman was grabbed by a man who wrongly believed she was wealthy, then killed to silence her.

His views were supported to the extent that Catherine

Headland and Ann-Marie Sargent were dumped naked while Bertha Miller was fully clothed.

The original investigators found nothing, other than the area where they were dumped, to link the three victims. Miller, however, believed one man — and possibly more — who could have known all three, committed the murders.

After more than a decade of retirement Miller refused to enter public debates on police matters. At a farewell dinner a good friend and colleague of more than thirty years presented him with a feather duster. It was a private joke on a much-repeated Millerism that you are 'A rooster one day and a feather duster the next'.

But when the elder statesman of the Victoria Police spoke, current senior police listened. When he approached the then Chief Commissioner, Neil Comrie, with his thoughts on Tynong North in late 1998, there was little doubt the case would be reopened.

It was perfect timing as police had decided to progressively work through some unsolved homicide cases and the Tynong mystery was high on the list.

Miller spoke with the then Assistant Commissioner (Crime) Graeme McDonald, a former homicide investigator, and the case was handed to a group of detectives who had become self-taught experts at trying to solve old mysteries and finding any hidden embers in previously raked old coals.

The case had been given to the group of homicide-trained detectives who spent three years reinvestigating the 1984 death of Jennifer Tanner, a young woman who was shot twice in the head in her Bonnie Doon farmhouse.

The original botched police investigation in the Tanner case suggested suicide, while Taskforce Kale, as the reinvestigation was named, provided evidence to an inquest that she was murdered by her brother-in-law, the since retired policeman, Sergeant Denis Tanner. Tanner still protests his innocence to anyone who will listen. Few do.

The team's new investigation, codenamed Lyndhurst, required detectives to check boxes of evidence, old notes from detectives long retired and look at statements from witnesses, some who had since died.

Friends of some of the victims, who were school kids at the time of the abductions, were in their late thirties when the case was re-activated. They were to be asked to recall minor details of events they had tried to block out of their minds for years.

WHEN homicide detectives were called out on December 6, 1980, the Tynong killer was well ahead of the posse. When the first three bodies were discovered the murders were already months old – the victims had been abducted in August and October in 1980.

Mick Miller always felt the initial investigators may have been overwhelmed with the task.

In homicide cases, trails can go cold in hours. Now police had to try to find fresh leads nearly two decades after those women were abducted and murdered in still unexplained circumstances. But they had one new asset – DNA technology. If there were any remains that could point to the killer then, they could now be tested.

In 1980-81 six women were abducted while waiting for public transport or from the street. Four bodies were found at Tynong and a further two at Frankston. Police tried to find whether two serial killers were operating in Melbourne at the same time or if one man was connected with all the cases.

The seven detectives from Operation Lyndhurst were briefed to concentrate on the four Tynong victims, but on the clear

— RATS —

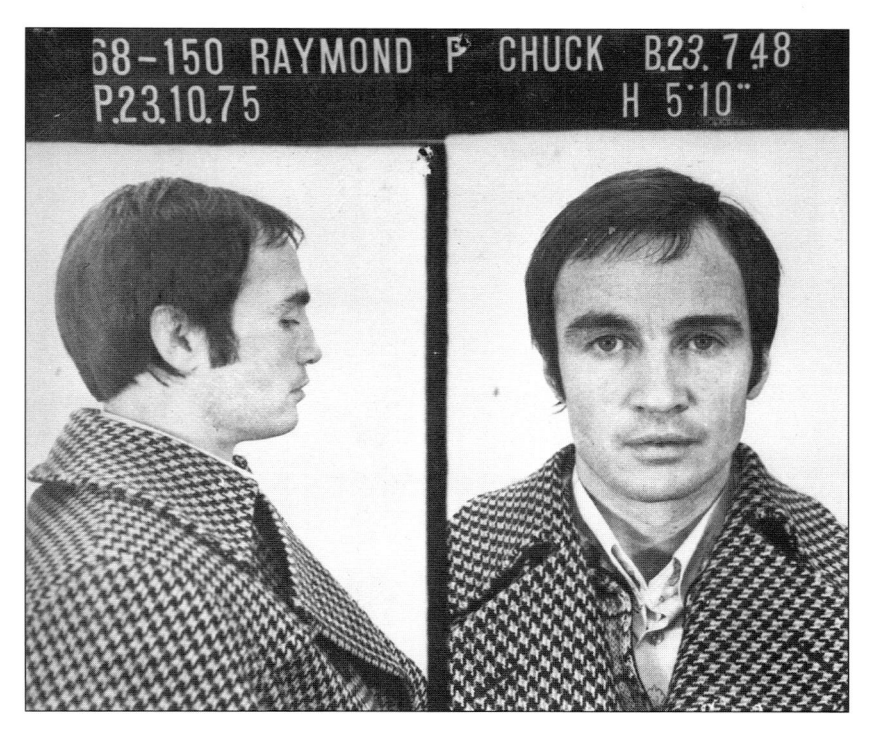

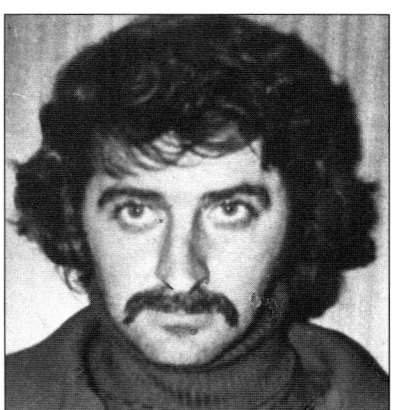

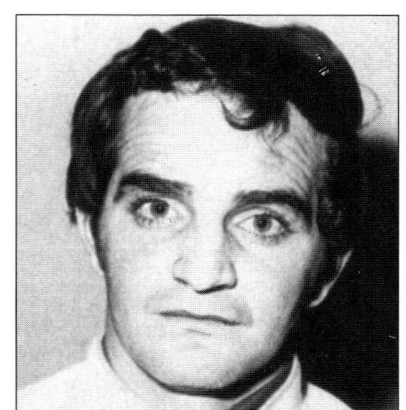

Dead men tell no tales ... Raymond Chuck (a.k.a. Bennett), Les Kane (left) and Brian Kane.

RATS

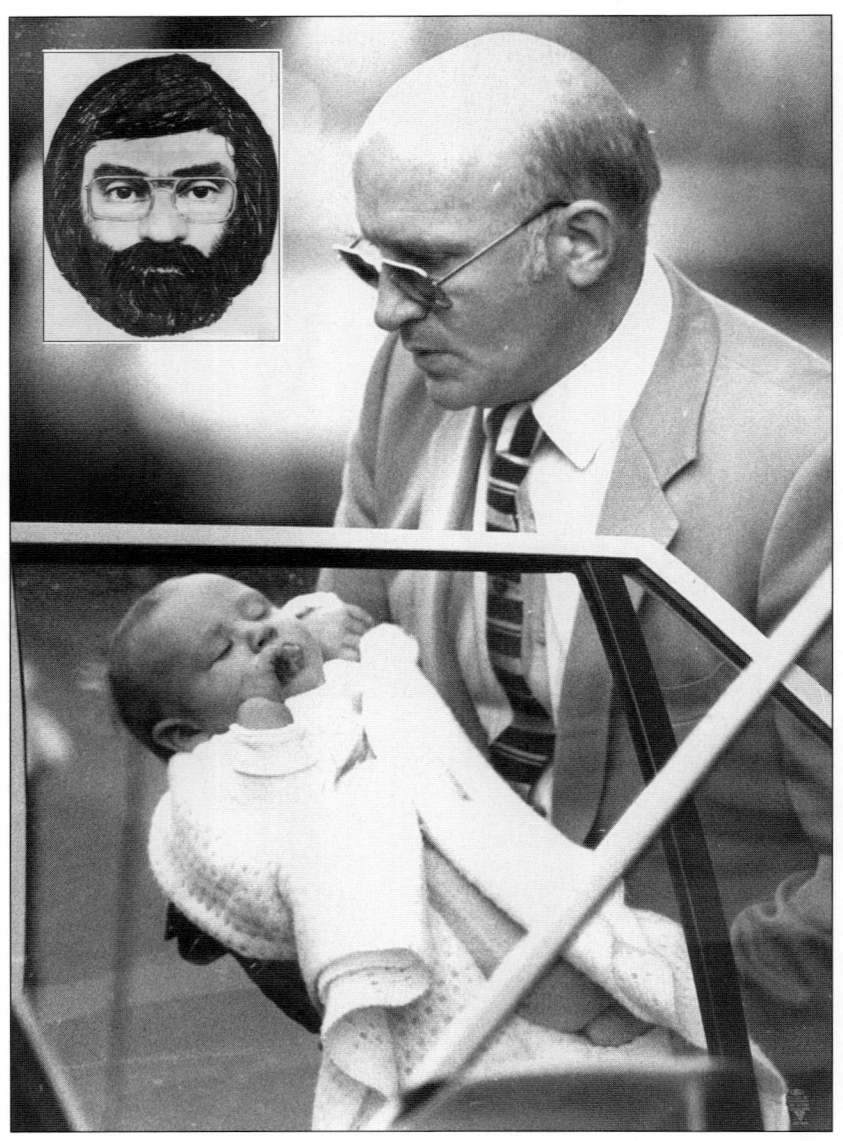

Straight shooter ... Brian Murphy carries the baby. Inset: An artist's impression of the courtroom killer.

RATS

Tough cop turned scriptwriter ... Gordon Davie rides shotgun after Ray Bennett's murder.

RATS

Under the pumpie ... police looking for the courtroom killer. They didn't find him.

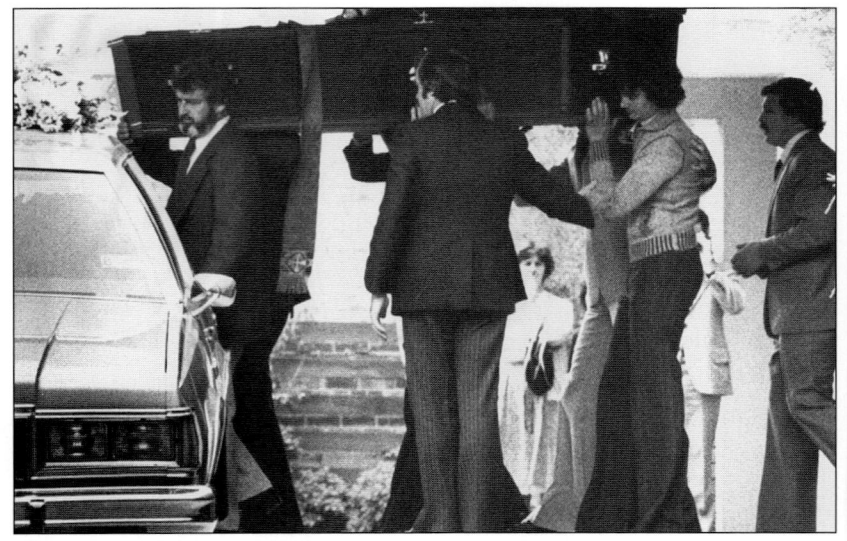

RIP ... the gunman's ultimate occupational hazard: his own funeral.

RATS

Outside the Supreme Court ... two months earlier there was saturation security for Bennett. What happened?

He went that way ... reporter Tony Wright and a much younger author, Andrew Rule, outside the court.

RATS

A hole in the story ... the final exit in a dream getaway for the courtroom killer.

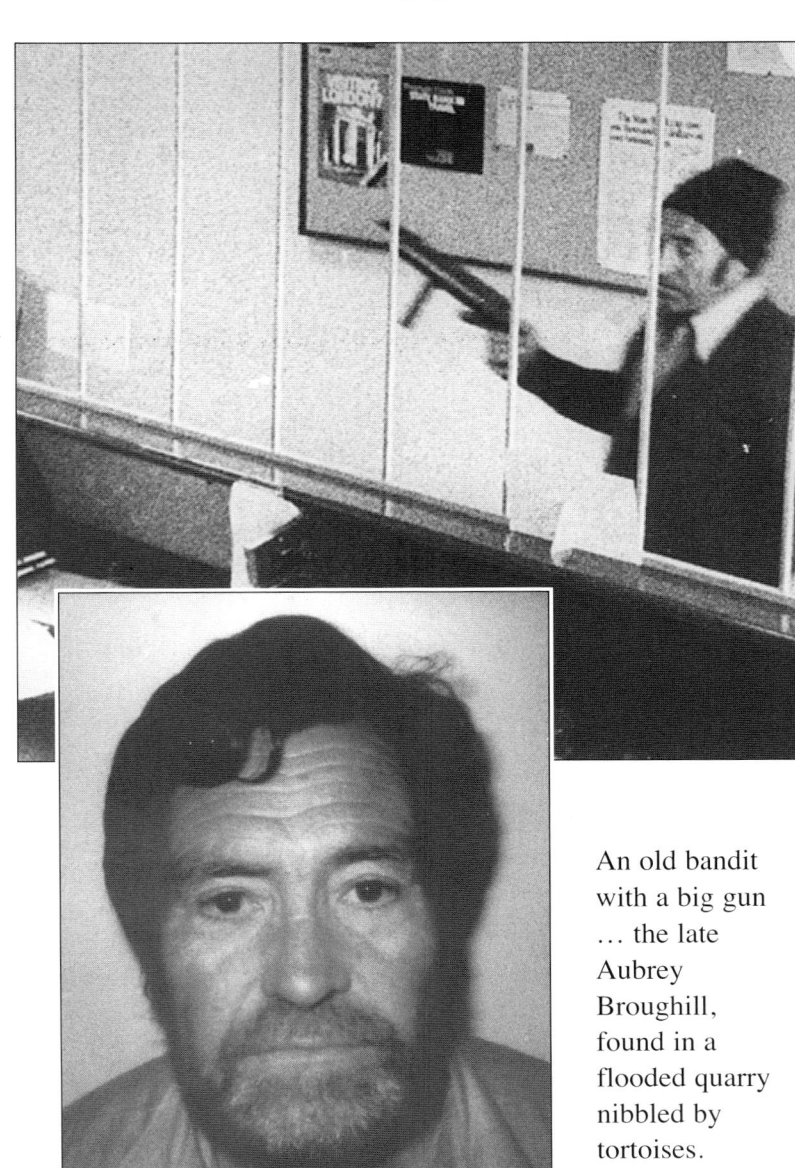

RATS

An old bandit with a big gun … the late Aubrey Broughill, found in a flooded quarry nibbled by tortoises.

RATS

Broughill as a young robber ... his death is a mystery. Turtles (inset) unable to help with police inquiries.

RATS

Happier days ... Aubrey in jail, intact.

RATS

RATS

Denis John Tanner ... no comment in court and no comment to investigators. What does he know?

RATS

Adele (born Paul) Bailey with relatives in the 1970s ... remains were found in a mineshaft near the Tanner property in 1995.

RATS

Rocky Iaria ... buried twice, six years apart.

RATS

Tynong victim Bertha Miller (above) ... aunt of Chief Commissioner Mick Miller.

Another Tynong victim ... Narumol Stephenson

RATS

Chief Inspector Paul Delianis and veteran homicide investigator Jim Fry at Tynong North in 1980.

'Brenchley reversed the ute between two trees ... and saw what appeared to be a body.'

RATS

George Brown ... when he worked as a strapper in Melbourne. Murdered, but on whose orders?

understanding the investigation could be expanded if they found evidence showing links to any other unsolved cases.

FOR every similarity between the cases there is a dissimilarity; every suspect has a possible alibi and every thesis has its doubters.

The case is riddled with unexplained coincidences, intriguing possibilities, viable theories and possible suspects. What is lacking is hard evidence.

The murders are broken into two groups: the Tynong murders – four bodies found in scrubland; and the Frankston murders – two women found off Skye Road. To make matters even more complex there was a seventh murder that police now believe may be connected – the death of a woman abducted in 1975 from Box Hill.

Police who have looked at the Frankston and Tynong cases since 1980 have theories without proof. Two Victoria police expert analysts, who examined all available material five years apart, have come to differing conclusions.

One believes one man is likely to have committed at least five of the murders, while the second thinks there are three separate killers.

Then Mick Miller came up with a name, one that was discarded by the original homicide investigators. The question facing the Lyndhurst detectives was, did the initial investigators discard it too quickly?

ALL murder investigations start off the same – with a victim. Operation Lyndhurst had seven – not cases represented by dusty files, yellowing transcripts and deteriorating court exhibits, but real people who were abducted from Melbourne streets and killed, possibly at random.

The passage of time does not make the crimes any less outrageous. You can't simply shrug your shoulders at murder. The victims were all women, aged from fourteen to 73. Three were mothers, two were teenagers, two were struggling back to health after serious illnesses and one was a highly respected churchgoer.

They seem to have only one thing in common – the violent way they died, possibly at the hands of the one man.

IF only Allison Rooke's twenty-year-old EK Holden hadn't been playing up on the second last day of autumn in 1980, she would never have been on the list.

If only she had given up on the idea of going into Frankston after it took five attempts to get the old car started about 10am that day.

If only she'd made other plans when she drove back to her unit fifteen minutes later when she realised the still spluttering car probably wouldn't get her to the real estate agents to pay her corporate fees.

If only she hadn't decided to catch the Frankston-Dandenong Road bus. But she did.

Allison Rooke was a woman determined to enjoy life. She was comfortable without being wealthy, owning her home and having $6000 in investments.

In good health and aged 59, she was a regular at bingo and enjoyed going to hotels with her daughter to listen to her son-in-law play country and western music every second Friday.

Rooke had moved to her unit in Hannah Street, Frankston, in September 1979 after selling her Cranbourne home following the death of her husband five years earlier. She had three children – one daughter lived in Seaford, a son in Moorabbin and the second son, Ivan, was a policeman in South Australia.

On Friday, May 30, 1980, when her car started to misfire on the trip to Frankston, she returned, had a cup of coffee with her neighbour and friend, Albert Hodren, then left around 11am to catch a bus that travelled along the Frankston-Dandenong Road. She told Hodren: 'I'll only be gone an hour or an hour and a half.'

She planned to go to Ritchies Supermarket to order groceries to be delivered and to Wal Jones Real Estate Agents to pay maintenance fees for the unit.

The regular bus driver on the route could not recall picking her up at the stop opposite Hannah Street. She did not place her grocery order and did not make it to the real estate agents.

Several people claim to have seen her at a lunchtime bingo session at the Bay City complex that day. She was alleged to have attended with a male friend, known only as 'Robert'. One witness said she arrived with Robert around 11.30am, but she was probably mistaken because she could not have left home at 11am and been at the bingo thirty minutes later.

Well-meaning but mistaken witnesses help lay a false trail for investigators seeking the real killer.

A neighbour believed she heard someone in the backyard of Rooke's unit between 5pm and 6pm on the day she disappeared. There were five bottles of beer in the fridge – more than usual – leading police to speculate she may have been expecting a friend to visit on the night or over the weekend. There were two sets of keys to the unit. Neither was ever found.

Her daughter, Elaine White, rang repeatedly that day looking for her mother. They planned to go to a hotel where Elaine's husband, Herbert, was playing with a country and western band that night. When she didn't get an answer, she rang her brother, Kevin, and they both went to the unit, fearing their mother may have collapsed alone in her home.

Kevin climbed through the window and found the place undisturbed, with an empty bottle of beer that Elaine had drunk with her mother the day before still in the sink.

It was a mysterious disappearance until the body was found on July 5, 1980, hidden in scrub beside McClelland Road, approximately three kilometres from where she was last seen.

IT was to be Joy Carmel Summers' first trip on her own to Frankston. Mrs Summers, 55, suffered from arthritis and had had a stroke. She usually went shopping every Friday with her partner, William Cotter, but he had a series of medical appointments that day.

The trip to Frankston should have been simple – the bus stop was less than 100 metres from the Norfolk Court, North Frankston home they'd bought just four months earlier.

On October 9, 1981, Joy had her normal breakfast of coffee, toast and eggs around 7am. She planned to go into Frankston to buy a side of lamb, and although she disliked travelling alone, she also insisted on personally picking her meat from her preferred butchers, Woodwards in Wells Street.

'I think this was the first time that she had been to Frankston by herself. Joy was scared of traffic,' Bill Cotter said later.

She had $66 in cash, but she also took her bank book with a balance of $1990 because she was thinking of buying a small television set for her bedroom. She had only partial use of her right hand and suffered some memory loss following her stroke two years earlier.

Cotter left home about 12.05pm to keep a doctor's appointment and when he returned nearly an hour later, the house was deserted. He found a note in the lounge room: 'Bill, taken string bags. Love Joy.'

The closest stop for the bus was at Chile Street on the

Frankston-Dandenong Road, where she was spotted around 1.20pm.

No bus driver could recall picking her up and she did not place her meat order. Bill Cotter remained convinced she would not have accepted a lift from a stranger.

On November 22, 1981, local residents collecting firewood in scrub beside Skye Road, Frankston, found her body. It was near where Rooke's body was discovered fifteen months earlier.

BERTHA Miller, 73, lived in Kardinia Street, Glen Iris, for more than 25 years in the house she shared with her brother-in-law, William Ross. She was an alert, active woman, in good health, who did not look her age. She had a large group of friends and was heavily involved in church activities.

About 10.15am on Sunday, August 10, 1980, Miller called out to Ross, who was in the shower, that she was off to church, would be late home and not to wait to have lunch.

She would usually take a tram from High Street, Glen Iris, to her church in Prahran. This time she didn't make it.

One of her good friends was Jessie Moore, who lived nearby in Burke Road. They were both members of the Spring Wesleyan Street Mission in Prahran. 'Beth' was the longest-serving member of the Mission, having first joined in 1932. She worked at the Sunday school and had served as the church treasurer.

'Beth Miller was a very kind woman. She took a strong interest in the Mission and was a very helpful woman. I feel that I was a close friend of Beth,' Jessie Moore said.

For the previous ten years, the two women had caught the same tram to church every Sunday – the 10.47am along High Street. Bertha Miller would board at the terminus and Jessie Moore would join her at the Burke Road stop.

But Bertha Miller was not on the tram. Her friend assumed she had caught the 10.15am tram to deal with church business with the pastor. Friends say she was not the type who would accept a lift from a stranger. The weather was quite mild for a late winter's morning, with a top temperature of eighteen degrees, making it even less likely she would accept a ride rather than take her normal tram.

'I arrived at church as normal on that date and Beth was not there,' her friend said. 'Usually if Beth did not attend the Mission on a Sunday, she would ring me the following Monday. I waited about home on Monday, but of course, I didn't receive any phone call.'

Her body was found off Brew Road, Tynong North, in December, 1980.

LIKE most fourteen-year-olds Catherine Linda Headland would have preferred to hang around with her mates rather than work part-time during her school holidays. But she owned a horse and her parents, not unreasonably, felt she could contribute to its upkeep.

The family emigrated from Lancashire in 1966, when Catherine was one, and had lived in Allan Street, Berwick, for five years. Catherine was popular at school and loved competing with her pony in local gymkhanas.

For three weeks she had worked part-time at the Coles supermarket at the Fountain Gate shopping centre and Thursday August 28, 1980, was to be her first mid-week shift – from noon until 4pm. Her mother, Hazel, was employed at the same supermarket and arranged for her to work extra shifts during the August school holidays. Hazel left home at 8.30am, leaving her daughter 70 cents for the bus fare.

At 9.30, Catherine left home to see her boyfriend, John

McManus, who was at his house in High Street with friends. They were both students at Berwick High – she was in form three and he was one year senior. John McManus could remember the exact day they became boyfriend and girlfriend – May 14 that year.

Like many teenagers with a schoolyard crush, they couldn't get enough of each other, going to school together and then spending two hours together after the last bell. Twice a week they would catch up after family dinners, but even that wasn't enough. John didn't want Catherine working during the school holidays and she told friends that while she didn't mind working, she was thinking of quitting to spend more time with them.

After more than an hour with her boyfriend, watching morning television and listening to records, it was time to head for work.

A friend at the house said Catherine sat on John's knee looking out the window for the bus to take her to the supermarket so she could wait until the last possible moment to leave. She saw the bus go past towards Beaconsfield at 11.10am and knew she had five minutes to get to her stop at the corner of Manuka Road and the Princes Highway.

'When she got to the letterbox, she turned and waved and said, "I'll see you tonight",' John said. She expected to be back by 5pm. Police say it should have taken her two minutes to get to the stop.

A bus driver was adamant he picked up a girl fitting Catherine's description and a blonde girl at the Peel Street bus stop, 800 metres from Manuka Road. But police found 'there is no evidence that she caught the bus'.

Friends claimed to have seen her and a blonde girl at Narre Warren about 2.30pm that day, but the blonde associate was never identified and police were to treat the Narre Warren sighting as unreliable. But if she had gone to Narre Warren and had only 70 cents, she may have decided to hitchhike home, a common practice in the area at the time.

The regular bus driver in the area told police he believed he had seen Catherine hitchhiking along the Princes Highway on previous occasions.

When Catherine said goodbye to her boyfriend to catch the bus, she was wearing a thin leather strap on her ankle. A group of girls from Berwick High wore the straps made from one of their father's leather bootlaces, as a sign of friendship.

Police used that friendship strap to help identify the body when she was found at Tynong North more than three months after she disappeared.

ANN-MARIE Sargent was eighteen years old and like so many teenagers in the area, struggling to find a career. Her father, Fred Sargent, described her as 'a happy-go-lucky girl' with 'a lot of mates'.

She went to school at Cranbourne, but started to struggle in second form after developing a serious illness. She underwent urgent surgery on December 15, 1977, to insert a device in her skull to drain fluids from her brain. 'After this was done she was normal and bright,' her father remembered.

When she left school, she worked in a toyshop, a poultry processing plant and a supermarket, but by April 1980, she was unemployed.

On Monday, October 6, 1980 she stopped at her mother's home at Cranbourne Drive, on her way to the Dandenong CES office and said she would return later that day to collect some clothing.

She lived nearby with family friends in Railway Road,

Cranbourne, and after three months without work she tended to hitchhike or walk because of her chronic lack of cash.

'She could have had money from home for a bus but she said she would rather walk because she loved walking. On the day she went missing, I knew that she had to hitchhike into Dandenong because she never had money to get the bus,' Fred Sargent said.

She did get to Dandenong, as she lodged a form at the CES office that day, but was not seen again. Her body was found with the remains of Bertha Miller and Catherine Headland two months later She was identified through the shunt in her skull and a catheter, code 01-66-0100.

IF it hadn't been for a flat tyre and idle curiosity, the remains of Narumol Stephenson may never have been found.

Former Essendon and North Melbourne footballer Barry Davis was driving along the Princes Highway to a college camp when a tyre on the trailer he was towing went flat about 11am on February 3, 1983.

When his mate went off to borrow a jack, he decided to stretch his legs. 'Whilst waiting for the tyre to be mended, I decided to take a walk up the bush track. I walked up this track for approximately fifty metres and came to a dead end. I then turned around to walk back and noticed a bone on the ground.'

Most people may have just ignored the find, but Barry Davis was not an average stroller. He was a senior lecturer in anatomy and physiology at the Phillip Institute of Technology, and immediately recognised it as a human thighbone.

When he walked into the Warragul police station with his find, the police would have known it was a matter for the homicide squad the moment Davis said where he found it. Tynong North.

NARUMOL Stephenson, 34, was struggling to settle in her new country and was having doubts about her decision to move to Australia.

She married Victorian dairy farmer Wayne Stephenson in Thailand in July, 1978, and followed him to Australia in August, 1979, leaving her two children in the care of her parents.

The newlyweds were reunited in Darwin, lived in Cairns and Mission Beach and then travelled through Lismore, Sydney, Wollongong, Lakes Entrance and Melbourne before heading to the lush pastures west of Melbourne in Deans Marsh.

The heavy rain and numbing cold of the surrounding Otways must have seemed like another world to a woman brought up in the heat and humidity of Thailand. She was homesick and friends said she was deeply unhappy.

The couple returned to Thailand in May, 1980, for a month to visit her family and it took a great deal of persuasion by Stephenson to convince his wife to return to Australia.

On November 28, 1980, the Stephensons and another couple from Deans Marsh, went to Melbourne to see a George Benson concert.

They stayed overnight with friends at Hartwell. The next day, Saturday, Narumol went to the Camberwell market to buy ingredients for a Thai meal she intended to cook that night.

The other three went out and didn't come back until 9pm and she became upset when told they were all going to visit a friend in Park Street, Brunswick.

When they got there Narumol, known to her friends as Dang, refused to go into the flat and stayed in the car. The other three people went into the flat to drink wine and coffee.

Stephenson went down to check on his wife at least three times. The second time he found her walking down the street from the direction of a 7-11 shop. The third time she had been talking to a man in a car who spoke 'Thai with a European accent'.

'I saw her talking to a guy in a car just up the road a bit. I walked up to her and saw that the front passenger-side door of the car that she was talking to the guy in, was open,' Stephenson said.

He said she returned to their car and he talked to his wife until nearly dawn, then went upstairs and fell asleep. Shortly after 6am, he had a shower and went downstairs to find her missing.

IT had been a difficult pregnancy for Margaret Conroy, and her best friend Margaret Elizabeth Elliott looked 'thrilled' when she visited the new baby and proud mother at the Box Hill Hospital on April 15, 1975.

The visitor, 26, had left her two young children and husband at home in Brisbane Street, Berwick, and expected to be home before 8.30pm.

Her red Mazda was later found in David Street, Box Hill, with blood on the seat and car door.

Her body was found in Gardiners Creek, Glen Iris, just near High Street.

Police said the Mazda had been driven between 140 and 170 kilometres, well over the thirty kilometres from Berwick to Box Hill.

The sump of the car was clean, indicating it had recently been driven over long grass.

Her family home in Berwick was one street away from where Catherine Headland would later live. A suspect in the Tynong murders also lived in the area.

Margaret Elliott's body was found a few hundred metres from where Bertha Miller lived and within sight of where Miller had intended to walk to the tram terminus on High Street on her way to church on the day she disappeared. Perhaps just another coincidence, or is it more?

To know the offender, you have to look at the crime.
Mindhunter, John Douglas, FBI Serial Crime Unit.

POLICE have looked at the six cases involving Tynong North and Frankston to try to find possible links. All were female; all were abducted waiting for public transport or from Melbourne streets.

The Rooke, Summers, Headland, Sargent and Miller murders have obvious similarities. All were last seen between 10am and 3pm. All were taken in the east of Melbourne. Both Frankston victims were abducted while waiting for a bus on the Frankston-Dandenong Road on a Friday around lunchtime.

Miller was taken after 10am on a Sunday. Headland disappeared just after 11am on a Thursday and Sargent on a Monday.

All five were taken in a seventeen-month period in 1980-81 and four lived in the line from Frankston, Cranbourne and Berwick.

Stephenson was different. She was taken from a car, at night, outside the killer's beat, yet she was abducted at the time the murderer was active and her body was found at the Tynong North dumping ground.

According to a 1985 police analysis of the crimes, never before published: 'There is nothing to suggest that the offender(s) selected their victim because of specific characteristics common to the women. It appears that each of them was selected at random. Who they were was not the criteria for their selection, but where they were: i.e. at a bus stop alone, or hitchhiking, on a major road.'

All the analysis can tell us about the possible offender(s) is that he/they:
1) Would have access to a motor vehicle.
2) Either did not work, was a shiftworker, or maybe on annual leave.
3) Had a good knowledge of the area bounded by Dandenong, Frankston and Beaconsfield and may have lived in the area.
4) Was an opportunist.

Most victims of organised offenders are targeted strangers; that is, the offender takes out or patrols an area, hunting someone who fits a certain type of victim that he has in mind.
Whoever Fights Monsters, Robert Ressler, FBI Serial Crime Unit.

MURDER victims cannot tell detectives who killed them, but their bodies can often do the next best thing. No matter how carefully a murderer covers his tracks, there are always clues left at the scene. The bodies of Miller, Headland and Sargent were all found within metres of each other in the bush west of Brew Road, near a disused sand quarry. Stephenson's body was found a short distance from the Princes Highway, about 800 metres east of Brew Road.

Rooke, Summers, Headland, Sargent and Stephenson were all found naked. Miller was clothed. 'It may be that the offender(s) baulked when they realised her age, or fear and stress engendered by her situation may have brought on a heart attack,' the 1985 crime analyst suggested.

Few personal items were recovered at the crime scenes indicating the killer(s) tried to hide the victims' identities. A wedding ring worn by Rooke and earrings and a leather ankle strap worn by Headland were the only items found.

There was nothing to indicate a struggle at the scene. 'Marks found in the soil beneath Headland's body suggested that she had been dragged into that position by her shoulders,' a police forensic expert concluded. All of the bodies had been covered by local vegetation, although some were hidden better than others. 'The branches used to cover Miller had been sawn off, whereas the branches and saplings used to cover the other bodies had been broken away or picked from the ground,' police reported.

Miller, Sargent, Headland and Rooke were lying on their backs. Summers was on her right side. Miller and Sargent had their right hand on their chest with their left hand beside the body.

The 1985 Bureau of Criminal Intelligence analysis supported the theory there were two, or even three, separate killers responsible for the six deaths. But the investigator felt that one person killed Miller, Sargent and Headland.

'Even though Miller was clothed and Sargent was naked the fact that they were placed in exactly the same position shows the same person placed them there. Headland being in such close proximity to Miller and Sargent would indicate the same person(s) placed her at that site, also. Such care was not shown in the placement of the bodies of the other three victims; Rooke, Summers and Stephenson.'

The analyst came to the chilling conclusion the cold-blooded killer of the three Tynong victims probably carefully selected the spot to dump the bodies even before the first abduction – that he grabbed his victims because they were vulnerable and he was able to trick, or drag them into his car.

'The person(s) who placed the bodies at the Brew Road site was also more particular in selecting a site at which to dispose of the bodies. An isolated site, off a little-used road, considerable distance from the nearest main road was selected. He/they were prepared to take the victim a considerable distance from where he picked them up before disposing of the body. This could indicate that the offender(s) responsible for the deaths of the three women at Tynong North had given some thought to how and where they might dispose of the body and suggest that he may have planned to commit a particular offence if and when the opportunity arose.

'The bodies of the remaining three victims, Rooke, Summers and Stephenson were all within 50 metres of a major road. This suggests that the three were placed at the first available suitable location known by the offenders. Their bodies were not placed or positioned with as much care as the three at Tynong North. These observations alone suggest that there were at least two different people or groups of people responsible for the deaths of the women.'

Then what of Narumol Stephenson? She was dumped naked at Tynong North and covered with branches near Brew Road like the others and was abducted just over a month following Sargent's disappearance.

It could not have been a copycat killer, because the first Tynong body was not found until a week after Stephenson was taken. But she was taken from well outside the killer's normal beat. Could it be just a coincidence that her body was left so close to the others? How many men were abducting women at random and dumping bodies at the time?

None of it makes sense, but if it did, the crimes would not remain unsolved almost 25 years later.

In an investigation that could hardly be more confusing, yet another unexplained murder has become linked – the abduction of Margaret Elliott in 1975.

She was not waiting for public transport, no great efforts were made to hide the body and she was apparently taken in Box Hill, well outside the killer's territory. But she lived in Berwick – part of the murderer's beat of Frankston, Cranbourne and Berwick and she lived one street from where the Headlands would later move. A major suspect for the Tynong case also lived around the corner from the Elliotts.

A coincidence? More than likely, but the body was dumped in Gardiners Creek, Glen Iris – less than 500 metres from Bertha Miller's Kardinia Road home and directly on the route the elderly woman would have taken on the day she was abducted five years later.

THE SUSPECTS
Sometimes, the only way to catch them is to learn how to think like they do. – John Douglas, FBI Serial Crime Unit.

A TAXI driver was known to offer women lifts in the Dandenong area and there were sightings of a taxi in Brew Road near the sand quarry area. He was identified and charged with a series of offences, but cleared of involvement in any of the murders.

ROBERT was a male friend of Allison Rooke who would go with her to bingo. Witnesses said they would often arrive at the bingo separately. He had offered several women at the bingo sessions lifts home, but Rooke had her own car and did not rely on public transport. That is except the day she was murdered. Despite a photofit being circulated, Robert did not come forward and has never been identified.

DESPITE screaming headlines and political hysteria designed to play on the community fears on crime, Australia remains a safe country and, according to some statistics, Victoria is the safest state in the nation. The murder rate sits around 70 a year in Victoria and few victims are picked at random.

There have been few serial killers identified in Australia – men who stalk and murder to a pattern – Paul Charles Denyer, who killed three women in Frankston, 'the Granny Killer' John Wayne Glover, who killed six women in Sydney, and Ivan Milat, the backpacker killer, who dumped six young hitchhikers at the Belanglo State Forest.

But there is a fourth man who police believe is a serial killer, although he has been convicted 'only' of a double murder that was committed years before the FBI term 'serial killer' became part of law-enforcement language.

RAYMOND EDMUNDS is known in the media as 'Mr Stinky'. Edmunds murdered Shepparton teenagers Abina Madill and Garry Heywood in 1966, but was not arrested for the murders until 1985.

Police believe he was responsible for at least 32 rapes and a series of unsolved murders in the nineteen years before he was caught.

Because of the law on police questioning at the time, detectives could talk to Edmunds for only six hours, hardly sufficient to question him about the Madill-Heywood killings, let alone crimes where the evidence was not as strong.

Thousands of questions on sex crimes Edmunds is suspected of committing have never been asked.

He is the prime suspect in at least one unsolved murder – that of Elaine Jones of Tocumwal in 1980.

Edmunds has refused to speak to police but over the years prisoners tend to talk to each other and the convicted double-killer is no exception.

He confided to a fellow sex offender that he had killed 'dozens' of women.

In 1989, the then Chief Commissioner, Kel Glare, received a letter from Pentridge taunting detectives about their lack of progress on Tynong North.

The inmate has since been released from prison. 'I have done some terrible things and I have taken some responsibility for them. He (Edmunds) was a very bad machine. One of those Tynong girls was only fourteen. I had to speak up.

'He has left bodies wherever he lived. He shows no remorse and he'll never change.'

The former sex offender said Edmunds once confessed to him: 'If I told them everything I've done they'd neck (hang) me.'

'The enormity of his crimes is terrible. Society should know what happened.'

Certainly Edmunds knew the areas in question, having worked and lived on farms at Nar Nar Goon and Officer directly in the Tynong dumping area, and one in Chelsea Heights, not far from Frankston. But he moved to NSW in April, 1980, and would have had to return to Melbourne regularly to have committed the crimes. Possible but unlikely.

THE Miller suspect knew Bertha Miller and Catherine Headland and may have known Ann-Marie Sargent through mutual friends. In the 1970s and '80s, he lived in Pakenham and Berwick, inside the murderer's triangle.

The original investigating police believed this man had an airtight alibi. He was working at a factory when Headland and Sargent were abducted. But Mick Miller came to believe the airtight alibi had a slow leak.

Each worker at the factory had to punch a card into a time-clock, but there was no way of proving who actually placed the card into the machine. A worksheet, filled in by hand, showed when workers were on leave or sick.

Operation Lyndhurst detectives wanted to establish if another worker could have filled out the worksheets, which were then completed by the suspect at another time, or if the man could have slipped out of work during the day.

The Miller suspect, then aged in his twenties, did not have a reputation as a good worker. He stayed in the job for only around seven months and often reported in sick.

There have been suggestions that supervision at the factory was poor at the time and worksheets were not checked daily against staff present. Some later admitted they would slip out for a few hours' sleep in their cars at quiet times.

However, there was only one exit from the factory, manned by a guard. Staff had to hand in their passes before they could leave. The suspect would have had to slip out, commit the murders and then return. Alternatively, he did not attend work on the days Headland and Sargent disappeared.

He knew Catherine Headland, moved in a social circle that probably put him in contact with Ann-Marie Sargent, and had contacts with Bertha Miller.

Intriguingly, he once lived in the next street to Margaret Elliott, the woman whose body was found in Glen Iris in 1975.

The 1985 police review found the man and members of his family were 'unlikely to be involved'. But that conclusion was based on the so-called perfect alibi.

Eventually Lyndhurst detectives briefed Mick Miller on what they had discovered on his suspect. They told him that the weight of evidence suggested he was not involved. Miller, a realist who was trained to act on evidence, accepted their conclusion.

BACK in 1985, at the Tynong North inquest, a court order was issued to suppress the name of the main suspect for the multiple murders. But decades later the suspect, by now a spritely man in his 70s, admits that he is the one that many police remain convinced is the Frankston-Tynong North predator. His name is Harold Janman and he maintains his innocence.

When first interviewed by homicide detectives in the 1980s, Janman tried to give the impression he was a prude whose strong religious beliefs made him a loyal husband and dedicated father to his three children. But police found the film projectionist to be a man of two parts, and one of them was exceedingly unpleasant.

Co-workers would comment about Janman's supposed moralistic bent and how he would turn girlie pictures to face the wall in the projection and staff rooms. He was quiet, pleasant and seemingly devoted to his wife, two daughters and son – but there was something distinctly odd about him. He was a member of a fundamentalist church that believed the mainstream Christian religions had strayed from the true teachings of the Bible.

But the religious prude was also a regular visitor to sex shops, a purchaser of pornographic magazines and a gutter crawler who liked to pick up prostitutes.

While none of these habits mean that he is a serial killer, there was one other quirk that makes him figure in the shortest of short lists when it comes to suspects for Tynong North and Frankston.

He liked to pick up women while they waited for public transport, often approaching them at bus stops on the Frankston-Dandenong Road, the same road where Allison Rooke and Joy Summers were abducted seventeen months apart.

Homicide squad detectives are trained to try to find links between where a body is found and any possible suspect. They know that most killers dump their victims in an area they know, perhaps an old fishing spot or a childhood camping site.

Before Janman worked as a projectionist in the city, he worked at the Frankston drive-in off Skye Road, the very road where the bodies of Rooke and Summers were dumped.

Janman's family home was between where the two victims lived.

All three lived within 1500 metres of each other and all lived on streets connected to the Frankston-Dandenong Road.

If the police have a series of five murders that demonstrate the same MO (modus operandi), *we advise looking most closely at the earliest one, for it will most likely have 'gone down' closest to the place where the killer lived or worked or hung out. As he becomes more experienced, the killer will move the bodies farther and farther away from the places where he abducts his victims. Often the first crime is not thoroughly planned, but succeeding ones will display greater forethought.*
– Robert Ressler, FBI Serial Crime Unit.

JANMAN often offered women in the Frankston area lifts in his black Corolla panel van. He said he made the offer to women and sometimes men because he didn't like seeing people waiting for public transport.

He worked shifts and on Friday, May 30, 1980, when Rooke was abducted, and Friday, October 9, 1981, when Summers disappeared, he was on afternoon shift, from 4pm to 2am. The women went missing between 11.30am and 1.30pm.

Several women gave statements to police that they had been approached by a man in a black van offering them a lift. One said she was waiting for a bus on the corner of Mahogany Avenue and Frankston-Dandenong Road. When she refused he said, 'You don't know what you're missing.' It was a Friday in May, 1980.

Another woman said she was approached at the same stop, again on a Friday. Another Frankston woman said she saw the van parked outside her home and when she refused a lift from the driver, 'he appeared upset and turned his car around and in doing so screeched his tyres'.

A man in a black van approached a schoolgirl on her way home early after an exam and offered her a lift, which she wisely refused. It was a Friday.

At 1.30am on October 21, 1981, two detectives went to interview Janman at the cinema in Collins Street where he worked. At this time Joy Summers had been missing less than two weeks and her body had not been found.

The police told him they were investigating the disappearance of Mrs Summers and had information about a man driving a car similar to his, offering people lifts in Frankston-Dandenong Road. He replied, 'I often stop and offer people lifts along there.' He said he picked them up 'sometimes at the bus stops in Frankston-Dandenong Road, sometimes when they are walking along the street'.

He said he picked up males and females, 'but mainly elderly ladies if they will get in with me'.

Asked why he offered people lifts, he said, 'Just to be friendly, and have someone to talk to. Some women have to wait at the bus stop for a long time and I help them by giving them a ride. You never know what will happen next. All the schools have got drugs in them now and the young kids are causing trouble.'

About twelve hours after being interviewed by police

Janman's memory seemed to improve. He rang the Frankston CIB office and spoke to Senior Detective John Kiely. He rang to volunteer that on the day Summers went missing he had driven to Frankston. 'About 12 o'clock that day I went to the bank with my wife to get some money. We would have drove down the Frankston-Dandenong Road but I didn't see anything suspicious, or else I would have remembered.' His loyal wife later supported the story. It would have been the perfect alibi if true. But it wasn't.

The bank manager later gave evidence to the Coroner that no money was withdrawn or deposited into the account on that day. Bank records show a withdrawal the day before, twenty kilometres from home.

After the body was discovered on November 22, Janman was upgraded from a run-of-the-mill suspect to a prime target.

On December 3, three homicide squad detectives arrived at Janman's Frankston house.

When asked if he was aware of the death of the two women, he responded, 'No, I don't read the papers or watch TV'.

Janman repeatedly lied to police when interviewed. Was this because he was the killer, or because he was simply frightened? He was found to have lied over an alibi. He denied knowing the location of Skye Road, even though he worked as the projectionist at the drive-in on that very street.

He first denied ever being anywhere near where Summers and Rooke were dumped, but he later admitted being in the area on his way to the local tip.

Detectives took him to where the bodies were found. Police had levelled areas and cleared scrub looking for clues. Yet when Janman arrived, he carefully avoided the exact areas where the bodies had been dumped. '(He) became nervous and sweated a lot. He walked around the sites as asked, but at no time did he walk in the immediate vicinity of where the bodies had been lying. Extensive areas around the sites had been cleared of bush and scrub by the police crime scene searchers and the investigators stated that 'without some prior knowledge it would not have been possible to tell exactly where the two bodies had been lying', according to a police analysis.

One investigator said his 'gut feeling' was that Janman was about to crack and confess when he started to chant religious statements and virtually went into a state of self-hypnosis. He told police he had only ever offered 'one or two' women a lift because 'I don't like to see people walk'.

He maintained he did not know that two local women had been murdered. When reminded that police had interviewed him only six weeks earlier, he said, 'I, I just forgot, I guess'.

He was then interviewed by Detective Sergeant Col Florence of the homicide squad.

Florence: *Our information shows that you pick up a lot or offer lifts to only women.*

Janman: *Yes, I get knocked back mostly.*

Florence: *So you do offer lifts to ladies?*

Janman: *Yes.*

Florence: *Mostly elderly ladies?*

Janman: *Mostly.*

Florence: *Ever younger women?*

Janman: *Mostly older women.*

Detective Sergeant Jim Fry then asked: *Have you ever given Miss Summers a lift in the past?*

Janman: *Sir, I may have, I honestly may have, but if I did I didn't kill her. I wouldn't do anything like kill anyone.*

Fry: *Have you ever made advances, sexually, to any of these people?*

Janman: *No sir, no. I never play around at all or do anything like that. Sex is sacred and the Bible says it should be with your wife ... I am not a sex maniac, I never play around and I resent the implication that I ever would.*

Fry: *On the 24th of October, 1979, did you appear before the Prahran Court?*

Janman: *Look, yes, but it is not how it is sir.*

Fry: *This is for soliciting for the purpose of prostitution was it not?*

Janman: *All I felt like was a cuddle. I was lonely.*

Police took Janman around the district to point out where he tried to pick people up.

Fry: *Do you know where Skye Road is?*

Janman: *Where sir?*

Fry: *Skye Road.*

Janman: *No sir. I've never heard of it.*

Fry: *So what you are saying is that you've never been in or heard of Skye Road?*

Janman: *I don't know where it is. I've never been there.*

IN his statement, Janman said: 'When I stop to offer lifts to people, I just ask them if they want a lift and that is all. I never force myself on them and when they refuse I just drive off. I would say that the majority of people I offer lifts to are female. I would say that I would have offered females lifts exclusively over the last twelve months. I cannot recall when I last offered or gave a lift to a male in my car. The age group which I ask for lifts in my motor vehicle is usually around the middle ages to older groups but I have offered lifts to younger females around the twenties and thirties ... I would estimate the number generally, over the last eighteen months, to be fifty or even more. Most people do not accept lifts from me and I would say that my success rate is about two or three per cent. Over the past eighteen months, about six females have accepted lifts from me.'

Was it just a coincidence that six women had accepted lifts – the same number to be dumped at Tynong and Frankston? He had lived in his Frankston home for fourteen years, yet he began offering lifts around the same time as the first victim disappeared.

After the homicide squad released him, he sensibly sought legal advice. The following day he returned to the Frankston police station with his wife and lawyer to say he would no longer answer questions. Two weeks later, he was interviewed again and stayed true to his word. He was asked a series of questions and responded with a straight 'no comment' to each.

But then came another twist. On December 6 – the first anniversary of the discovery of three bodies at Tynong North – Janman returned to the Frankston police station.

Senior Constable Michael White was working at the watch-house at 7pm on a quiet Sunday – the day most devout Christians go to church – when Janman walked in, uninvited. He said he wanted to speak to police to tell them he was not involved in a series of rapes in the Ferntree Gully and Olinda area.

Then he said something that has never been fully explained: 'You know I was brought in about two murders in Frankston, well why haven't I been asked about five murders instead of two?' White responded: 'Which other ones are you talking about?' He said: 'The ones at Tynong.'

Intriguingly Janman did not talk of the four murders at Tynong North, just three. While publicly the four bodies were linked, many police believe that the one killer was responsible for the murders of Catherine Headland, Ann-Marie Sargent, and Bertha Miller while another person killed Naromol Stephenson.

Perhaps Janman shared that view, or perhaps he just couldn't count.

Some offenders attempt to inject themselves into the investigation of the murder, or otherwise keep in touch with the crime in order to continue the fantasy that started it.
– Robert Ressler, FBI Serial Crime Unit.

Police in Victoria know serial killers can try to find out the state of the investigation into their cases. Paul Charles Denyer, the man who abducted and killed three young women in Melbourne, contacted the Cranbourne police and falsely claimed to have been interviewed by police over the murders. He wanted to know if he was still a suspect.

WHILE there is no doubt that Janman remains the red-hot suspect for the Frankston murders, was there anything to suggest he could also have been involved in Tynong?

If he was dumping bodies near his home, why would he drive to an area more than 40 kilometres from his patch? Investigators needed to know if there were any connections between Janman and the scrub off the Princes Highway.

Like the killer, they didn't have to dig too deep.

Janman lived in Garfield, the area adjoining the killer's dumping ground, in the late 1950s and early '60s and used to work at the Tynong Hotel.

During the time that Miller, Sargent, Headland and Stephenson disappeared, he was a regular in the area and his black van was often seen parked outside an old friend's home in Garfield.

He had one other job in the district before he moved from the area.

He worked in the sand quarry off Brew Road – the very one where the bodies of three victims were later to be found. Is it yet another coincidence? Police remained divided. The 1985 police analysis concluded: 'It would be possible to formulate a reasonably sound argument linking Janman to the deaths of the four women whose bodies were found at Tynong North. However, whilst there is little information available about the circumstances of their deaths, what is available is sufficient to show that person(s) was not Janman.'

The analysis found Janman remained a strong suspect for the Summers murder and as the possible killer of Rooke.

'The dearth of physical evidence and eyewitness accounts linking him to either of the (Frankston) victims means that it is unlikely that he will ever be charged with any offence or eliminated as a suspect.

'The only conclusion I can draw is that the person(s) responsible for the deaths of Rooke and Summer at Frankston is/are not the same person(s) responsible for the deaths of Miller, Headland and Sargent and it is most likely that a third person or persons was responsible for the death of Narumol Stephenson.'

But with no hard evidence, no confessions, no witnesses and no conclusive causes of death, even experts could not be sure.

A second Bureau of Criminal Intelligence report conducted in 1990 came to a different conclusion from the one conducted five years earlier.

This time, Janman was described as a 'viable suspect with weak or non-existent alibis'.

'On the balance of probabilities the same person or persons were responsible for the murders of Allison Rooke, Bertha Miller, Catherine Linda Headland, Ann-Marie Sargent and Joy Carmel Summers. On the information available Janman is the best nominated suspect for the offences.'

If Janman killed the two Frankston women and was not involved in Tynong, then two serial killers were abducting women from streets at the same time. Even more baffling is that both stopped around the same time and do not appear to have struck again.

Janman was not working when Miller, Sargent, Rooke and Summers went missing, but was rostered to work 11am to 11pm on the day Headland was abducted. If the alibi is right, he is not involved in any of the Tynong murders at the quarry site as there can be no doubt Miller, Sargent and Headland were killed by the same man.

But what if it is wrong?

The sequence of the killings adds to the mystery. Rooke was abducted and her body discovered three months before the first Tynong victim was grabbed.

Joy Summers was abducted ten months after the Tynong gravesites were found. Is it possible that after the killer's first dumping area in Skye Road was discovered, he had to find a second spot he knew well? Then after the Tynong spot was discovered, he returned to his original base, safe in the knowledge the police interest in the area had waned.

Organised killers learn as they go on from crime to crime; they get better at what they do, and this shows in their degree of organisation.
– Robert Ressler, FBI Serial Crime Unit.

IN August, 1997, police conducted a routine gutter-crawling operation in St Kilda, codenamed Elista. In the early hours of the morning a 65 year old man, dressed conservatively in a suit and tie, approached a policewoman working undercover as a prostitute. He asked for sex.

He was just one of seventy men nabbed in the regular clean-up but he caused fresh interest when he volunteered to police that he was 'the prime suspect in the Tynong North killings'. It was the religious prude who liked to offer women lifts in his car – Harold Janman.

The head of Operation Lyndhurst, Detective Senior Sergeant Clive Rust said in 2001: 'It is fair to say that we now believe that one man is responsible for the Tynong North and Frankston murders. We are confident we know his identity. We are focusing on the one suspect.'

Janman agreed to undergo two lie detector tests in relation to the murders. Police say he failed both. Janman says the results were inconclusive.

• In 2005 Harold Janman and his loyal wife Vivalesi told *The Australian* newspaper that he was no killer.

'You know, we have been, all of our family, to hell and back. I know in my heart of hearts that Harold did not do these horrible things. I would not be here now if I had the slightest doubt. If he did do them, I would be as guilty as him, and God knows – He knows – that Harold is innocent,' she said.

Mrs Janman is loyal, but occasionally forgetful.

Nearly 25 years earlier, she told police she was with her husband on the day that Joy Summers was abducted in 1981, that they had gone to their bank together. The alibi was false.

Janman maintains he is an innocent victim of monstrous circumstances. He says, 'I just know that one day I will be vindicated.'

── CHAPTER 18 ──

It's Payback Time

They thought they got away with pack raping two 15-year-olds they were sure would stay silent forever. They were wrong.

THE leader of the pack is out there, in the suburbs or some country town. He's in his 40s now, probably with a family of his own. If he has teenage daughters, you can bet he's careful where they go and who they're with. He knows bad things can happen – he and his mates used to rape girls that age in the 1970s. It was sport to them, like wild dogs killing sheep.

Maybe he thinks about it sometimes when he's mowing the lawn or washing the car, or when a schoolgirl walks past. Or last thing before he goes to sleep.

No one outside the gang knows exactly how many girls they lured into cars, abducted and violated. There were a lot of gang rapes in the 1970s, and not all were investigated, let alone solved.

Often, the victims and their families became part of a conspiracy of silence – gagged by fear, shame and the prospect of blame.

And so the gangs got away with it until something stopped them: they were caught, or close enough to it to be scared off, or they tired of their brutal game. A few of 'the boys' might have committed other violent crimes and ended up in jail, but the rest faded back into suburban anonymity. Family men with secrets. It would be a lot to presume that many, if any, feel remorse about what they did. But they must wonder in quiet moments whether the past can ever reach out for them.

The answer is that it can. This is the story of how a terrified schoolgirl has become a driven and determined adult, hunting a gang of men who raped her when she was 15.

She has traced the man who betrayed her by delivering her and her friend to the gang.

This time, she guesses, he will betray the same gang. He just doesn't know it yet. Nor does he know that a detective who has worked on the case for ten years has been watching him for weeks.

ON the first Tuesday of November, 1976, the rest of the world was watching the United States presidential election: Jimmy Carter versus Gerald Ford in a cliffhanger. But in Australia, the Melbourne Cup pushed the White House off the front page. Even the worst Cup Day weather in memory couldn't stop the race that stops a nation. More than 78,000 turned up at Flemington.

It was a day of portents, humid and oppressive, as if the tropical wet season had strayed south. By early afternoon, thunderclouds blacked out the sun. Anxious drivers turned on headlights even before the first cloudburst hit. Hundreds of cars were stranded in flooded streets. The wind uprooted trees and

IT'S PAYBACK TIME

stripped roofs. Then the rain hit again, turning Flemington into a paddy field of ruined shoes and shattered hopes.

It was the wettest Cup in history. The deluge would stick in people's minds for years. The betting ring was swamped with money for a New Zealand mudlark called Van Der Hum, a dour plodder backed to favouritism who duly splashed his way into racing folklore by winning the slowest Cup in decades.

Hundreds of police were rostered to watch the race crowd. One was Richard Parsons, a 26-year-old constable in uniform, seconded from Footscray. Twenty-six years later, as a veteran detective, he remembers how wet it was and that he found a warm welcome and a few drinks when he finished his shift, at a party hosted by Melbourne socialite Peter Janson in a double-decker bus.

There were other attractions on that public holiday. At Festival Hall in West Melbourne, not far across the industrial sprawl between the docks and the muddy Maribyrnong River, thousands of teenagers queued to get into a concert, Cup Day Rock.

The old boxing stadium was a primitive but popular venue. Just nine days earlier, some of the biggest Australian acts of the 1970s had packed the hall for the annual Rocktober concert. Now it was full again. The Cup Day concert featured Mark Holden, a clean-cut pop idol who tossed carnations into the crowd and drew adoring teenage girls who'd seen him on *Countdown*. Where girls go, boys follow. Not all of them clean-cut.

The concert ended about 5pm. Ushers opened the back doors into Rosslyn Street to ease the crush around the main doors at the front. The crowd poured into wet streets under a sullen sky.

Among them were two girls, schoolmates who'd caught the train in from the eastern suburbs. They were in third form at high school and had not long started going out by themselves. Donna, curly-haired and vivacious, was dressed in jeans, T-shirt and a blue Lurex cardigan. Angela opted for the hippie look: 'treads' sandals, a long skirt, earrings. They were friends, but not best friends.

Waiting in the street were three youths in a station wagon. Donna had first met two of them at the Rocktober concert nine days before. The shorter, better-looking one she knew as Wayne Thompson. He was fair, with browny-blond hair, cut short in a modified version of the sharpie style. He wore the uniform of the time: a polo shirt with a penguin logo and tight Staggers jeans.

Wayne's mates were both called John. The one Donna had met twice before had pale skin and dark hair with longer 'tails' at the back. The three were in the front bench seat of the fawn station wagon, probably a Holden, the back packed with tools and building equipment. At 18, they were working men with adult tastes in alcohol, cigarettes and sex.

Donna knew the car. It was the one in which the obliging Wayne had given her a lift to Flinders Street station after the Rocktober concert. The same car that, a few nights later, he had driven all the way from the western suburbs to Box Hill to meet her. She had skipped a ballroom dancing class to meet him and one of the Johns that night – and had agreed to meet them the following Sunday, October 31.

That Wayne would drive across town to see her impressed Donna. He was older, had a car and money, and came from somewhere else: among her peers, that made him desirable. She didn't realise it might also make him dangerous.

But there were clues. During the week, a stranger, calling himself 'Tony', telephoned Donna at home asking her to a party.

IT'S PAYBACK TIME

He said Wayne had given him her number. This confused her. She wondered why Wayne would hand out her number. She refused.

On October 31, she took the train to the city. Wayne met her at Flinders Street station. With him was his supposed 'brother', John, who, Donna later found out, was not related to Wayne at all. This tendency to fudge names puzzled Donna but did not make her suspicious.

They then drove west, across the Dudley flats and the Maribyrnong River and beyond, through suburbs she had never seen. To a deserted picnic area, where there was a public toilet block near a creek, some boulders and scrubby trees. There they met friends of Wayne's, including one called 'Tony'.

It was a trial run, Donna was to realise later. She was naive. She half expected to have sex with Wayne, as she thought of him as her 'boyfriend'. But when he pushed her to 'turn it on' for Tony, she was upset.

Tony forced himself on her and Wayne took photographs, as if she was a trophy. She was angry and humiliated but not scared. She did not yet grasp she was being set up as a target for the gang by being branded a 'slut'.

Which is why, two days later, when Wayne got out of the station wagon outside Festival Hall, she listened to him when he apologised for his behaviour. He said he would make it up to her by taking her and her friend to a party.

At first, Donna played it cool. She said, 'I know what your parties are like,' referring to the Sunday incident. But Wayne was persuasive and plausible. That was why, as she realised much later, it was his job to 'chat up' vulnerable girls picked out of the crowd at concerts. It was the gang's *modus operandi*.

Donna took the bait; she and Angela agreed to go. As soon as he closed the deal, Wayne smoothly switched things: he said that as his car was already full, the girls could get a lift with his friends. He assured them his mates were trustworthy.

On cue, a gleaming red Torana pulled up next to them. It was a two-door manual with black bucket seats, a billiard-ball on the gearstick and a transfer with the word 'Torana' in big white capitals across the top of the windscreen. Four young men were in the car. The driver wore a hat. A big man leaned forward in the passenger seat and unlatched it so Angela could climb in between the pair in the back. Donna realised she was expected to sit on the big man's knee in the front. She was taken aback at first, but having to squeeze in seemed so clearly uncomfortable and temporary that it reinforced the impression that the party was nearby.

Wayne assured her he would drive ahead and lead the way. She believed him – and Angela trusted her. It was all organised. In seconds, the situation had changed from the girls going with three people Donna had already met to being in a car full of strangers.

The first thing she realised was that the four men belonged to one ethnic group. They were dark-haired and spoke with the same accent. She thought they were Greek or maybe Italian. In itself, that didn't matter to her. Donna and some of her five siblings were born overseas – to a Canadian father and Northern Irish mother – and the family had been all over the world before immigrating only a few years before, so she knew what it was like to be an outsider.

What made her uneasy was that these strangers knew things about her: which concerts she had been to; that she liked dancing; where she came from and which school she went to.

'They were kind of laughing but in a sly way,' is how she put it later. 'We were being "interviewed" but I didn't know it. They were looking for someone who fitted their criteria: who came

IT'S PAYBACK TIME

from a different area and had no idea who they were or where they were taking us.' The men avoided using each other's names. They called each other 'mate', although she heard the name 'Joe' and one mentioned working in a garage.

What the men knew about her was harmless enough, but the fact they knew it unsettled her. Donna glanced in the rear-vision mirror and caught the eye of one of the men in the back seat. She didn't like his stare. He was sizing her up.

The longer they drove, the stranger the situation seemed. For the second time in three days, she was driven into the western suburbs. When both cars pulled up at a service station she was uneasy. The one she called the 'big guy' got out and spoke to Wayne secretively.

It was as if they were discussing a drug deal.

It was a deal. But not drugs.

THE big guy was boss. He was broad-shouldered, thick-set and had a strong accent. Donna noticed the distinctive crease across the bridge of his nose.

By the time they left the service station, Donna was spooked but didn't know what to do. Even if she got away, Angela was trapped in the back.

Soon, they left the houses behind and passed open country – the rifle range at Williamstown – then turned off on to a rough dirt track that led into wasteland between the Altona beachfront and a row of huge fuel or chemical storage tanks. In the distance she saw the orange-tiled roofs of a new housing development, but the wasteland was deserted. Thunder rumbled as the cars stopped near a patch of stunted scrub.

Everything was wrong. Donna jumped out of the Torana and ran to Wayne's car, checking over her shoulder that Angela was behind her. 'What's going on?' she yelled at Wayne.

'What's the problem?' he answered, and one of the two with him said something odd: 'We're doing a deal.' An admission.

She heard a thud, a sudden exhalation of air and a scream. She jerked around to see that the big guy had knocked Angela to the ground and was dragging her, like a hunter with an animal carcass. Angela's face was contorted with fear. (Years later, when Donna saw Edvard Munch's painting *The Scream*, it reminded her of the way her friend looked at that moment.)

Donna turned back to Wayne and the two Johns and begged them to do something. One mumbled something about going for help. They got back in their car and drove off.

She never saw them again. It was a set-up.

The big man threw Angela into the Torana. Donna ran at him and jumped on his back, clawing at his neck. He grabbed her and tossed her into the back seat with Angela, who was sobbing. The other two men were still outside, leaving the driver and the leader in the front.

The other two walked off, as if they had rehearsed their movements. The driver sped off, bouncing over the rough ground, then stopped the car.

Donna was terrified, but she was still thinking. 'You don't want to do this,' she said, but the big guy interrupted.

'Why don't you just fucking shut up,' he said quietly, cold eyes staring into hers. Then she saw the glint of the knife in his hand, held low between the bucket seats.

That's when she knew there was no way out. But she couldn't imagine what was going to happen. How could she? She was 15.

IT wasn't until Donna was twice that age, an apparently successful and sophisticated woman living a long way from Melbourne, that she found the words to tell what happened that day.

IT'S PAYBACK TIME

She had worked hard and lived fast, a party girl running on adrenaline and deadlines, pushing herself to exhaustion so that she could sleep it off and do it all again, night after night. She left school and Melbourne soon after the rapes, started as a window dresser, moved to working in nightclubs and then theatre – steadily more frenetic jobs that kept body and mind busy. It was the mask she held up to the world, a way to keep nightmares at bay.

It didn't always work.

Once, in 1983, drunk in an empty club at 5am, she told a friend she'd been raped, but then fell silent. He did not hear the full story until years later.

After one failed relationship and a few false starts, she stayed single for years. Her family knew what had happened in Melbourne, but it was taboo. Her parents had opposed going to the police, moved interstate soon after the ordeal and 'left it behind'. Donna was implicitly encouraged to go along with an unspoken conspiracy to keep it buried for the same reasons many rape victims did and still do: shame, blame and fear. Not only fear of blame and fear of reprisals, but fear of being cross-examined in court and judged outside it.

In any case, for years she could not force herself to talk about it. Until one day in early 1992, when the past finally caught up and her mask cracked.

It happened with a chance sighting at a mailing house where she was approving theatre subscription brochures. A supervisor asked where she went to school, explaining that one of the men working there thought he remembered her face from a high school in Melbourne.

It was a harmless query, but Donna was rattled. Being recognised triggered a rush of submerged memories – and fears. From that day, friends noticed that her behaviour changed.

One of those friends was Tom McDonald, an Australian business lawyer then practising mostly in the United States but who often visited the city where Donna lived. He first met her in 1991 at the club she then managed. They became friends and he helped her with a legal problem. She repaid him by cooking him dinner when he was in town. To McDonald, Donna was 'sparkling company and a damned good cook', but their friendship was platonic. After one such meal in early 1992, they were listening to music and having a drink when Donna's breezy charm fell apart. She said she trusted him because he had never made a pass at her. Then she said she'd been having 'strange feelings'. Then she broke down.

The savvy club manager turned into a frightened girl. Crying and disjointed, she poured out a stream of raw recollections. 'It was so traumatic it made her physically ill,' McDonald recalls.

Afterwards, he felt 'ashamed to be a man for about five minutes'. Then he decided to help. He suggested psychological treatment – and legal remedies. One avenue was crimes compensation. The other was justice – searching for the attackers and seeing them punished. McDonald helped her launch a crimes compensation case that she eventually won. But mere compensation – about six months' wages for a dozen rapes and a ruined life – was never going to be enough to put her back together again.

In 1992, Donna's friends saw what one calls 'that sparky, mischievous, bossy girl' unravel. The workaholic could no longer work. Her stylish Art Deco inner-suburban house was a mess. She stayed indoors for days, curled in a ball, crying. On her first visit to a psychologist she handed over a tape recording of an interview she had recently had with a sexual assault counsellor. It was, the psychologist said later, 'a harrowing account of a harrowing crime'.

Another friend heard the story first-hand, with detail that shook him – 'all the filthy parts she needed to have said,' he says.

She finally went to the police on March 17, 1992, while in Melbourne for a conference. She went to Nunawading Community Policing Squad and started talking. It took 10 hours to finish the statement. A kind policewoman took it all down and shared a piece of boiled fruitcake with her, the only thing either of them ate from midday until 10pm.

She recalled every detail as if it were frozen in time. 'I have these snapshots in my brain,' she explained later. 'It unfolds like a film. A noir film.'

IT wasn't just the knife but the look in the eyes of the man who held it that terrified Donna. He dragged her out of the car, then got in the back seat and started to rape Angela.

Donna was in shock. The driver stayed in the car, watching. The other two men walked up. They pushed and abused her, working themselves up. They called her 'fucking slut' and 'stupid bitch' and 'hopeless c...' and grabbed at her breasts. They called her 'boutana' or 'puttana' – Greek and Italian variations of whore.

She refused to undress. 'Smart bitch,' one snarled, and they shoved her face down on the bonnet of the car and pulled her jeans and underclothes down, one holding her by the hair. What followed was obscene, violent and degrading.

She was numb with pain, fear – and concern for Angela, who was a virgin. And who, Donna thought guiltily, wouldn't be there except for her.

She could hear her friend whimpering in the car. It rained again. She tried to block out what was happening by concentrating on the sky, the refinery tanks and the raindrops on the windscreen. Forever after, a wet windscreen has jolted her into remembering these unspeakable acts.

The rapists laughed and taunted Donna as they zipped up their flies. She dressed herself and got in the car with Angela, thinking it was over. It wasn't. The Torana went a few hundred metres and stopped. Waiting was another station wagon, a metallic, mocha-brown Ford with curtains in the back. There were two men in it – a tag team. The big guy dragged Angela out and ordered both girls into the Ford. He got in, too, as if he owned them. They drove off. Donna didn't see the Torana again, except in bad dreams.

She had no idea where they were until she saw a Footscray Institute of Technology sign as the car turned down a sloping entrance to parkland beside the river opposite Flemington racecourse, still crowded after the races. It was quiet on the Footscray bank, but a family was nearby trying to have a picnic, despite the weather. The girls were raped again. Donna could see the picnickers through the fogged-up windows. She willed them to realise what was happening and rescue them.

They drove off again. The gang leader put his arm around Angela in a grotesque parody of affection, as if she was his girlfriend. When the car stopped at traffic lights, he whispered in Donna's ear, 'I know you'd like to run'. They drove under a bluestone bridge where water was lying across the road, almost knee-deep. They turned into cobbled lanes among warehouses and factories, somewhere in North Melbourne or Kensington, went up a steep lane and stopped in a car park underneath a building. It was dark and deserted, but suddenly the space was filled with the rumble of a V8 engine and male voices. More men.

Donna whispered to Angela to cling to the pack leader, 'Just stay with him – he won't let anyone else touch you.' She was

IT'S PAYBACK TIME

not sure this was true, or even if they would survive. She feared their ordeal was heading for some sinister climax: 'I was frightened we were going to be annihilated.' One by one, the newcomers raped Donna. Except the last one, the twelfth man to straddle her that day.

She saw his face. She thought one of the others called him 'Steve'. He was smaller and fairer than the rest and less sure of himself. She whispered to him, 'Help me get out of here.'

He quietly helped her get dressed, then called to the leader, 'Mate, it's getting late. Why don't we get rid of them?'

They drove. It was getting dark. Minutes later, the car pulled into a lane beside North Melbourne railway station. The girls were shoved out, like pieces of rubbish. They had avoided death, but their life sentences were just beginning.

DONNA'S police statement trickled through the system and across the city from Nunawading to Footscray CIB, a crowded office with stained carpet and strained resources in one of the busiest police stations in Australia.

The file was handed to a detective who was transferred soon after, then to another, who was too busy on recent offences to waste time on something that happened so long ago. And so, in mid-1993, the file passed to Detective Sergeant Richard Parsons, the constable at the 1976 Melbourne Cup.

Parsons had lived and worked in the western suburbs all his life and none knew 'the patch' better. He had seen a lot of bad endings but, unusual in his calling, that had not stopped him being calm and courteous. Only a fool would mistake this for weakness or lack of purpose. No policeman who has worked the Melbourne waterfront is a soft target – but it didn't stop him having a soft heart.

When Parsons read Donna's statement, it touched a nerve. He

remembered gang rapes in the district in the 1970s and it bothered him that some went unsolved. Besides, he had a daughter of his own. And when he spoke to Donna, they struck a rapport.

Without new leads, there wasn't a lot Parsons could do, but he did what he could. The starting point was the man Donna knew as Wayne Thompson and his friend John. Although Wayne had lied that John was his brother, Donna knew his real surname. What she didn't know was that Wayne had also lied about his own surname: it wasn't Thompson.

The day after the rapes, Wayne had called her at home and told her his telephone had been disconnected and she would not be hearing from him. She had no idea where he worked, except that he was probably a labourer or apprentice tradesman. He had vanished.

Sergeant Parsons soon found John, who still lived locally. He had a string of convictions – assaults, thefts and drink-driving – and had served time for armed robbery in the 1980s. The detective wasn't surprised when John denied having anything to do with Donna or the rapes.

On John's criminal record, Parsons noticed that one of his associates was called Wayne, though his surname was not Thompson. This Wayne (Wayne X) was the right age – 18 in 1976 – and had a record for assault, theft and burglary in the 1970s. He had served time in Turana youth training centre.

When Donna visited Melbourne in January, 1996, the detective showed her a series of mug shots of possible suspects, including a poor-quality photocopy of Wayne X. She paused over the picture and said the eyes reminded her of 'Wayne Thompson' but she wasn't sure.

Meanwhile, Parsons had traced Angela. Whereas Donna had left Melbourne soon after the rapes and had lived interstate ever

IT'S PAYBACK TIME

since, Angela had stayed. They'd written to each other briefly but the friendship had petered out. They had little in common except their ordeal, which each had tried to bury in her own way.

Angela had married, had children and moved to an outer suburb. Parsons arranged to meet her discreetly. Angela confirmed Donna's statement, but refused to be involved in any possible prosecution.

Her husband and children did not know about the rapes and she wanted it to stay that way.

It looked like a dead end.

IN June, 1996, Donna was going through things she had stuffed into a suitcase when leaving Melbourne 20 years before. She opened a satchel full of school English notes. As she put it down, something orange fell out.

It was a ticket to the 1976 Rocktober concert at Festival Hall. On the back was written 'Wayne' and a telephone number. She stared at it, then sat down and typed a fax to Parsons. 'You'll never guess what!' it began. 'I'm still shaking with excitement and amazement.' She was sure the old telephone number would lead to Wayne and unravel the rapists' identities. Eventually, it would, but for a long time the orange ticket was a red herring.

In the rush to computer databases in the 1980s and '90s, old telephone records and manual systems had not only been superseded, but destroyed. In 1976, a disconnected telephone number might have been used to trace someone who didn't want to be found. But in 1996, the same number seemed useless because it couldn't be crosschecked using modern data systems.

Months after finding the ticket, Donna saw an article about old telephone directories for sale. It gave her an idea. She asked the State Library of Victoria to look up Wayne X's surname in the 1976 Melbourne directory to see if any subscriber of that name matched the number she had. None did.

Donna either had to give up or look for a needle in a haystack. She decided to look. In June, 1997, she asked Telstra to let her search an archival copy of the 1976 directory. She spent hours every week at her state's Telstra headquarters, poring over it. She took four months and 655,000 names to find the number.

Again, it seemed like a breakthrough.

The name listed for the number was T. Fennell, at 175 Millers Road, Altona. Perhaps Fennell was a friend or relative of Wayne's family?

It had the allure of the unknown and it seemed to Donna and the detective that T. Fennell was the missing clue.

But when Sergeant Parsons went to 175 Millers Road, his heart sank. It was a block of flats that had been rented out to dozens of tenants over the years. No one knew of a T. Fennell. Parsons and Donna set up stories in local newspapers, appealing for help. None came.

The problem was that the 1976 telephone directory had been out of date. (In fact, respectable tenants called Tony and Doris Fennell had moved out of the Millers Road flat in December, 1974, but Fennell's name and outdated address and number had mistakenly stayed in the 1976 directory. Meanwhile, the number had been allocated to new subscribers: Wayne X's parents. There was no way of knowing this until the author finally traced Tony Fennell to a country district in eastern Victoria.)

For five years, however, it threw the investigation off course. Without Fennell, it seemed they couldn't prove a connection between the telephone number and Wayne X. As it turned out, when Fennell was found, he couldn't directly make that connection – but he provided valuable information by pointing

IT'S PAYBACK TIME

out that Donna had searched the wrong telephone directory. There was still hope.

In 2003, on a rare visit to Melbourne, Donna went to see Richard Parsons. Once more they revisited the crime scenes, from Festival Hall to Altona to the Maribyrnong riverbank to North Melbourne. This time, the detective had unearthed a good-quality photograph of Wayne X in the 1970s. Donna said it looked like the Wayne she had known – but she needed to be sure. Later, she went to the State Library and asked for the 1977 telephone directory. She eventually found the telephone number she had written on her concert ticket 26 years before.

Proof that 'Wayne Thompson' was really Wayne X.

Proof that the past can reach out.

THE last chapter of Donna's story has not been written because it has not happened yet. The ending she hopes for is that the net will tighten around the men who planned and committed the pack rape of two terrified teenage girls all those years ago.

She knows they are out there. Time has disguises – thinning hair and thickening waists – but it cannot alter some things. If he's alive, the leader of the pack will still be tall and broad-shouldered and have a southern European accent and a domineering personality ... and that distinctive crease across the bridge of his nose. Time cannot alter the fact he used to go around with his mates in a spotless red two-door Torana and that he knew someone with a dark brown Ford station wagon with vinyl bench seats and a column shift.

The Torana was the sort of car young men prized. Somewhere, photographs of it will be in an album. Somewhere, people will remember the car and who owned it in 1976. The rapists are not the only ones with secrets. Richard Parsons is sure Donna and Angela were not the only girls set up and raped who didn't go to the police because they felt compromised by the unspoken suggestion that they had somehow 'asked for it'.

Those frightened girls will be women in their early 40s now. Old enough not to be scared any more and to help each other fight back. Each will know something that counts. Some might even know who their attackers are or where they live.

Meanwhile, time is running out for the gang. The day will come when the patient Sergeant Parsons will knock on the door of a pale brick-veneer house in a suburb on Melbourne's western fringe. It's the house where Wayne X lives with a new woman.

The detective will pick his time – Wayne is a truck driver these days, and isn't always home.

What happens next is up to Wayne. He can help police. Or he can try to protect the members of the gang.

Wayne X knows what jail is like: he once did time for assault. He was young and reckless then. Now he has family reasons not to go back inside. Wayne's wife died recently and he has a young daughter to worry about. It won't be long before she's at high school and wanting to go out with boys.

• *Two women have come forward to tell police they were victims of the same gang. They identified several suspects as members of the gang and police established that two of the men have died since the rapes described in this story were committed. Inquiries are proceeding. Victims' names have been changed.*